Who Cares for Our Children?

THE CHILD CARE CRISIS
IN THE OTHER AMERICA

Who Cares for Our Children?

THE CHILD CARE CRISIS IN THE OTHER AMERICA

VALERIE POLAKOW

Foreword by BARBARA EHRENREICH

Teachers College, Columbia University
New York and London

Published by Teachers College Press, 1234 Amsterdam Avenue, New York, NY 10027

Copyright © 2007 by Teachers College, Columbia University

Lines from "Käthe Kollwitz" on p. 29 and "Ann Burlak" on p. 161 are reprinted by permission of International Creative Management, Inc.:

"Käthe Kollwitz": © 1968 by Muriel Rukeyser, from *The Collected Poems of Muriel Rukeyser*, Pittsburgh Press, 2005.

"Ann Burlak": © 1939 by Muriel Rukeyser, from *The Collected Poems of Muriel Rukeyser*, Pittsburgh Press, 2005.

Library of Congress Cataloging-in-Publication Data

Polakow, Valerie.
  Who cares for our children? : the child care crisis in the other America /
  Valerie Polakow.
      p. cm.
  Includes bibliographical references and index.
  ISBN 978-0-8077-4774-2 (pbk. : alk. paper)
  ISBN 978-0-8077-4775-9 (cloth : alk. paper)
    1. Child care–United States. 2. Children with social disabilities–United States.
  3. Poor children–United States. 4. Low-income mothers–United States. 5. Poor
  families–United States. 6. Child care–Government policy–United States. I. Title.
  HQ778.63.P65   2007
  362.71'20973–dc22   2006038068

ISBN: 978-0-8077-4774-2 (paper)
ISBN: 978-0-8077-4775-9 (cloth)

Printed on acid-free paper
Manufactured in the United States of America

14 13 12 11 10 09 08 07   8 7 6 5 4 3 2 1

For Jerry

*In the fragrant brushwood of the hills, in the waves of the sea,
under free skies, and in the custody of love.*
—Albert Camus

Contents

Foreword

When I was doing the research for my book *Nickel and Dimed*, I worked at low-wage jobs to the point of exhaustion, lived in grubby circumstances, and dined on fast food far too often. Still, compared to many low-wage working women, I had it easy, for one simple reason: I didn't have small children with me to care for and support. After *Nickel and Dimed* was written, I hoped that some young journalist with children of her own might undertake the same kind of project, if only to see how far entry-level wages would go in supporting a family.

But shortly after the book was published, I became a grandmother, and realized that no one in her right mind would take on a journalist experiment like that. It's one thing to put yourself through hard times; it's quite another to subject your children to shabby dwellings, inadequate food, and catch-as-catch-can child care. I wouldn't do it to my grandchildren—or any child, for that matter.

As a part-time caretaker for my granddaughters (ages 2 and 4), I'm reminded every day of how vulnerable babies and small children are. When my own children were small I had to patch together child care from many sources. One consequence for me as a working parent was perpetual worry. When my son was 2, I noticed that he seemed withdrawn and depressed when I picked him up at the home of a woman who took in two other toddlers. What was going on? Finally I figured out that her idea of "care" was to plop the kids down in front of TV with some sugary snacks. So I whisked him out of there and re-started the search for reliable, high quality care.

Without money, this is usually a fruitless search. One of my co-workers (in *Nickel and Dimed*), when I was working as a maid with a housecleaning service, was the single mother of a toddler. On a wage of about $7/hour, a licensed group day care center was out of the question, so she paid her boyfriend's sister $50 a week to care for the child. The trouble was, she didn't trust her boyfriend's sister, and ended up calling her several times a day to check on her daughter. I could see the tension on her face, and the rage she felt when we cleaned the home of a wealthy stay-at-home mom who had not only a cleaning service, but also a full-time nanny

Welfare reform plunged millions of single mothers into an impossible situation: In order to hold on to any benefits, they had to get out into the workforce, but the provision of child care for them has been inconsistent and unreliable. Only about 1/7 of the families which need child care subsidies actually receive them, and, as this book documents in painfully vivid detail, most poor working women have to turn to unreliable and often unqualified, caretakers–a family member who also works, for example. There are few options, since missing even one day of work to care for a sick child can lead to being fired. Many women end up leaving their children with an older child; some have to leave children home alone. The emotional cost to the mother is unbearable; the cost to her children, immeasurable.

Politicians on both sides of the aisle have hailed the "success" of welfare reform, and it has been successful in reducing the welfare rolls. But as a social initiative meant to reduce poverty, it has been a disaster. Without welfare-as-we-knew-it, low-wage women are left with an ugly choice: stay home and be what the middle class considers a "good mother," in which case you may soon have no home to stay in–or work long enough hours to support your children, in which case you may never see them. More and more women are forced into the latter choice, often working two jobs in order to pay for child care of dubious quality.

Who Cares for Our Children is one of the most disturbing books I have read in a long time. It should have a major impact on debates over poverty and social policy, as well as attracting a wide audience with its powerful stories. To read it is to know that, right now, somewhere, a child really is crying. Because she fell and there's no one to comfort her. Because she misses her mother. Because America just doesn't seem to care. . . . This has to change, and I thank Valerie Polakow not only for exposing the problem, but for pointing the way to achievable solutions.

–Barbara Ehrenreich

Acknowledgments

This book has been many years in the making, and, like a good cup of tea, it's taken a long time to brew. In all the work that I have done during the past two decades, advocating for and writing about the lives of women and children in poverty, child care has emerged as an *edge* issue—central to poverty, welfare, homelessness, low-wage working families, and their children left behind. And for years I have wanted to focus a book on child care and the crisis it presents for low-income mothers, telling their stories and bringing visibility to their lives.

The Center for the Education of Women at the University of Michigan—where I spent a summer as a visiting scholar in 1997 working with Peggy Kahn to document the impact of welfare "reform" on low-income student mothers—planted one of the early seeds for the book. This was followed by collaborative work on access to child care with Marjorie Ziefert, Peggy Wiencek, and John Benci at The Institute for the Study of Children, Families, and Communities at Eastern Michigan University and with Jennie McAlpine and the staff of Child Care Network. A sabbatical in 2003 and a Graduate School Research Fund Award from Eastern Michigan University helped support the interview phase of the study. The women whom I interviewed, and whose stories are at the heart of the book, taught me about the enormity of the child care crisis confronting low-income parents, as they spoke so articulately and passionately about their own lives and those of their young children.

Many other individuals have been central to the writing of this book. Cindy Guillean and Huayun Xu provided me with valuable research assistance during the early and final phases. A community of colleagues and friends sustained me with ongoing feedback and support and were always available to offer their help in so many essential ways. Special thanks and appreciation are due to Leslie Bloom, Martha Baiyee, Nkem Khumbah, Begoña Garcia, Vania Rasche, Joseph Meadows, and Peggy Kahn. In addition, Peggy has significantly contributed to this book in a myriad of ways, helping to shape its course through her wide-ranging expertise and incisive critique. At Teachers College Press I have greatly benefited from working with a remarkable director, Carole Saltz, and two outstanding editors, Susan Liddicoat and Karl Nyberg.

My sons Shael and Sasha, as always, have been strongly engaged and interested in my work. Sasha provided excellent suggestions about the international and human rights issues as I began framing the book, and reviewed the earliest chapters and meticulously read the final proofs. Shael read the completed manuscript, and his penetrating insights and critical questions challenged my thinking about the broader meanings and educational implications of the work. He provided me with invaluable support during the final, critical weeks of writing.

But in the end, this book is not only mine; it also belongs to my husband Jerry Weiser. It was Jerry who first inspired me to write about the child care crisis, and whose encouragement, involvement, and support were so central to my capacity to conduct the research and write the book. Until the final weeks of his illness, Jerry continued, as he always had done, to read and critique every chapter I wrote, constantly urging me as a writer to witness and document wrongs in order to set them right. He lived to see me complete the writing of the book, but not to celebrate its publication. Jerry's legacy as an educator is one of compassion, integrity, and a fierce and firm commitment to social justice and human rights. *Who Cares for Our Children?* is a tribute to Jerry's life and his courage to be.

Who Cares?

The neighbors seemed pleased when the babies smothered. Probably because the mint green Cadillac in which they died had annoyed them for some time. They did all the right things, of course: brought food, telephoned their sorrow, got up a collection; but the shine of excitement in their eyes was clear.

When the journalist came, Mavis sat in the corner of the sofa, not sure whether to scrape the potato chip crumbs from the seams of the plastic cover or tuck them further in. . . .

"This must be terrible for you." Her name, she said, was June.

"Yes, m'am. It's terrible for all of us."

"Is there something you want to say? Something you want other mothers to know?"

"M'am?"

June crossed her knees and Mavis saw that this was the first time she had worn the white high-heeled shoes. The soles were barely smudged. "You know. Something to warn them, caution them, about negligence."

—Toni Morrison, *Paradise*

Who cares about Mavis and her children? Mavis, the negligent uncaring mother. Mavis, the battered woman, crazed and desperate. Mavis, the Cadillac-driving "welfare queen." And who are her dead babies? Their lives, now gone, of immeasurable value in the post-tragedy media storm, but worth little as they spent their earliest months in a household scarred by domestic violence and state neglect. Mavis, poor mother-public, invisible until judged guilty. Mavis, a mother undone.

Who cares about women-as-mothers whose struggles and suffering float in the unnamed world of otherness? Women, single and partnered, survivors of family violence and neighborhood violence; women workers barely making ends meet in low-wage dead-end jobs; mothers on welfare and not; mothers stressed and stretched, juggling scant resources with household budgets that defy calculation; mothers with young children and no good place to turn, constantly settling for less, making bad, sometimes desperate choices as they confront the closed door: shut out from the quality and the stability of high-priced child care made for other people's children. And who cares for *their* children? There are the tragedies of course, but far more common are the casualties, the dailiness of young lives scarred by the worst of child care–harsh and dreary landscapes, disrupted attachments, shifting arrangements, unsafe spaces.

"What the best and wisest parent wants for his own child, that must the community want for all of its children."[1] But the community public that John Dewey called for in the early decades of the twentieth century is now largely privatized and gated. A wise *poor* parent desiring the best for her young child must purchase child care on the free market, where the best goes to the highest bidder, and the worst is doled out in the netherworld of informal, unregulated, custodial care. And so begins the early educational stratification of unequal life chances.

Clara is a special education teacher in New York City. She, too, struggled to find affordable child care for her son as a young, single, immigrant mother living on the edges (see Chapter 7). Now, from the other side, she sees the shape of the crisis for the mothers of the children she teaches:

> I tell people I know how you feel because I've been there. . . . What do you do? I mean, you cannot leave your children at home, and you can't take a day off and you don't have child care. . . . I mean, we just had two children that were burnt, that died in a fire. . . . Last year, we had one lady, she had to leave her son at home to go to work. . . . It's very sad. It's very, very sad . . . we say these children are our future, but we just throw them away!

Clara comments on the deplorable quality of child care that so many poor parents must settle for. Fearful of losing their jobs, they "choose," living in constant terror of what might happen to their young children left in the seamy underworld of child care. In her brief stint as a special education teacher, Clara has already seen the damaging consequences. She describes the situation of a mother of one of her students:

> Her daughter went to day care; she went from 8:00 to 2:30. It was four hundred dollars [a month], and she was getting a discount . . . and I would guarantee you, five, six times a month her daughter was taken to the emergency room. The day care was unsanitary, so she was constantly

getting sick. . . . And, if she stayed home, she [her mother] still had to
pay the entire amount of money. . . . It's like a no-win situation. Your
child is getting sick, you still have to pay. Eventually she had to leave.
She had to stop working and take her daughter out. . . . It's very very
sad because, especially for minorities, the situation is so horrible. It is
terrible. . . . The 12-year-old was staying home watching the 3-year-old
and the one-year-old. . . . and I mean, just so many things so mother can
go to work! . . . Child care is a huge, huge problem—Sometimes I mean
you're working on a job and what do you do?

There is little that the United States does do for parents, and in particular for low-income women, in terms of family policy that would ensure
that mothers can be both nurturers and providers for their children. The
right to care for one's children and the right of children to be cared for
are both existential and pragmatic policy issues. What does it mean to
care when the viability of the family may rest on the fortunes or ravages
of an unfettered free market? And when the care and education of the
young is constructed as a private rather than public responsibility, the
health and well-being of children is purchased at an increasingly high
cost; while "cheap" children, 13.5 million of them, continue to inhabit
the other America.[2]

The history of public provisions for women and children has always
been premised on the question of who constitutes the deserving poor,
and the moral conduct of its recipients–where poverty is viewed as a
private pathology not a structured system of inequality based on the politics of distribution.[3] The ideology of motherhood, intersecting at critical
national moments with an emergency need for child care, has produced
a two-tiered history of child care provisions–custodial and educational,
untrained and professional, day care and nursery school–differentiated
by discourses about class, race, and moral imperatives about the poor.

CRITICAL MOMENTS IN THE HISTORY OF CHILD CARE

In the latter part of the nineteenth century, in contrast to the progressive
nursery school and kindergarten movement influenced by classical European pedagogues such as Froebel and Pestalozzi, day care was developed
to provide custodial care for the children of poor working mothers, many
of whom were immigrants. During the 1800s, there were few options
for young children whose parent(s) labored in factories or worked long

hours in the service sector.[4] Indenturing children to be fostered under the tutelage of persons of "good moral character" was seen as one alternative to the undue influence of the almshouses where thousands of street children were sent.[5] But, more common were boarding institutions, "orphan asylums" that served both child rearing and child care functions. They were segregated institutions run by Black and White charities and were particularly important for African-American women, who worked primarily in domestic service that required mothers to live at the homes of their employers; hence, if no extended kin were available, boarding for their children was a necessity. Such orphanages, which were generally fee-paying, for both Black and White children, became widespread in the mid-nineteenth century, and the number of half-orphans (children who had one parent living) actually exceeded the number of full orphans in most orphan asylums.[6]

Day nursery founders, inspired by the French example of the well-functioning crèche system, campaigned for the establishment of day nurseries for working mothers, which was viewed as a "a more humane and less expensive" alternative to the orphan asylums.[7] Hence day nurseries, emphasizing cleanliness (children were stripped on arrival and given nursery smocks to wear while their own clothes were disinfected) and moral training, began as philanthropic charity institutions to provide for the care and social welfare of the children of working mothers, widows, and those abandoned by their husbands and, with the rapid influx of immigrants at the turn of the century, the children of immigrant parents. Day nurseries were open six days a week, twelve hours a day, caring for infants as young as 2 weeks through 6 years old, with some providing after-school care for young school children. The day nurseries were largely run by White upper-class women whose "noblesse oblige" created an avenue to extol the virtues of family preservation and, while lamenting the necessity for poor and fallen women to work outside the home, saw day nurseries as temporary havens for the moral socialization of poor children, who would be "removed from the unhappy association of want and vice, and (be) placed under better influences."[8]

By the 1900s, the National Federation of Day Nurseries (NFDN) saw its explicit goal as the Americanization of immigrant children through the provision of temporary assistance to wage-earning mothers. The support for poor working women was conditional on their poverty or an emergency domestic crisis and was never premised on women's rights to paid employment, but rather was perceived as a saving strategy—saving children from vice, and saving poor and defective mothers from abandoning their children and from descending into the moral turpitude of prostitution. The African-American day nurseries, on the other hand, run by middle-class Black reformers of the National Association of Colored Women (NACW), viewed maternal employment as a necessity—a permanent, rather than temporary, way of life for Black urban families. As such, poor Black mothers were viewed in a far more sympathetic light by their African-American benefactors.[9]

While some day nurseries were lavishly endowed, the "typical charitable day nursery was a dreary, highly regimented institution reeking of carbolic disinfectants . . . a place to which no middle-class mother would consider sending her children."[10] Run by matrons, who were drawn from working-class backgrounds and viewed as little more than "glorified housekeepers" by their employers, the day nurseries were the embodiment of class stratification—where upper-class volunteers ran the board meetings and managed the nurseries, allowing no input from matrons, staff, or mothers. Staff training and educational development were absent, and the day nurseries were criticized by social reformers such as Jane Addams, who questioned the "double edged implement": as the meager wages of poor women barely enabled the family to survive and the conditions of the nurseries "were neither encouraging nor reassuring."[11] It was during the Progressive era that day nurseries fell out of favor, as the movement for Mothers' Pensions (subsidy payments to mothers who lacked male breadwinner support) gained momentum. Julia Lathrop, who became the first head of the federal Children's Bureau in 1912, was joined by other social welfare reformers and maternal feminists of this period in questioning the high costs to poor mothers of ill-paid jobs with no protective labor laws and long hours away from home. The day nurseries were inadequately staffed, lacked good child welfare provisions and protections, and provided little in the way of educative care for their young charges.

Hence it was the advocates for women and children during the Progressive era who were instrumental in quashing the nascent public day care movement, arguing that poor mothers' employment led to child delinquency.[12] Instead, the social welfare reformers pushed for the passage of Mothers' Pensions, and between 1910 and 1920, 40 states enacted Mothers' Pension laws, but by 1934, only three states specifically included single unmarried mothers. The "suitable home" provision, which made women's conduct and her childrearing a condition of eligibility, served as a racialized and "moral" exclusionary mechanism for unmarried mothers and African-American mothers, as well as immigrant mothers. Not until the Social Security Act of 1935 did poor women gain access to a federal welfare entitlement, Aid to Dependent Children (ADC), as part of Roosevelt's New Deal reforms, although, in practice, many jurisdictions continued to restrict access to women of color.[13]

The War Years and Day Care Provisions

The emergency mobilization of women workers during World War I led to the proliferation of day nurseries, particularly at sites where defense industries were hiring female workers. However, the NFDN, led by its founder, Josephine Jewell Dodge, campaigned against the establishment of industrial nurseries on the grounds that this led to the exploitation of women for war purposes—despite the fact that many working women stood to benefit from higher-paying skilled jobs. Buttressed by the domestic ideology of motherhood and separate spheres[14] and the generally stigmatized view of the day nurseries, a critical moment for the expansion and public support and investment in a national system of child care was lost.

After World War I, the clinical casework perspective that dominated social work increased the stigmatization of poor working mothers, whose children were viewed as inevitably maladjusted because their mothers worked. Maternal employment—not low wages and deplorable working conditions, nor the overcrowded conditions in day nurseries, nor domestic violence, nor the teeming tenement neighborhoods—was to blame for wayward children and delinquency. Mother's vocation was at home, and only aberrant mothers absented themselves; so that "a mother's decision to work came to be seen not as a rational—if regrettable—response to poverty but as evidence of psychopathology."[15]

In the intervening years between the two world wars, the class differences that had differentiated the middle-class nursery school movement, with its focus on child pedagogy, from the largely custodial day nurseries became even more evident. When the Great Depression took hold, the federal government, under the leadership of President Roosevelt, elevated child care to a national need, and Emergency Nursery Schools (ENS) were established under the New Deal policies. The ENS planners looked to the progressive educators in the early childhood nursery movement for guidance, and not to the established day nurseries, which already had a history, albeit checkered, of serving poor families in crisis. The ENS programs, often based in schools, operated from 1933–1943 and expanded to 43 states, offering early educational programs to low-income children, as well as parent education, and serving thousands of working mothers who held Works Project Administration (WPA) jobs. Often called the WPA nurseries, the ENS programs were the first federally (and state) funded child care programs and were notable for their educational emphasis, in contrast to the custodial "social hygiene" focus of the day nurseries.

While New Deal relief programs, including the WPA nurseries, lost federal support in the early 1940s, many of these same nurseries were transformed during America's entry into World War II, as the large-scale mobilization for the war effort overrode the ideological opposition to maternal employment. With a substantial public investment targeted to the provision of war-time child care services made possible by the passage of the Lanham Act, more than a million and a half children were in day care by 1945.[16] The famous Kaiser Child Care Centers at the Kaiser shipyards exemplified the best of what could be accomplished by well-trained staff, led by progressive educators offering affordable high quality care around the clock, with take-home meals prepared for mothers when they picked up their children! But the Kaiser centers were unique, both for their innovative designs and for their wraparound family services; and the wartime effort and public support for working mothers was short-lived.[17] As the war ended and the returning soldiers reclaimed their jobs and benefited from the GI Bill's promise of higher educational opportunities, women were displaced, and their children were sent home.

In the immediate aftermath of World War II, the 1950s ideals of female domesticity and the traditional nuclear family were reinforced by the dominant psychoanalytic theories of the time, emphasizing the vital significance of mother-infant bonding and secure stable attachments.[18] Mother absence through maternal employment was viewed as inimical to the healthy development of infants and young children. The dominant ideology of motherhood was once more at center stage and, with it, the care of children as a private and uniquely gendered responsibility. Yet, the reality behind the motherhood discourse was that during the 1950s large numbers of women were already in the labor force, with particularly high labor force participation by African-American women.[19] In 1953, 22% of working women had children under 18, and of this group 1.5 million had children under 6. The demand for child care far outstripped the supply, and facilities in urban centers, documented by the Women's Bureau, were found to be inadequate, unaffordable, and overcrowded.[20] Another decade would pass before any major child care and education initiative was to emerge.

Head Start: An Ambitious Federal Early Childhood Initiative

During the War on Poverty in the 1960s, as part of Lyndon Johnson's Great Society initiative, a massive antipoverty early intervention program was implemented. Head Start, funded by the Economic Opportunity Act, was designed as a comprehensive and compensatory public intervention, early childhood program that addressed children's health and nutrition, as well as their cognitive and social development, and included parent education and social services as integral components. Head Start grew out of an era of optimism and change, and the belief that early intelligence was infinitely malleable if children were provided with a stimulating and rich environment. The original founding philosophy reflected the clinical deficit assumptions about poor families that were prevalent, and early intervention was premised on the need to interrupt the cycle of poor parenting (i.e., poor mothering). Robert Cooke, one of Head Start's founding members, summed it up well as "the nearly inevitable sequence of poor parenting which leads to children with social and intellectual deficits, which in turn leads to poor school performance, joblessness, and poverty. . . ."[21] The deficit assumptions about poor women and poor children were pervasive and permeated every welfare and educational service provided during this era.

Nevertheless, Head Start was an ambitious federal initiative that enriched the lives of generations of poor children and supported their early development at critical moments. It has served more than 22 million children since its inception, targeting 3–5 year-olds, and serving a small percentage of toddlers and infants through Early Head Start.[22] At the same time Head Start programs have always been racially and economically segregated because they are targeted to poor families, who were (and are) disproportionately represented among racial and ethnic minorities. Forty-one years later, Head Start remains the only federally supported national early childhood program in the United States!

A National Child Care Plan Defeated

The attempt to create a universal child care system that included all children was led by a broad coalition of early childhood advocates, feminists, labor, and civil rights leaders during the Civil Rights era. The Act for Better Child Care, sponsored by Democrats Senator Mondale and Congressman Brademas, was a radical piece of legislation that passed both the House and Senate and proposed free child care for low-income families, with sliding scale fees for middle- and upper-income families. The Act was the first comprehensive piece of child care legislation in the history of the United States and its provisions were dedicated to the development of quality child care for all children. However, in 1971, the Mondale-Brademas Bill, a landmark effort to create a national child care system, was vetoed by President Nixon on the grounds that it would "commit the vast moral authority of the National Government to the side of communal approaches to child rearing"![23]

After the defeat of the Act for Better Child Care, subsequent attempts to promote the establishment of a national child care system were derailed, and, in its wake, limited Title XX funds were targeted to child care for welfare recipients, who were required to participate in work and training programs as part of the Work Incentive (WIN) program. The conservative backlash against poor women on welfare during the 1970s created fertile ground for a ferocious discourse against any public benefits, including child care. In his 1976 primary campaign for the presidency, Ronald Reagan immortalized the image of a Cadillac-driving welfare queen defrauding the nation: "She has 80 names, 30 addresses, 12 Social Security cards and is collecting veteran's benefits on four non-existing deceased husbands. And she is collecting Social Security on her cards. She's got Medicaid, getting food stamps, and she is collecting welfare under each of her names."[24] Reagan's sustained assault on the welfare state reached its zenith when the Omnibus Budget Reconciliation Act (OBRA) was passed by Congress in 1981, leading to major social service cuts, including drastic reductions in welfare, food stamps, Medicaid, and child care. During this same period, in an effort to encourage the private sector to enter what appeared to promise a lucrative child care care,[25] tax breaks became the main source of federal support for c'"federal and ironically, from the mid-1980s to the end of the 1990 ent funding government lost more money through tax breaks tha grams"![26] public child care programs or subsidizing commun'

CARING FOR CHILDREN: A PRIVATE C RESPONSIBILITY?

In 2004, 77.5% of women with c'7, 62.2% with children under 6 years old, and 57.3% w'under 3 years old, were in the
labor force.[27] However, th'dearth of family support policies
available to working r'ornick and Meyers point out, "This
exceptionally priv'of family life leaves American families

to craft individual solutions to what is essentially a social dilemma: If everyone is at the workplace, who will care for the children?"[28] The United States stands alone among all major industrialized countries in failing to provide paid parental leave, child care, and health care for all its children. As mothers are the primary caregivers for children, child care is indeed a woman's issue where economic independence, autonomy, and social equality are directly linked to access, availability, and affordability of good quality child care. Far-reaching changes in the structure of families and women's employment have, in the past decades, increased the need for child care and there has long been a "care deficit" for working mothers, both married and single.[29]

The Care Deficit

Under the 1996 Personal Responsibility and Work Opportunity Reconciliation Act (PRWORA) welfare legislation, the need for child care expanded exponentially as poor single mothers were coerced, under threat of sanctions and benefit cutoffs, into the low-wage labor market, leaving infants as young as 12 weeks old behind.[30] Paradoxically, poor women's care for their own infants or young children does not count as a legitimate work requirement, and their rights to make decisions about their own children's nonparental care is severely undermined by the inflexibility of the welfare-to-work mandates. The underlying assumptions behind this legislation are that poor mothers are work-aversive, dysfunctional parents, and unfit to care for their own children. Such legislation impugns their dignity and "repudiates them as mothers."[31] Although welfare "reform" has dramatically increased the demand for care, particularly for infants and toddlers, the public supply is grossly underfunded, leading states in a child care race to the bottom for the cheapest of publicly subsidized care subsidy. At present there are long waiting lists in over 20 states, and only one in [ ] income-eligible children actually receives any child

While universal public education exists for all children in the United States, there is no entitlement for young children to an early childhood education. Although ten initiatives have been [ ] the past decade, state-funded prekindergar- has resulted in restricted [ ] nted in 38 states, but lack of funding Head Start still serves only [ ] poor quality in many programs.[33] wide, and most programs do n[ ] income-eligible 4-year-olds nation- parents. From public preschool in [ ] wraparound care for working [ ] rograms, licensed private

and community-based centers and family day-care homes, religious-affili-
ated centers, employer-sponsored child care, for-profit chains, to license-
exempt care and the vast unknown informal care sector—child care is a
patchwork of uneven quality and market-driven provisions demonstrat-
ing the glaring inequities in child care services for young children.[34] As
child care costs between $4,000 and $10,000 a year, low-income families
must often compete with families on welfare for scarce child care subsidies. In 20 states a family earning $25,000 a year is not even eligible for
child care subsidies. Subsidies also do not pay the full cost of care, and
in the majority of states, the reimbursement rates are based on outdated
market surveys.[35] When state reimbursement rates are low, many child
care providers are reluctant to accept children whose parents cannot pay
the difference in copayments, which may run as high as $200 to $300 a
month, further exacerbating the stratified system of care.

Under the Bush Administration's 2006 budget, domestic discretionary spending has been decreased by $152 billion over the next five years,
with steep cuts in education, training programs, social services, and health
care—tax cuts for the wealthiest amid a myriad of public services slashed:
Medicaid, child care, after-school care, and welfare.[36] These are far-reaching attacks on the public good and further contract the spaces for care,
leaving low-income families in often desperate straits. Hence, the care
deficit ricochets with alarming costs for the well-being and healthy development of children. Gornick and Meyers argue that there is an urgent
need for new public policies that would redistribute the costs of caregiving.[37] While affluent working mothers compete to enroll their toddlers in
the "baby Ivies" paying up to $15,000 a year,[38] how does a food-service
worker mother earning $6 an hour at her local Taco Bell purchase quality
care? If she lives in New York City, where there are 38,000 children on
waiting lists for subsidized care,[39] she has few options open to her other
than the cheap informal care sector.

Making choices in the best interests of one's child is arguably a vital parental responsibility. But low-income women have few choices.
And the poorer they are, the less autonomy they have as providers and
caregivers. Why should poor women in the United States not have the
right to make choices about the care of their own children? While con-
servatives continue to urge middle-class mothers to choose the traditional terrain of a stay-at-home motherhood, in order to raise their own
children and "preserve the family," poor mothers are still located in
the space of a marginal motherhood, and family values for *them* are constructed as something entirely different. Neither the extensive psycho-

logical literature on early development nor the array of studies pointing to the importance of high quality child care experiences appear to have influenced the design of welfare "reform" and its underfunded, made-on-the-fly inferior child care provisions. Mothers working just beyond the edges of poverty find that they, too, must settle for *less;* less than what they choose and less than what they want for their children, as the increasingly privatized child care market creates dangerous disjunctions between quality care and affordable care.

It is paradoxical that the youngest and most vulnerable members of our society are shut out from the only two universal public systems that exist in the United States–the education system and the social security system. A free public education system–albeit riddled with "savage inequalities" and segregated schooling–is still an entitlement for 6 to 18 year-olds.[40] Social security for elderly Americans, although under increasing attack from the right, is still considered an earned entitlement and functions as an important antipoverty measure for low-income seniors. But a social security system for children (which, in turn, would depend on benefit transfers to their parents) forms part of a completely different conversation because parents, specifically poor mothers, are seen as undeserving of government support. The prevailing discourse about poor mothers, like that of the nineteenth century, is couched in "moral" and "personal responsibility" and "productive work" refrains, despite the fact that most low-wage jobs are not productive in material terms. In 2001, 27 million workers earned poverty-level wages, with women still occupying a disproportionate share of the low-wage economy.[41]

Investing in Child Care

A cost-benefit rationale for investing in child care in the United States is a far more politically palatable argument than one that frames child care as a right and an entitlement.[42] And from a cost-benefit analysis, it is indisputable that investment in the early lives of young children has clear demonstrable payoffs–individual, social, and economic. The human capital benefits of investing in high quality child care programs point to increased student achievement, improved health, greater family stability, and young adult productivity. High quality child care appears to have a particularly beneficial impact on low-income children's educational achievement. The Abecedarian project conducted in the 1970s and monitored for two decades demonstrated long-lasting positive effects on academic achievement, with higher numbers of participants finishing high school and attending college. Longitudinal research on the High/Scope Perry Preschool Project over four decades consistently points to positive outcomes, including education, employment, health, and family relationships, with an estimated economic return of $17.07 per dollar invested.[43] While the gains to young children's development are substantial, the economic benefits to families and communities are also significant (see Chapter 8). One immediate consequence to the family of providing stable quality early childhood care is the support provided to working parents, and specifically working mothers, whose need for public early childhood programs is acute.

Nancy Folbre argues that children should be viewed as public goods.[44] The unpaid labor of parenting—usually women's work—also contributes to the development of human capital. Caring for one's children—good mothering—is, too, a public service that provides immense social benefits as healthy children have the capacity to become productive, engaged citizens who contribute their intellects, goods, and services to future generations. These "positive externalities" ultimately result in long-term benefits for their families and communities and contribute to building the human capital of the society. But woman's unpaid care work has long been undervalued and becomes a particularly acute problem when mothers are also earners in the labor market, yet there is no social care and early educational infrastructure in place to support them and their children. In a postindustrial globalized world, in which the male breadwinner/female homemaker family form has been superseded by an earner/carer society, the family/work conflict creates a domestic crisis of far-reaching impacts.[45] As long as caring and educating the nation's youngest children remains a uniquely private responsibility, the poorest and most vulnerable families will pay a disproportionately heavy price.

A QUESTION OF LOSSES AND RIGHTS

While the human capital and economic investment arguments are part of an ongoing discourse about the value of investing in family support policies and providing quality early childhood care to sustain young children's development, there is another more fundamental issue that concerns rights: The rights of all mothers, of all parents, to public support for their roles as providers and nurturers, earners and carers. Children, too, have rights to a safe, protective, nurturing place away from home that envelopes their developing being and celebrates their growth, fosters their curiosity, engages their minds, and provides them with a healthy social milieu in which to interact with peers and adults—in short, a landscape of care and trust and possibility. Such child care landscapes do exist, and they are wonderfully formative and enriching, but unfortunately poor children experience the loss of such rights far too frequently; for how do we create landscapes of care and early enrichment for all our children if this most delicate and formative phase of life is left to market forces?

In contrast to Scandinavia, Western Europe, Canada, and other industrialized nations, the United States has not chosen to create family support policies that benefit the most vulnerable, and with neither paid parental leave nor national child care policies in place, poor children's development will always count for less. Perhaps Grubb and Lazerson are right that, in the United States, we "lack any sense of public love for children."[46] As downsizing, outsourcing, and the proliferation of low-wage odd-hour jobs become the face of the leaner, meaner, economy, working mothers are expected to go it alone and silently cope with the disappointments and constant anxieties of inferior child care or, worse, the terrors and consequences of dangerous child care. Consigning millions of infants, toddlers, and young children to a diminished childhood is commonplace in the other America. Legislative indifference to public policies that actively harm children at their most formative stage of development creates neither moral panic nor public alarm.

In E. L. Doctorow's *Waterworks*, set in the late 1800s, the destitute children of New York City are described as "losses society could tolerate." The narrator continues, "Our city was spendthrift and produced enough wealth to take heavy losses without noticeable damage. It was all a cost of doing business as the selection of the species went relentlessly forward."[47] How many more losses we need ask, is this society prepared to tolerate as private greed, sordid profiteering, and government deregulation destroy the remaining vestiges of public infrastructures and support services? How do we begin to think about mothers' and children's rights to care in the context of free-market fundamentalism and the relentless pursuit of a privatized life, liberty, and happiness?

This book is about who cares *for* and *about* poor young children and the child care crisis their mothers confront in the United States. Social suffering is most often a consequence of a lack of rights. Rights denied demand that we bear witness. *Who Cares for Our Children?* seeks to understand and document the lived realities of the child care crisis from those who have experienced it up front—low-income mothers.[48] The heart of the book lies in the narratives of individual life circumstances—narratives of particularity that portray and make visible the worlds of poor mothers and their children; their daily child care struggles, their terrors, and their tragedies, as well as some remarkable triumphs. By making visible the texture of mothering and caregiving lived out on the margins, and confronting the losses—another vision of the possible may be articulated.

NOTES ABOUT THE ORGANIZATION OF THE BOOK

Chapter 1 presents the story of Jasmine, a young mother and her son, isolated and alone. Jasmine's story illuminates the care deficit and raises the broader question of rights within the frameworks of social citizenship, gender, human capabilities, and human rights. Chapters 2 to 6 present the resilient struggles and the distress of 15 diverse low-income mothers across four states—Michigan, Iowa, New York, and California—all of whom have encountered a crisis of child care that threatened their family viability. Poverty, domestic violence, housing insecurity, low-wage odd-hour jobs, intransigent welfare-to-work mandates, immigrant status, multiple and makeshift child care arrangements, dangerous and damaging care, emotionally destabilized children, lack of access to affordable quality care, social isolation, as well as the power of advocacy networks, are threaded throughout these five chapters; as these mothers, married and single, welfare-reliant and working poor, insert themselves into the larger narrative of care and what it means to live and to be *without.* Chapter 7 chronicles the "wonderful and different change" that occurs in the lives of five mothers when high quality child care is accessible and available and how lives are transformed when child care works.

The concluding chapter positions the U.S. child care crisis in a larger international context and analyzes the costs of inaction and indifference to the plight of millions of poor young children and their families. Public policy arguments and proposals for investing in child care are examined and juxtaposed against a human rights framework. The existential and developmental consequences for children, and the well-being of families, are framed as necessary and overriding arguments for universal child care as a human right for all our children.

CHAPTER 1

Whose Rights?

Jasmine Thomas and her toddler son, Che, live on the outskirts of a minimal life. Theirs is a tenuous, day-to-day existence. Being a poor single mother in the United States, at barely 20 years old, Jasmine, a Michigan high school dropout, may as well live in an impoverished community of the Third World. Out on the streets at 15, in group foster homes until 18, Jasmine became pregnant in eleventh grade, and with scant help or encouragement from her teachers to complete her schooling, she joined the ranks of America's swelling numbers of dropouts and "pushouts,"[1] temporarily moving in with her boyfriend and his aunt while pregnant. That arrangement proved precarious after the baby's birth, when Jasmine's boyfriend became violent, and she was forced to seek a protection order against him for domestic assault. Attempts to obtain monthly cash assistance and housing support from the Michigan Department of Human Services' Family Independence Program (FIP), proved futile, as Jasmine was sanctioned for her failure to attend mandatory Work First training when Che reached the age of 12 weeks.[2] Jasmine recalls her initial desperation: "I didn't know what to do . . . I couldn't find someone to watch my baby."

With her cash assistance cut, and no place to live, Jasmine sought help from a former caseworker at a nonprofit community agency. Only with the community caseworker's persistent intervention and advocacy on her behalf were Jasmine's food stamps reinstated, and soon after she received a subsidized apartment. As public housing goes, the apartment is clearly better and safer than most, located in a small, pleasant-looking complex set down in the midst of a wealthy college town neighborhood. Here, in a sparsely furnished two-bedroom apartment with a TV and an empty refrigerator, Jasmine and her 10-month-old son try to make a life.

Jasmine begins to search for jobs along a nearby strip mall in walking distance and along a bus line. She applies at a drycleaner and in the housekeeping division at a hotel chain—both places located close to the strip mall. She applies for child care subsidies from FIP but is denied because she does not yet have a job and has not attended the mandatory Work First orientation. She temporarily makes up with her abusive boyfriend (despite the protection order in force), and he watches Che while she searches for a job. A part-time job at the drycleaner comes through, and Jasmine begins working 9:00 a.m. to 1:00 p.m. each day. Again she applies to FIP for subsidies, again she is denied, ostensibly on the grounds that she has not attended the mandatory Work First orientation and is only working 20 hours instead of the required 40 hours per week. After the arrangement with her boyfriend collapses, Jasmine's sister, a high school senior living in a neighboring city, comes to help during her winter break. However, when her sister returns to school, Jasmine loses her job after missing several days of work, all the while desperately trying to piece together makeshift child care arrangements that continually fall apart.

Jasmine's former caseworker has advised her to seek child care for Che in the licensed sector, and for more than a month she has been fruitlessly searching for a licensed family day care home in the area, because without a car, she has limited options. "It's been so hard," she says, "I been looking and looking for child care. If it's not the area, it's the amount of money. If it's not the amount of money, it's the transportation." Still jobless and reliant on her abusive boyfriend and his aunt for sporadic sums of emergency money, Jasmine returns to the hotel chain near the strip mall, and as luck would have it, there is an opening and she is hired on the spot. She calls her sister, who takes time off school once again and temporarily moves in to help with Che's care, while Jasmine continues to work and search for a permanent child care arrangement. Jasmine again seeks out her caring former caseworker who assisted her earlier, and she refers Jasmine to a regional agency of the Michigan 4C Association.[3] Jasmine receives support and encouragement (in contrast to the inflexible treatment by Michigan's FIP program), and the 4C agency offers her a partial child care scholarship and gives her a list of licensed centers and family day care homes to contact. However, without an actual child care slot, the scholarship cannot be activated. Jasmine has her hopes pinned on a family day care home that she locates in the neighborhood. She has only seen the outside, "which looks nice and clean," and has talked with the lady on the telephone. When she thinks about the kind of provider she wants, she describes her as "respectful, trustworthy . . . just someone nice, sweet, that likes kids, that knows about kids, that have kids of their own, that are experienced." Jasmine has not observed the child care setting nor met the provider, but it's the only one that she has been able to find in close proximity that is cheap enough for her to afford with the help of the child care scholarship. Jasmine is told that a spot will open up in the next few weeks.

Meanwhile, Jasmine's $7.50 an hour job hangs by a thread as she tries to piece together stopgap arrangements; her boyfriend's aunt says she might be able to help one day a week, another friend offers to "maybe do a day every now and then," a neighbor who had volunteered to fill in for a few weeks has changed her mind, and the only reliable person in Jasmine's milieu is her sister, who has already missed over three and a half weeks of school. Jasmine is becoming desperate. She becomes even more alarmed when she is informed that after her training period in housekeeping is over, the 9:00 a.m. to 3:00 p.m., Monday-to-Friday hours will, in fact, change. She will be required to work some weekends, and her schedule will vary from week to week, so she cannot make a consistent child care arrangement. Despite these mounting obstructions, Jasmine still has hopes that things will work out as she thinks about the future: "I'm going to go back to school and I'm going to get my diploma (GED). And I want a car so transportation wouldn't be so hard and a better-paying job to be able to pay day care."

Another week passes, and Jasmine still has not heard from the "day care home lady." Her child care scholarship expires and is offered to the next parent on the waiting list, although Jasmine is told that she can reapply once she secures a child care place. With panic mounting, she again looks to enlist her boyfriend's mother, grandmother, and aunt; but they are all poor and single, and they are all working low-wage jobs with little time flexibility in their lives. Her sister has now missed a month of school and tensions are building in the household. Jasmine's sister leaves to return to school, still hoping to graduate, despite a month of unexcused absences. A friend of Jasmine's, who is passing through on her way to Milwaukee, arrives for a few days to help out. And after that? "I've just been trying to go to work and trying to pretend it's not even there. When I come home, I still call [child care providers], but I mean nothing's changed. I feel like I ain't getting nowhere."

Two young lives on the edge—loss of a job, eviction, and homelessness looming; a young family's contingent survival threatened—Why? Why should Jasmine have to suffer such chronic instability for herself and her baby, the crisis of child care that throws her fragile household into such turmoil? It is clear for Jasmine, as with so many other millions of low-income mothers, child care is the tipping point, and that without safe, affordable, accessible, and decent quality child care, family viability is on the line. And what are the costs? As Jasmine struggles to hold onto a low-wage, no-benefits, odd-hours job that, despite full-time work, will keep her young family mired in poverty–the best she can hope for is safe, cheap, but likely inferior quality child care, if she ever finds that coveted slot for her baby son. At worst, her son will be shuttled between multiple unreliable care arrangements, ranging from dangerous to indifferent, with friends and family members whose own lives have been marred by poverty, substance abuse, and violence, and cheap unregulated caregivers in the informal sector.[4] Why, in fact, should Jasmine not have the choice to take care of her own infant?

As a poor mother with a young child having the misfortune to be born in the United States, Jasmine can expect little in the way of social citizenship rights, such as universal child care, paid maternity and parental leave, employment supports, and child allowances. Rather, the United States stands alone among all major industrialized nations in its "exceptionalism,"[5] failing to provide what Martha Nussbaum terms "a basic social minimum," a social threshold below which "truly human functioning is not available to citizens."[6] Why should Jasmine not have the right to child care, which would provide her son with a caring stable environment where his well-being is foremost and his development nurtured in a safe, regulated, high quality child care setting? Such social citizenship rights are available in most industrialized democracies, codified in the European Union Charter, and directly addressed by the International Convention on the Rights of the Child, which the United States has not yet ratified.

SOCIAL CITIZENSHIP AND MOTHERHOOD

Social citizenship rights undergird what British sociologist T. S. Marshall referred to "as an absolute right to a certain standard of civilization." He argued that social policy had a vital role to ensure that all had "a claim to be admitted to a share in the social heritage." "What matters," he said, "is that there is a general enrichment of the concrete substance of civilized life, a general reduction of risk and insecurity, an equalization between the more and the less fortunate at all levels . . ."[7] Social citizenship comprises not only political and civil rights, but social and economic rights, creating a "positive state" that guarantees citizens economic and social security, as well as the positive freedoms of individual opportunity and individual development.[8] Marshall's principles of social liberalism are embedded in the social and economic rights of modern welfare states in Scandinavia and Western Europe. However, in a "residual welfare state," such as the United States, market sovereignty serves as the basis for the argument that the state should play a minimal role in the distribution of social resources and that individuals are essentially responsible for contracting their own welfare. Esping-Anderson has characterized social citizenship rights in welfare states by their degrees of decommodification—the extent to which citizens are *not* dependent on the vicissitudes of a market economy—but rather are able to rely on a generous set of social entitlements in their society.[9] The greater the degree of decommodification, the greater potential there is for social inclusion, poverty alleviation, and social equality. Hobson and Lister[10] and other feminist social theorists point out that decommodification has to be understood in terms of the very specific struggles that women confront (child care, labor market discrimination, and so forth) and argue that both universal entitlements *and* gender-differentiated rights are necessary in a postmodern and post–male-breadwinner era if the "positive state" is to be realized for women and mothers. It is clear that a social care infrastructure is a fundamental condition for achieving gender equality, and that women's economic independence in the labor market is also heavily dependent on the existence of "universally accessible child care as a public service."[11] Furthermore, argues Mahon, because child care is a key social citizenship right for women, it is also a politically charged "gendered" issue.

In contrast to the social democratic states of Scandinavia, which offer generous and comprehensive social safety nets and universal systems of child care, and societies such as France and Belgium that provide family supports and universal child care, social policy in the United States has never emphasized a social care infrastructure, and the right to receive or give care has been completely absent from the concept of citizenship. Mothers are seen neither as caregiver-citizens deserving benefits and services for child rearing and caring for their children (as in the Netherlands) nor as parent-worker citizens (i.e., working caregivers) requiring benefits and services to reconcile work and child care (as in Sweden and Denmark).[12] Gornick and Meyers' comparative analysis of social policies indicate that the most sustainable and successful family policies are inclusive and offer broad-based social provisions and supports to all families, thereby avoiding the stratified, means-tested, stigmatizing benefits that are characteristic of the United States, exacerbated by "deep racial and ethnic cleavages and resistance to policies that redistribute across these divides."[13] In countries where social citizenship rights are strong, with high quality public child care systems, there are lower rates of child poverty and the life chances for children improve dramatically, with positive emotional, social, and cognitive outcomes.

The four Nordic countries–Denmark, Finland, Norway, and Sweden–emerge as the most successful in eliminating child poverty in the Organisation for Economic Cooperation and Development (OECD) countries. Among households with children in 2000, Denmark comes out on top with a poverty rate of 2.1%, while the United States and Mexico rank last at 18.4% and 21.3%, respectively.[14] In addition to the well-resourced, inclusive, social provisions and public child care available in Scandinavia, France, and Belgium–most of Continental Europe, Australia, and Canada's model Quebec province have also established public child care systems and family support policies that play a large part in eliminating child poverty. Because child care plays a pivotal role in supporting women's employability and education, particularly for single mothers, it forms an indispensable ingredient of family stability. The burden of unpaid care work across the life cycle–for children, aging parents, and other family members–still disproportionately falls on women creating "one of the most entrenched and consequential components" of gender inequality.[15] As there is no paid parental/maternity leave in the United States, the lack of safe, developmentally supportive child care for infants and toddlers creates even more acute needs for low-income working women.

In the absence of a nationally subsidized child care system, child care, for most parents, must be bought on the private market. Costs are prohibitive, and low-income mothers spend an average of 18.4% of their income on child care, with some low-income mothers spending as much as 25%, compared to 6.1% for mothers in upper-income households.[16] As more and more low-income mothers of infants, like Jasmine, are forced to enter the labor market and work longer hours as part of the escalating work requirements of the 1996 federal welfare legislation, there is a growing national crisis of unmet need: Inferior quality, unstable, makeshift arrangements, and the worst and the cheapest of care for the poorest of children. Multiple studies point to critical concerns about the quality and provision of care, and national reports on child care have documented unsafe, unsanitary centers, poor quality care, lack of regulation, closed access, and chronic unavailability to low-income families; with particular concerns raised about substandard and dangerous care for infants and toddlers.[17] What does it mean to children who are the recipients of inferior and developmentally damaging child care? What are the costs as their early lives are made cheap: lives not considered worth investing in nor protecting as part of our public responsibility? What does it mean to low-income women, like Jasmine, whose dual role as caregiver and marginal earner place her and her son in constant situations of fear and instability, while her own opportunities for education and viable employment are shut down? Clearly Jasmine would fare better if she and her son lived in a society that accorded her social citizenship rights by providing public child care and a set of social care provisions that would promote the health and well-being of her baby, and enable Jasmine to further her own education and find a stable job with a living wage, standard hours, and benefits.

Yet, despite the shameful record of the United States in failing to provide for the fundamental needs of millions of its poorest citizens, including the youngest and most vulnerable, social citizenship almost had its day in the United States. It is FDR's little-known Second Bill of Rights that laid a foundation for as yet unrealized affirmative social citizenship rights in this country and, at the same time, became "a leading American export."[18]

FDR'S SECOND BILL OF RIGHTS

[The nation] cannot be content, no matter how high that general standard of living may be, if some fraction of our people—whether it be one-third or one-fifth or one-tenth—is ill-fed, ill clothed, ill-housed, and insecure.[19]

FDR's 1944 State of the Union Address proposed a Second Bill of Rights, which Cass Sunstein points out is a vital yet "widely neglected" part of America's constitutional legacy and the foundation for a different vision of the country and its future. In laying out a framework for a set of social and economic rights that included the right to social security, to remunerative employment, to adequate food, shelter, and clothing, to a decent living, to medical care, to unemployment insurance, and to a good education, Roosevelt's Second Bill is closely aligned with the Universal Declaration of Human Rights. Adopted by the United Nations in 1948, the Universal Declaration was, in no small measure, brought to fruition under the leadership of Eleanor Roosevelt. The Universal Declaration of Human Rights stands in sharp contrast to the American Constitution that enshrines political and civil liberties but not social and economic rights.

In the Second Bill of Rights, Sunstein argues that Roosevelt went far beyond the New Deal to propose a new conception of rights in response to social and economic injustices. This set of "constitutive commitments" was designed to provide every American fundamental security in the face of social risks so that "the states of poverty and deprivation are denaturalized."[20] Roosevelt's belief that desperate economic conditions were and should be preventable and that good government has a vital role to play in the regulation of wealth and property, implicitly embodies a social citizenship approach, particularly in his arguments for redistributive justice that he outlined during the New Deal period and later conceptualized in the Second Bill of Rights. Some of his public statements are remarkable for their prescience–"The thing that matters in any industrial system is what it actually does to human beings. . . ." and "Necessitous men are not free men."[21]

If we consider the harsh postindustrial and globalization impacts on those whose rights to a decent life are violated–from the *maquiladoras* in Mexico to the sweatshop laborers in China and Indonesia, to minimum wage maids, like Jasmine, in corporate U.S. hotel chains–we see "necessitous" women with invisible children in their shadows, women who cannot be free without adequate social provisions for the care of their children. Roosevelt's proposed Second Bill of Rights did not confront the racialized welfare policies of the New Deal, nor the patriarchal control and surveillance of mothers on welfare, nor the urgent gendered needs for child care grown ever more acute for working women as the World War II nurseries shut down. Nevertheless, the Second Bill embodied a core moral sensibility, contending that those who live in "want" cannot be free and that "want" should not be seen as inevitable but rather as "a product of conscious social choices that could be counteracted by well-functioning institutions directed by a new conception of rights."[22] The vision of a new conception of rights is part of what Sunstein describes as Roosevelt's "Unfinished Revolution." Six decades later, that vision finds new forms in an articulation of human capabilities and human rights that ground women's social equality in the distinctive supports and affirmative obligations necessary for the "fundamental functions of a human life."[23]

THE HUMAN CAPABILITIES APPROACH

Martha Nussbaum makes a compelling argument for using a Human Capabilities Approach when attempting to understand and advocate for women's rights in a context of social and global justice. In framing the human capabilities approach, Nussbaum points out that women in all nations face distinctive problems because of their sex, and that their material and social circumstances must be understood in the context of their daily concrete realities. If human beings are to be treated with dignity and respect, there are certain universal norms of human capability that should form the basis for a set of constitutional principles that citizens have a right to demand from their governments. The principle of each person's capability implies that persons should be treated as ends, not means, "seeing them as agents, each with a life to live, deserving of both respect and resources."[24]

According to the Annual Human Development Report of the United Nations, using measures of life expectancy, wealth, and education, there is no country that treats its women as well as its men, and in developing countries this disparity is starkly apparent.[25] In the United States, a country already rated rock bottom among the industrialized First World in terms of the provision of social insurance policies that would primarily benefit women and children, mothers face competing demands for work and parenting, with few external supports, as they navigate a labor market unfriendly to the notion of mother as worker. Low-income women face substantially compromised lives as they work at unstable jobs with inflexible time demands and wages that keep many impoverished, and they lack the freedom to make child care choices in the best interests of their young children. Impoverished women in the United States, like women in the developing world, experience unremitting obstacles to their human capabilities, as the geography of poverty and gender inequality spreads across a global terrain. For women, there is always a fundamental common denominator that affects their lives, best summed up by Nussbaum: "unequal social and political circumstances give women unequal human capabilities. . . . When poverty combines with gender inequality, the result is acute failure of central human capabilities."[26] How then, might we understand the failure of human capabilities in the context of Jasmine's young family? Nussbaum's criterion of a minimum social threshold, below which truly human functioning is not available to its citizens, is certainly true in Jasmine's situation. Because she lacks fundamental economic and human resources–she has no money, no time to take care of her own child, no time to attend to her own development in terms of education, no child care, few social networks that function, and she faces certain eviction and homelessness if she cannot maintain her job–she lives well below a minimum social threshold. Her son, Che, by extension suffers the same lack of a basic social minimum, compounded by his needs as an infant for stable and secure care from nurturing caregivers with whom he can form a stable attachment.

The significant question to ask about Jasmine's life is what is she "actually able to do and to be?"[27] To be a successful mother and a successful earner, to create a stable family, she needs an infrastructure of social supports that include child care, health care, affordable housing, and the right to living-wage employment. Central to her needs as a single mother is stable, affordable, and quality child care, without which neither she nor her son can attain their human capabilities.

Public monies cannot make Jasmine and Che happy and healthy, but they can lay the foundation for healthy development and healthy human functioning, because they create possibilities for development and remove so many of the obstacles that litter the pathways of poor families. The current American discourse of private responsibility negates the moral principles underlying the notion of a public space: the public responsibility of a society to ensure that a minimum social threshold exists as a starting point for individuals; an opportunity to make a life and care for one's children with dignity; and not to be treated as the stigmatized object of an ownership society–a society in which Jasmine, as a single, young, and poor mother, has no stake. On the bottom rung of the low-wage labor force, Jasmine's life is not considered worthy of social investment by her employer (the hotel chain) nor her government, and she is merely an exploited means to an end–outsourcing, streamlining, greater profits in a globalized economy from which her family reaps no benefits. In short, Jasmine's dignity is violated and her labor exploited in a market economy that locks hundreds of thousands of unskilled female workers into marginal and gendered jobs, and "that is at the core of what exploitation is, to treat a person as a mere object for the use of others."[28]

In that sense, basic human capabilities cannot be realized without actualized social and economic rights–rights deferred under Roosevelt's "unfinished revolution"[29] and still glaringly absent from the American constitution.

CHILD CARE AND HUMAN RIGHTS

Jasmine's son, Che, is one year old; yet in his short life he has experienced multiple makeshift arrangements in the informal care sector: Jasmine's boyfriend's aunt, Jasmine's boyfriend's mother, Jasmine's boyfriend's grandmother, Jasmine's sister, several of Jasmine's friends, one or two neighbors, and occasionally Che's father, although there is a restraining order in place preventing him from contact with Jasmine. On one occasion Che was left unattended by one of his caregivers who was sleeping, and he tumbled down the stairs from a second floor landing, luckily escaping with only a few scratches and bruises. Jasmine's desperate search for infant child care has been fruitless, despite good support from two caseworkers at two nonprofit community agencies. She has received no public child care subsidy assistance and was literally pushed into the low-wage work force when Che was 12 weeks old by the provisions of Michigan's welfare-to-work regime. She has been sanctioned for failing to attend Work First orientations and for failing to work 40 hours a week, which, in her complicated young family life, were all but impossible to do, given her unstable existence and her lack of reliable child care. What she needs for Che is simple and clear: good quality subsidized child care. However, because there is no universal child care system in place in the United States, the care of her baby son is her private responsibility, her own private "problem," and, increasingly, her own desperate dilemma. Jasmine's life–as an emotionally troubled but resilient teen, a victim of family violence, a child inadequately mothered living in a destitute household, a runaway spending her adolescence on the streets and in group foster care–epitomizes how "'private' problems create social costs."[30]

How should we understand Jasmine and Che's life chances? Accept their destitution as one of the inevitable losses society can tolerate? It is clear that they, together with millions of other poor families, reap scant benefits from the privatized distribution of ample resources in their globally dominant nation, which ranks next to last on most social indices, including poverty alleviation. Ultimately public policies transmute into existential questions. What does it mean to be *without?* It is after all a question of daily worlds diminished–a question of losses and rights, a question of whose rights count?

How should we think about Che's rights? Good quality, stable child care, together with health care, food, and housing, constitute his most basic needs–living as he does in an impoverished household embedded in a society with staggering wealth. Why is his policy-induced destitution and impaired development not deserving of the most urgent and serious attention? Child care *could* and *should* be seen as one of his basic human rights. High quality child care would create the possibility for developing his human capabilities so that what he "is able to do and to be" may turn on a very different trajectory.

Martha Davis argues that it is time to develop a new and different framework for the lack of rights experienced by poor women and their children.[31] Viewing child care through a framework of human rights and using international covenants and international law to spur domestic policy changes exposes American deficits to international scrutiny. The Convention on the Rights of the Child (CRC), The Convention on the Elimination of All Forms of Discrimination against Women (CEDAW), and the International Covenant on Economic, Social and Cultural Rights (ICESCR) all recognize the centrality of child care and family support policies for parents and children. The United States has not ratified any of these international human rights treaties, which exert considerable moral pressure on governments to reexamine and change their policies to align with the stated goals of the treaties. In addition, the Joint Report on Social Inclusion covering the 25 European Union (EU) member states aligns with the three treaties and explicitly emphasizes those policies that promote social inclusion and access to resources and rights that combat poverty and support families: parental leave, child allowances, and child care.[32] All these measures affirmatively recognize children's rights to public child care (see Chapter 8).

Child care in a postmodern globalized world represents a new frontier, where family support policies are accorded critical importance for the well-being of mothers and children and, hence, their families. Child care as a human right makes public what heretofore has been framed as a private failure–the fundamental need for family supports to alleviate the care deficit that working mothers confront. This care deficit is thrown into dramatic relief when the United States' shoddy record on child care and parental leave is compared with other nations that have implemented universal child care and parental leave provisions for infants. The United States is clearly out of compliance with Article 18(3) of the CRC, which mandates child care assistance for working parents.[33] Turning to international law to create a visible and public discourse about the United States' domestic policy deficits and advocating for child care as a human right moves child care from a private responsibility to a very public and international human rights agenda.

Ultimately, however, rights and wrongs emerge in the ordinary daily lives of people, of women and their children, whose human capabilities create for them an open world of possibility or a diminished world of crushed hopes and battered opportunities. Shifting the discussion about women and children and the right to child care from abstract discourses to the ground on which they stand is vital. For to understand what child care (or its lack) means for a particular woman in a particular time and place, it is necessary to listen to those who have grappled with the absence of rights–whose own human capabilities, and those of their children, have been eroded. Jasmine's story, in this chapter, begins the chronicle; other mothers' stories follow, illuminating what many have chosen not to see.

> What would happen if one woman told the truth about her life?
> The world would split open.[34]

CHAPTER 2

Young, Vulnerable, and Poor: Confronting the Child Care Maze

In this chapter the lives of three young women and a grandmother are portrayed as they tenaciously attempt to access social supports and child care. One of the young women is from Michigan, and the others live in New York City. Distinctive to their lives is the constant struggle to make ends meet, while confronting an intransigent welfare-to-work regime that creates continuing obstacles. Bizarre Kafkaesque situations trap the young women and their children in a child care maze of policies and practices that harass them and violate their rights and human capabilities. As they struggle to care for their young babies in an eroded welfare system, each confronts an acute child care crisis caused by mandatory welfare-to-work requirements, lack of public resources, and denied access to good quality subsidized child care.

ANNETTE AND NICHOLAS: AGAINST ALL THE ODDS

> I've never had any experiences of day cares or anything like that
> before . . . I couldn't just throw him in any day care you know, because
> that's my son, you know. I'm not going to let somebody else hurt him.

Nineteen-year-old Annette is the White mother of a baby son born five months ago. The oldest of three children, growing up in a small town in rural Michigan, Annette suffered continuous physical abuse from her own mother and was removed from the home at 14 years old. She has spent time in a juvenile facility, two foster care placements, as well as an independent-living situation in a group home. One credit short of graduation, she dropped out of high school in twelfth grade when she became pregnant. With nowhere to go, she reluctantly moved back to her abusive mother's home, where her two younger siblings still live. After the birth of her son, Annette feared that her mother would once again become abusive towards her, saying, "I didn't want us to be there . . . I could tell it was going to get to that point again. . . . She hates me."

After she leaves her mother's home, Annette, now homeless, applies to a shelter in a well-resourced county in southeast Michigan. Savvy about how the foster care and welfare bureaucracies work, Annette is aware that by living in a shelter, she will be placed on a priority list for subsidized housing in the county, and she hopes to find an affordable apartment to rent after her 90-day stay at the shelter. Annette finds a $6-an-hour job at a local grocery store, applies for state child care subsidies, and begins to search for child care for her baby son. However, as she leaves the shelter one morning, she is hit by a car as she crosses the road. With a broken pelvic bone and injured shoulder, she is hospitalized, and with no other ready network of friends or relatives to help, Annette reluctantly sends Nicholas back to stay at her mother's home. Meanwhile, because she has moved from one county to another in Michigan, the new FIP caseworker has not yet transferred Annette's Medicaid coverage, and after she is discharged from the hospital, she cannot get an appointment to see the orthopedic surgeon. In constant pain, with no prescription drug coverage, she receives a bill of $40,000 for medical costs! With neither food stamps nor a welfare cash grant in place, Annette, now destitute, picks up her baby from her mother's home and returns to the shelter. She seeks out her grandfather for help, and he gives her his old car and some extra money to pay for diapers.

In order to be eligible for child care subsidies in Michigan, Annette must either be employed or attending a Michigan Work First program.[1] Yet how does the mother of an infant begin a job without first obtaining child care? The distorted logic of the welfare-to-work program only gets worse: Annette cannot access child care subsidies because FIP has still not opened her case in the county where the shelter is located. She seeks out help from the local nonprofit Michigan 4C child care agency and applies for a child care scholarship, while she desperately searches for child care that can accommodate the late afternoon and evening hours of her job. Using her mother as a temporary caregiver, despite her own childhood abuse, is not easy for Annette, but she has no other options open to her, short of leaving the baby in the car while she works.

Annette's ongoing saga with her caseworker at the FIP program is almost beyond belief. As a homeless teen mother with an infant, Annette has been waiting for more than four months for her own Medicaid activation (the baby's coverage was not interrupted), for child care subsidies, and a cash grant. The case manager at the shelter has called on her be-half, but to no avail:

> The caseworker doesn't return my calls. . . . She doesn't return their calls here, she doesn't do her job, and I've been waiting since, I applied on February 2nd for the cash assistance, and I still haven't seen anything . . . FIA won't even call the case manager [at the shelter] back.[2] And now I get food stamps, but that's it. And he [the baby] gets Medicaid but it's still open through [the former] County, but my Medicaid got shut off, and she can't turn my Medicaid back on until his is switched to [this] County, and that's still not done, and that's been over a month and a half, two months. . . . So I don't have any insurance . . . I went to a su-pervisor [at FIA] and she just acts like it's no big deal. She said there's nothing you can do about it, and I'm like what?

Because the FIP worker is unreachable and unresponsive, Annette has not been able to file a child-support case against the father of her baby either, saying, "If my FIA worker would do her job, I would have filed." Annette's complaints are confirmed by both the shelter and the 4C com-munity agency case managers who have tried repeatedly to intervene on her behalf. Annette is in a holding pattern, unable to access services to which she is legally entitled:

> I've complained, obviously it didn't do any good because she still has not called me. It has been probably two months since I talked to her. Yeah, two months since I last heard. And I was calling her almost every day, leaving her a message. Going up to FIA almost every day trying to talk to her . . . I'm sick of dealing with all this crap. I just want people to do what they're paid to do. . . . And, if I had a choice, I'd not go there, but he's got to have Medicaid and I've got to have whatever they decide they want to give me. I guess you have to take what you can get!

Annette is also entitled to state emergency relief (SER) because she is homeless, and the SER would enable her to pay a security deposit on a subsidized apartment for which she is now at the top of a waiting list. With her meager earnings from her minimum-wage job trickling in, Annette's resources are stretched very tight, and the 90-day maximum-stay period has expired at the shelter. The case manager has permitted her to stay for an extended time due to her recent car accident and, no doubt, to her young and desperate situation. Annette has now been at the shelter for five months. Apart from the gift of an old car at a critical moment from her grandfather and some sporadic cash from the father of her son, who refuses to pay any regular child support, Annette is the sole provider for her baby as she struggles to keep afloat.

With the help of the 4C child care agency, which provides Annette with a child care scholarship to pay for child care costs while she waits for the FIA to process her application, she finds a child care place at the home of a licensed family day care home provider who is willing to take Nicholas while she works an afternoon and evening schedule. With relief and high hopes that things will finally work out, Annette is anxious about leaving her baby but feels comfortable with the child care arrangement. Unfortunately, however, it is short-lived—after a few weeks the provider tells her she cannot take care of Nicholas any longer, and Annette is faced with a crisis: "She didn't give me a good explanation. She didn't do anything. . . . She tells me 'tomorrow's the last day I can babysit him . . . I'm sorry, I just can't do it anymore.'"

Annette's fragile world is suddenly destabilized again. Where to find another provider who will do odd-hours care? She has just found a new job, which pays $9 an hour at a data statistics firm, and without child care she is stuck. The baby goes back to her mother, which creates enormous stress for Annette: "I mean, what was I supposed to do? He had to go to and stay with my mom because I didn't have day care . . . The job I have, if I miss any hours, if I can't make them up, I get demoted to part-time. So I have to be there."

Annette's new work hours are Sundays 3:00 p.m. to 11:00 p.m. and Monday to Thursday 4:00 p.m. until midnight. She embarks on another urgent search for child care and describes the second provider who charges $250 a week:

> I had an extremely bad feeling when I left. And, I mean, she had children in high chairs that were, not old enough to like, be by themselves. She didn't go check on them or nothing. . . . And she showed me around the house, and it wasn't clean. And the bathroom, there was dirty diapers all over the counter, and I just left with a really bad feeling. And I called the complaint line, and she had a couple complaints, so then I sent out for her little complaint record, and I got it back and I would never take my child there.

While Annette is young and inexperienced as a mother, she is astutely aware of safety and quality-of-care issues, and she conscientiously follows all the advice she has been given by the local 4C child care agency in

terms of checking up on licensed providers. Her years of emotional abandonment and childhood abuse at the hands of her mother and an adolescence spent in foster care have made her suspicious of any caregiver.
Despite the urgent need she has to find another placement for Nicholas,
she turns down provider number two, citing one of the complaints that
particularly disturbed her:

> A parent walked in to pick her child up, and one of the assistants, was
> yelling at a child saying, "No, I don't love you today.". . . That got me
> right there. . . . Because no matter how old a child is, a child knows what
> I love you means. And you don't tell a child I don't love you today. That's
> horrible!

Annette continues to visit licensed providers on a list she obtains from the
4C agency. She locates a newly licensed provider who lives fairly close to
the shelter and is willing to provide evening care up until midnight. She
enrolls Nicholas and the first few days go well:

> She does what I ask. She feeds him when I ask . . . I actually got an okay
> feeling from her, but it was a little rough on the first night. He cried a
> little bit, and then the next night, his second night, he just smiled at her
> when we walked in the door. And it seems like they get along good. . . .

Annette's first impressions of the provider continue to be positive, and
she makes her expectations very clear, telling her:

> I want my child stimulated. I don't want my child sitting in a walker all
> day. I don't want my child sitting in a swing all day. I want him to be
> taught to, paid attention to, sang to, read to. Even though he's 5 months
> old, he still needs to be read to. I want him to feel like he is at home, and
> I told her, if you don't think that you can't handle that, let me know be-
> cause I don't want to waste my time. Because after the first two [provid-
> ers] I went to, I don't sugarcoat it. And she seemed perfectly fine with it.
> You know, she was like "I'm glad you let me know."

Annette worries constantly about the fact that Nicholas has "been
bounced around so much, and that he could end up having bond issues and might not be trusting," so she repeatedly questions the provider
about her long-range plans, saying she would like Nicholas to stay and
form a relationship with one caregiver, and is partially reassured by the
provider's stated commitment to stay in the child care business. While

Nicholas seems to adjust well to his new provider, Annette continues to monitor everything with concern and some mistrust, saying, "So far it's okay. I've resorted to counting how many diapers he goes with, knowing how much formula she was giving and all that, because they just, sometimes they just don't do what they're supposed to do." The new provider charges $150 a week for Nicholas. Meanwhile Annette, still dependent on the child care scholarship from the 4C agency that has been a godsend for her, continues to wait for the FIA child care subsidy, to which she is entitled and for which she has now been waiting *four* months, to be approved and activated.[3] With her current earnings of $9 an hour, Annette will still need to make a child care co-pay of $86 a week[4] when and if her child care subsidies come through, as the child care scholarship is a temporary support. As Annette thinks about a future beyond the shelter, she worries further about how she will manage to provide for her family: "I've got insurance to pay. I'll have the child care bills to pay. I'll have all that. It's going to be hard. I mean, it's going to take all the money I have, but I'll have to do it because, you know, he needs a place to live. He can't live in no shelter all his life."

From the cold world of demographics, Annette is just another statistic—a teen mother and a high school dropout, an abused child, a juvenile detainee, a foster-care youth—all the odds appear stacked against her. Yet she displays a courageous tenacity that is rooted in her deep attachment to her baby:

> I mean, I wouldn't give it up, but then again, I'd rather it be a little bit easier and a little bit later in my life because it would be easier. But when I look at him, and he smiles at me, it's all better again. Every time it gets bad, I just sit and play with him, and it all changes. It's not like it's horrible any more, because for a while you get really down. And you're like God, this sucks; this is horrible, and then you know . . . you just look at him and he smiles and you're like, it's all for him. It's not like it's just for me anymore. . . .

Annette plans to complete her GED; however, due to state funding cuts of adult education, not many places offer high school completion programs.[5] Annette hopes to enroll at a community college that offers GED completion, and then apply to the college to become certified as a medical technician. She believes that a hospital career will mean higher earnings and good benefits. Annette has grit and determination and very badly wants to make a better life for herself and Nicholas; a life she never experienced with her own mother, saying, "I gotta keep it together for him . . . he is everything to me. He's my inspiration."

A few weeks later, however, when Annette arrives at the child care provider's home at midnight to pick up Nicholas, no one comes to the door and the house is in darkness. Repeated knocking and banging and shouting bring no results; Annette panics, and hysterical from fear, calls the police. They arrive and find the provider and Nicholas asleep. Relieved that her baby is safe, but angry and mistrustful of the provider, Annette takes Nicholas and embarks on yet another urgent search for child care. This time she keeps Nicholas with her and calls in sick at work—and the dreaded circle of instability begins anew.

The ongoing saga of Annette's frantic search for good child care and Nicholas's disrupted child care placements is, unfortunately, not an unusual phenomenon in Michigan, or the rest of the states. The inability of Annette to access child care subsidies, as well as obtain Medicaid for herself and the cash grant to which she is entitled, is part of the routine indifference to low-income parents' needs that characterizes the welfare climate in Michigan. In earlier case studies of low-income welfare-reliant mothers conducted in 1999–2000, Kahn and Polakow found the same systematic neglect of clients' needs, improper denials of child care subsidies, long waits for actual child care subsidy payments, and a hostile climate that does not support education and schooling, but rather coerces young parents into low-wage and, ultimately, unstable jobs without ensuring access to decent quality child care.[6] Annette, as a young teen mother in Michigan, should be completing her high school diploma, but instead she is left to fend for herself as she and her child flail around in the private child care market. Homeless, recovering from a car accident, still without health insurance, denied the right to take care of her own baby, Annette has great difficulty finding stable infant care that is both affordable and of decent quality.[7] There are 460,000 young children under 6 in Michigan with parents in the labor force, and of those, almost 40% are living in single-parent families; yet there are currently only enough licensed slots to serve 75% of the state's children in need of care,[8] and the needs are particularly acute for infants and for those children needing odd-hours care. Average prices for full-time infant care in licensed family day care home settings in Michigan average $120 a week, but costs are considerably higher in southeast Michigan where Annette is located.[9] In addition, not all providers will accept children who are on subsidies. Only 47% of licensed centers and just over 50% of licensed family child care homes in the state accept subsidies.[10] Without the temporary lifeline offered by the 4C scholarship, Annette would be unable to keep her baby.

For teen mothers such as Annette and Jasmine (see Chapter 1), there are few existing supportive public infrastructures in place, and without the interventions of overextended nonprofit agencies that have helped them, their fragile family units would collapse. The fact that Adult Education in Michigan has been steadily eroded and that class offerings have been reduced by 50% in a state hard hit by massive budget cuts to K–12 education,[11] points to the public neglect and the lack of human capital investment in young women with children who desperately need an education in order to have any chance of making it out of poverty.[12]

Annette's urgent need for stable odd-hours child care, housing, and educational opportunities are all necessary prerequisites for her to develop a stable family with a chance of making it. Without those public care and education provisions in place, Annette and her baby remain in jeopardy. Repeated disruption of child care placements will take their toll on Nicholas, a problem that Annette, because of her own destabilized childhood, is fighting to avoid. With a former boyfriend who refuses to take any responsibility for his son and an abusive mother, Annette's only supports have been the shelter and the child care agency. However, they are temporary and cannot be long-term solutions. Annette's experience as a poor young mother in Michigan is not unusual: there are ready parallels across the country.

FRANCESCA AND TAMERON: A KAFKAESQUE QUEST

It's child care, child care, child care. . . . I go to the caseworker with all the information, keep going back, keep going back. "Oh come back this day, come back, come back, come back.". . . I called numerous times. No one got back to me. I didn't get to speak to anyone. . . . I didn't hear anything about my case, then I am denied. Why am I denied? "Oh, we don't know. If you want you can reapply. . . ."

Francesca is a 21-year-old former community college student with a 10-month-old son, Tameron. Originally from the West Indies, she came to the United States with her mother as a young girl and has grown up in New York City. Francesca was in the second year of an associate's degree, with a major in computer programming, when she became pregnant. She left school and a part-time medical records job, where she was earning $11.50 an hour, just before her baby was born. In March 2003, soon after Tameron's birth, Francesca went to apply for child care subsidies so she could return to school and to work, but for the past nine months she has endured a never-ending stream of bureaucratic errors, delays, and denials from the Human Resource Administration (HRA) in New York City. When pregnant, she became eligible for Medicaid health coverage, but her coverage was cut after the baby was born, despite the fact that she was legally entitled to receive it. Although eligible for food stamps, Francesca never received any until late November, nine months after her son was born, and then only because of the intervention of a legal-aid attorney.

Francesca has been fighting the "system" now for nine months, and in the process has had to move into her mother's small one-bedroom apartment because she and her son were on the verge of homelessness. For Francesca, responsible for a baby she cannot support, doubled up in her mother's tiny apartment, the way out of her predicament is access to affordable child care, as without it, she can neither work nor go back to school. "My situation is right now, I'm unable to, you know, go out and find a job or go to school because I have no one to take care of my son to do so."

Francesca's mother works full-time, attends community college classes at night, and works at an internship all weekend, so she is unable to assist with child care. Tameron's father refuses to take any responsibility for his son, but his paternal grandmother, who has multiple health problems, has helped Francesca out financially from time to time. Francesca's grandfather is 87 years old and too frail to take care of an active baby. Her friends are all working and in school, and apart from occasional babysitting, cannot help either. Francesca is stuck:

> I get really frustrated. Because I'm like, Oh, I have a young baby and I can't do anything for him. You know, I see things out there that I want to get for him, and I can't. I have no one to watch him. I want to get back, you know, start back working. I want to go to school. It's really frustrating. I'm like, I'm a single mother. You know, I at least I thought I would have help from the father . . . but he is another story in itself—he's not doing anything to help!

Francesca went to court to try and get court-ordered child-support payments from her son's father, describing him as "a lost cause," and someone "I can't depend on." The child support took months to work through the system, and the father has recently been ordered to pay $50 a month in child support. But Francesca has not yet seen a penny, and if she succeeds in getting any form of public assistance or child care subsidies, the child support money will be used by the HRA welfare agency to recoup any public subsidies, "so basically," says Francesca, "the money is not going to be coming to me." She describes her long and frustrating saga of trying to get public assistance and child care subsidies:

> The first time I went [to the welfare office] they said, "Oh, you cannot, you cannot get any help, you have your mother." Like, I'm over age, you know, I'm 21. "Oh, well, we can't help you." I'm like "okay." I went back and researched. I went back. I kept going back. I mean my mother, yes, she helps me out, but she cannot do everything. I need a little help. I paid my taxes, so I feel I deserve my help. I need help. I deserve to get some right now.

Informed about her rights, and determined to access food stamps, Medicaid for herself, public assistance, and child care subsidies, Francesca persists, but it is only when she has to go to the emergency room in the summer of 2003 for an eye infection and receives help from the hospital social worker, that her Medicaid coverage is reinstated. Inexplicably, she had been cut off after the birth of her son, although he continued to receive services. Francesca describes the motions she is put through each time she applies and reapplies for services:

> It's very frustrating, to go back over and over in the space, and they always tell you to come back. You go today to fill out an application, they tell you come back next week. You gotta come back, come back, and you stay there the whole day. . . . The whole day they keep you there. You are waiting. They give you appointments. Oh, an 8:30 appointment, you end up leaving 4:30. Or you might just get called at 4:30, after the whole day. You know, they're taking advantage of people . . . they treat you bad, they're very nasty . . . they're not respectful at all . . . I don't know why these people have jobs. . . . You know the phone rings, no one answers the phone, no one knows who the supervisor is. . . . What's really going on? I have other things to do. I don't want to stay here all day. I just came for you to tell me what's going on with my child care!

Francesca finds herself caught in a New York system in complete disarray. Former Mayor Giuliani's much publicized welfare reform plan to rid the city of " dependency" in the late 1990s led to a string of lawsuits that accused the HRA of willfully preventing eligible clients from obtaining any form of public assistance.[13] In March 2003, when Francesca did try to access public assistance and child care subsidies, she found herself confronting that same institutional culture of refusal and indifferent regard for clients' legitimate needs:

> I mean, I went there, I said I need help with child care, that's my main concern right now, so I could actually go out there, try to find me a decent job, try to get back in school, to take care of my responsibilities. . . . In order for me to do anything, I need help. I need someone to be able to watch my child. I can't afford to pay for a babysitter, if I have no job! Before I went there, I researched different child care providers and, you know, got the information so it would not take such a long process. I did everything. I provided all information they asked me for, and up to this day, I got no response.

After Francesca fills out the first child care subsidy application, she hears nothing. After calling the caseworker repeatedly, several weeks pass with no response, and Francesca becomes increasingly frustrated. She pays many visits to the welfare office and leaves a string of messages. After two months, in June 2003, the caseworker calls her and tells her to come in to the office to see her as more forms need to be filled out:

> I went in, and spoke to the receptionist. They don't let you speak to the person in the back, only the receptionist. Spoke to them, I said, "Well, Miss Smith told me to come here, and she needs to speak to me about the child care forms that I have to bring in." "Oh, just leave the forms." I said, "Well, she told me she needed to speak to me face-to-face." "Well, just leave the forms." I was like, "Um, no, I want to see her." The receptionist says, "Hold on, let me go in the back and see if she needs to see you." Comes back, she says, "Oh, she said to leave it in a envelope. You don't need to stay. Just leave the forms and you can go."

After Francesca reluctantly leaves the forms without ever making contact with the caseworker, she waits. Weeks pass and once again, she begins calling the caseworker:

> I'm calling her on her phone. The phone rings and no one ever answers. Ring! Ring! Ring! Ring! Ring! No one answers the phone. I am waiting, calling, calling, calling, waiting—no answer. No mail, nothing in the mail saying, you know, they denied the case—nothing. After going back

numerous times, that's when I find out that they closed the case, but no one told me they closed the case. And no on told me why they closed the case!

It is now September and Francesca finds herself caught in a classic Catch 22. She has found a job that she is qualified for at a medical records office that pays $11 an hour, but she cannot take a job until she locates affordable child care. She has found child care too, at a licensed family day care home. The child care costs $140 a week and Francesca clearly cannot afford it without partial child care subsidies, commenting, "That would be breaking my pockets." Francesca has done her homework in locating this child care setting. She has visited many and settled on this one because of its reputation and the quality of the care:

> A lot of people try to get their children there . . . like they want to have their child there because she's good. She's good—a very good lady. It's clean, the place is really clean, you know! I mean it's decent and it's expensive. . . . I went, I sat there, and I, you know, scoped out the place. Talked to her, she said she takes the program [child care subsidy program]. I made sure of all of that, and the hours, and, you know, fees—she's really strict. . . . There's only certain people that could pick up the child. If your name is not on the list, you can't. . . . Yeah, she's very careful with them. Safety is the number one thing for me, especially with my first child.

Francesca, now desperate to hold on to the child care slot and with a potential job at hand, goes for help to a nonprofit low-income advocacy group in the city. They provide her with a legal-aid attorney who promptly demands a hearing on Francesca's behalf. Francesca is sent a hearing date and waits the whole day to be called, but no one meets with her. The attorney files again, and a court hearing is set to force the welfare department to explain why Francesca has been denied public assistance, Medicaid, and child care subsidies. The attorney's intervention brings results:

> And, you know, they said, "Oh we have no information here stating why the case was denied. We don't know why that happened," and you know, they want to adjourn the case. But I found that I won, and they sent me a letter. I got a letter stating that I won the case, and that the public assistance office is supposed to contact me. I just received the letter last week.

After Francesca receives the letter, she is told to appear in court a week later, and she finds out, to her relief, that the case indeed has been decided in her favor and that she will receive food stamps and child care subsidies, as well as some cash assistance. Unfortunately, it is now already December and the job that Francesca hoped to obtain has already been filled, and there is no available slot at the child care setting she carefully selected in early fall. However, Francesca is hopeful that she will be able to enroll her son after the New Year, if any slots open up. Meanwhile she needs to reapply to the community college for spring and search for another job and for another child care place as a backup. She still hopes to find a job in a hospital working with data entry or medical records, as she has a good prior work record in that area.

During this period Francesca continues to live at her mother's one-bedroom apartment, which she describes as "not healthy" and "very rough," particularly now that her son is so active and walking. Her mother works very long hours, and the cramped living situation is taking a toll on mother and daughter, creating stress and strain in their relationship. Through it all, however, Tameron has been a source of constant joy for both mother and grandmother. He has a sunny disposition and appears to be a bright and healthy baby who is already saying his first words. So far, to Francesca's credit, he has emerged unscathed from his mother's ordeal.

As a young woman who has had to put her life on hold since the birth of her son and as a mother who wants the best possible child care for him, Francesca is angry about the treatment she has received at the hands of the welfare bureaucracy and cannot understand why she was initially denied child care subsidies. When asked to reflect on the past 10 months, she replies:

> Me, personally, I don't want to be on public assistance, to sit home, and, you know, collect small bits of money. . . . I want to work for my own, I want to work for way more than they want to give me to take care of myself and my child. If they would have a heart, and actually go through a day or a week of what we single parents who don't have it, go through—then they would look at things differently. And maybe they'd actually say, "Well, we should do more to help them get on their feet, do better for themselves." I mean, I heard stories, I heard stories before, people complaining about the system and the child care, and they can't get this and they can't get that, and I always thought, Oh, man! But me going through it myself? Then I actually can say I walked in their shoes. I know.

As one who has always prided herself on holding a job, even through high school, Francesca has found the whole process of applying for assistance demeaning and emotionally exhausting. The surreal experience of going around in circles trying to access public assistance supports that she was legally entitled to, initially losing both a job and a child care slot on the grounds that she should be working and therefore was not entitled to assistance, has left Francesca bitter and frustrated about the wasted months and ongoing incompetence and mistreatment. Now that Francesca has succeeded in obtaining court-ordered child care subsidies and public assistance with the help of her attorney, she has a single-minded vision: complete her associate's degree, find a decent-paying job, and move to an apartment with her son. She credits her son for inspiring her to persistently fight for her rights, and for *his* rights, during the long 10-month battle with a seemingly intransigent system:

> Giving up on doing this is like giving up on my son, and I can't do that. I have to work hard and fight hard too, you know, to take care of him and get what I need. I used to work, I paid my taxes. So it should be not just me taking things—I mean I should be getting back from what I put in, what I've been working for. My son deserves that!

Francesca's tenacity has finally paid off, and she fully intends to take advantage of every benefit coming her way: the vital child care subsidies as well as food stamps, Medicaid, and cash assistance, so "I can get back on my feet." With determination, a strong work ethic, clear educational goals, and an unwavering commitment to find good child care for her child, Francesca faces the daunting challenges ahead.

And the challenges most certainly are daunting. Characterized by the Welfare Law Center as a child care system "badly broken" and "in crisis,"[14] the city's plethora of contradictory rules and regulations creates innumerable obstacles for parents and their children. Although New York City runs the largest child care subsidy system in the country, it is dysfunctional and fragmented, with the Agency for Child Development (ACD) administering public funds for child care subsidies, including Head Start services, for low-income parents *not* on welfare, and the Human Resource Administration (HRA) operating a separate child care subsidy system for welfare recipients. In addition, there is also a prekindergarten program serving 4-year-olds with priority ostensibly given to low-income children, and these programs operate from community-based centers that often house other separately subsidized programs. Lack of access is a chronic problem, and because there is no unified, centrally coordinated system, parents encounter multiple barriers as they run from agency to agency to submit applications, often missing work or school or both, while experiencing misinformation, frequent inexplicable denials, and long delays in receiving subsidies.[15] There are currently 38,000 children on child care waiting lists for subsidized child care in New York City, and Francesca's son, Tameron, is only one of them.

Chaudry's ethnographic study conducted in four of New York City's poorest neighborhoods also points to the crisis of care in New York City[16]–a crisis that has been exacerbated since the passage of welfare "reform," as welfare-to-work programs have forced low-income mothers to work at low-paying, unstable jobs. Chaudry chronicles the survival strategies of low-income mothers as they struggle to work and find child care for their young children in New York City. Like most of the nation, New York has opted for cheap child care provisions for poor children, while their parents, mostly single mothers, are coerced into the low-wage labor force. The informal care sector, where most poor children land, is notoriously inferior,[17] and yet welfare "reform" across the country has focused on promoting child care policies that favor nonprofessional informal, custodial-care arrangements. The mothers in Chaudry's study experienced great difficulty locating subsidized slots in licensed child care centers; hence most of their infants and young children were relegated to "care that is cheap, and often of dubious quality,"[18] experiencing fragmented and disrupted child care arrangements, with the majority of children going through five or more primary child care placements in their first four years of life. Many of these placements were terminated because of the mothers' concerns about child care quality and the conflicts they had with unsatisfactory child care providers.

With tens of thousands of children on New York City's waiting list for child care subsidies, it is clear how a fragmented and dysfunctional bureaucracy, operating in tandem with harsh and punitive welfare policies, threatens the well-being of infants and young children whose development is impaired by inferior and unstable care. In the following story, Carmina, a mother and a grandmother, resists a work placement and fights for the right to take care of her baby grandson so that her teenage daughter can complete high school.

CARMINA, MICHELLE, AND THE BABY:
A GRANDMOTHER FIGHTS FOR THEIR RIGHTS

> I just wanted to take care of my grandson so my daughter can finish high school . . . and my [welfare] worker tells me, "We're going to pull you back in, and we're going to give you an assignment," and I was "No you're not. I need to take care of my grandson and I'll call for another hearing."

Carmina, a divorced Puerto Rican mother of three children, is a survivor of domestic violence, and now, at 40 years old, grandmother to her teenage daughter's baby son. With no child support to speak of, Carmina has raised her children alone, cycled on and off welfare, and worked at low-wage jobs, while always aspiring to complete her GED "so I could show my kids I did it . . . that I managed to get my diploma." Carmina currently volunteers at the office of a social and racial justice advocacy coalition in New York City. Carmina's 17-year-old son, Joseph, and 19-year-old daughter, Michelle, still live at home with her, together with Michelle's 7-month-old son, Matthew.

Since the birth of Matthew, Carmina has been battling New York City's HRA trying to secure welfare benefits for Michelle and the baby, as well as the right to stay at home and take care of her grandson while Michelle, in twelfth grade, completes high school. Carmina and Michelle's ongoing encounters with a hostile caseworker, and the continuing attempts by the welfare agency to coerce both mother and daughter into the Work Experience Program (WEP) have created enormous stress for the family. From her perspective as both grandmother and mother, Carmina is determined that her daughter will have the opportunity that she never had–to graduate from high school and go to college. Carmina is now unemployed, after being laid off from a factory job several months ago, and with her unemployment benefits about to expire, she has applied for welfare benefits for her family and the new baby. She relates what happened as she tried to plan ahead while her daughter was pregnant:

> I went to the [welfare] center when my daughter was pregnant and asked them, I tried to apply for child care money for her so we could be on record that she's having a baby. . . . So I explain that she wants to finish high school and I will do the child care.

The response of the welfare office is to track down Michelle and order her into a WEP placement, despite the fact that she is a high school student. Carmina is outraged:

> We received a letter saying to come in to BEGIN [the job training and placement program] and it was like, why you want my daughter? She's 18 years old, she's going to high school, and she's a full-time student. You can't touch her, that's illegal. They say bring me a note saying that she's a full-time student, this and that, and the other. I said, "Okay, fine." As soon as she became 19 they were after her again I was like "She is still in high school. You're not touching her; she's going to finish high school. I'm not letting you touch her. I'm not letting you destroy her life." So it's a battle. Yeah, it's been a big battle. Because they're doing this, taking out teenagers—they're supposed to be in high school, but if they're not doing good, they take them into the WEP program.

After the birth of the baby, Carmina returns to the welfare office seeking benefits for herself and her daughter. She is informed that she will now be required to enroll in a WEP placement in exchange for welfare benefits. Carmina protests, arguing that for Michelle to finish high school, she needs child care and that *she* (Carmina) should be permitted to take care of the baby:

> I told them I can't because my daughter just finished giving birth, and I had to take care of my grandson. They tell me I need to be assigned to a work assignment, or to do something. I need to be enrolled in something—you know, the HRA programs. At that time I kept going back and forth with them to get out of this because I didn't trust anyone with my grandson.

Carmina's previous WEP placement was picking up trash and weeds on an interstate highway in return for welfare benefits. Now, with her daughter obviously in need of child care, she would like to be approved as the child care provider, thereby fulfilling her work requirement and ensuring her grandson is well taken care of. Michelle and the baby have not received any benefits yet, because the welfare caseworker tells Carmina that, as head of household, she is the only one entitled to benefits for the family. With her unemployment benefits at an end, Carmina knows that they cannot manage on monthly welfare benefits of $400 a month plus food stamps, as the rent on her apartment alone is $501 a month. But the caseworker informs Carmina that her daughter cannot live in the same household and receive her own benefits; nor can Carmina get paid for child care and count that as her mandatory work activity.

> My worker tells me, "We're not paying because you fall under the same rules and it's the same budget.". . . And then she's saying I cannot get paid to take care of my grandson because we're in the same household, and "We're going to pull you back in to a WEP assignment.". . . I was like, "No you're not. I need to take care of my grandson, and you're not. I'll call for another hearing. Because my grandson comes first." There's a lot of crazies out there and there's been a lot of, you know, horror stories over here about people taking care of your kid and suddenly they wind up dead. "No," I told her, "I want him, I want to take care of him!"

Fearful of being denied welfare benefits, in need of extra resources to support Michelle and the baby, and desperate to keep the baby under her care, Carmina reluctantly arranges for Michelle to move in with a relative she does not like or trust, but hopes that the move will be temporary in order to create two households with two sets of benefits that will allow her to register as caregiver. But Michelle is distraught away from home:

> My daughter was crying, she was very upset . . . and I would call her every night. . . . And it was hard for her . . . when you're living like this, stepping on their toes or in their way, it's like a lot of conflict. And there was a lot of cursing over there, and the baby would hear it, and she didn't want no cursing in front of the baby, and she felt very uncomfortable. . . . And that wasn't healthy for her, she wasn't eating right and stuff like that. . . . She was out of the house for about a month and half to two months. And it was hard you know!

During this time Michelle becomes very distressed, overwhelmed by the multiple demands of high school, teen parenting, and living away from home in an emotionally abusive relative's household; she develops bleeding ulcers and starts missing school. Meanwhile, the welfare caseworker, annoyed by Carmina's persistence, suddenly accuses her of "fraud" and threatens an investigation. With child care for her baby suddenly in question, Michelle anxious and fearful, begins to look for other options. She describes her fruitless quest:

> But welfare, they don't tell you, like, they don't tell you have a right to it [child care]. They're supposed to give you a book of the providers. They don't tell you nothing. They're supposed to give you that. They don't let

you know about things like that! . . . And I hear the horror stories, like on the news and stuff about what happens in day care and stuff and I don't want none of that. . . . So I was calling, calling, I was calling the father's mother and other people, I had no one to turn to . . . no help anywhere you turn, no help except for my Mom.

Anxious to keep her daughter from dropping out of school, Carmina continues to take care of the baby and returns to the legal-aid attorney, who tells Carmina that "Michelle's right is to go to school, she's still underage, move her back in, get her back in your apartment—I'm going to try and get you a separate suffix." Michelle moves back home and the attorney files for a hearing to request a separate suffix attached to Carmina's case number, which would allow Michelle and the baby to live with Carmina and receive their own benefits. When the hearing takes place, the judge orders the welfare office to create a separate suffix for Michelle so that she can receive her benefits. Carmina is relieved and triumphant but must still battle her caseworker:

She [the judge] said that, no problem, she can have her own separate suffix and you can take care of the baby because she's underage. She can be underage while's she's 19. When she's 21, she's considered of age. So I said okay, so we got the paperwork going, and now I'm starting to take care of the baby. But when I went to my worker, she tells me, "No, we're going to pull you back in, we're going to give you an assignment." And I told her, "You can't do that! We had a fair hearing, you can't put me on an assignment because I have to take care of my grandson. I already won my fair hearing!"

At this point Carmina has won an important victory: her daughter and baby can continue to live with her, and Michelle will receive separate benefits. As a consequence of the hearing, Carmina may be deferred from a WEP placement to take care of the baby until her daughter graduates from school in six months time. Still at issue is whether Carmina can continue to take care of the baby after her daughter completes high school. That will hinge on whether a judge at the next hearing decides that Carmina can be listed as her daughter's child care provider and be paid through the child subsidy program, because the caseworker has refused to approve Carmina as a child care provider for her grandson. Carmina wants her daughter to have the opportunity to go to college—a choice Carmina never had as a teen mother—and is determined to continue fighting for her right to take care of her grandson, to whom she is very attached, saying, "I don't want nobody else to take care of him."

Michelle, who has received no support at her high school, has suffered throughout the year's ordeal. After she temporarily dropped out of high school for three months, she had trouble gaining readmission and found out she had failed all her classes because of her three month absence. In order to graduate Michelle needs to retake her classes. She angrily describes the treatment she received:

> You get discouragement every which way you look. And my high school wanted to kick me out because I was getting of age, and being I had left, my grades didn't carry over, so because I had taken off those two, three months, my grades didn't really count. . . . But, it was like, so discouraging to hear that they wanted to kick me out. . . . It was like everywhere you go, people putting you down. My teachers were telling me I'm not going to make it, I'm not going to amount to anything. Teachers aren't supposed to do that to you. They're supposed to teach you. The counselor saying that I'm not going to make it and having a baby is harder to manage with school. . . . I was failing all my classes. Because I didn't care. But, now, because I'm doing it for someone else, I want to do it, I'm doing it for my son. I'm pulling those grades for him, because I stay up 'til 2 doing my homework.

Michelle, a smart student, has pulled up her grades and is back on track to graduate in June. She wants to go to college and become a veterinarian, which Carmina proudly supports. But she is under constant surveillance by the welfare office and has to offer proof that she is still enrolled in school each semester, and her caseworker threatens that she will be placed in a WEP assignment as soon as she graduates. Michelle feels the Panopticon gaze at her shoulder constantly:

> I worry about welfare so much. I wonder of ways to get out of welfare and stuff like that, because I know you need it, but I wish there was some way that we didn't have to have it, and still manage. After June comes, and I graduate, I guarantee that that day that school lets out, they're going to come get me . . . they're going to pick me up real fast.

Carmina, however, has other plans for her daughter. As an active member of a low-income parents rights coalition, she is well aware of the recent Davila class-action settlement that reversed the Giuliani Administration's intransigent position denying welfare recipients the right to count education as a work activity and coercing them into WEP assignments.[19] The Davila settlement essentially granted recipients the right to time-limited vocational or postsecondary education. Carmina wants Michelle to start college immediately after graduation, so she escapes welfare's reach. Michelle, encouraged by her mother, has already signed up for enrollment information at a number of community colleges, saying "I want all the help I can get out there . . . because you can't go anywhere with just a high school diploma." But her visceral fear of welfare as an omnipresent stalker, lying in wait to pounce, is a source of continuing stress:

> I want to be a vet. But I don't think welfare's going to let me. Because they keep trying to put me in (WEP) every six months. And they won't let my Mom take care of the baby. I don't understand why I have to find someone I don't know who could be real bad, when my Mom is right here and asked them to let her do it. And I don't know . . . I know there is supposed to be a way that I'm supposed to go to college. . . . But I don't know if they're going to let me because welfare doesn't like it when people go get educated.

With Michelle almost through high school and aspiring to college, and with her mother temporarily approved to take care of her son, Michelle has a six-month reprieve. Carmina, however, is readying herself for the next battle to come. She is actively working with the legal-aid attorney on her case, determined to assert her right to take care of her grandson and her daughter's right to go to college after graduation. As she puts it, "It's wonderful taking care of him and seeing him grow . . . why should I have to do a WEP placement when I can take care of the baby and help my daughter go to college?" And why not?

The distorted policy dynamics that emerge from Carmina and Michelle's life situation are disturbing. In order to promote family stability and provide Michelle with educational opportunities so that she has a fighting chance of becoming self-sufficient, it makes eminent sense for Carmina's plan to be implemented. With a college degree, Michelle would be able to obtain a professional job, and her son would be ready to enter kindergarten after a stable period with his grandmother. Yet under New York City's aggressive welfare-to-work program, multiple obstacles stand between her and a college education. Giuliani, who pledged "to end welfare by the end of this century completely," derided public assistance as a "perverted social philosophy."[20] As Jason Turner, Giuliani's Welfare Commissioner, put it, poor people need to "live on what you get, and if you run out, figure out what to do until your next paycheck"![21] New York City has effectively terminated a half million people (two-thirds of whom are children) from welfare assistance. In 1995, when Giuliani implemented his controversial policies, a year ahead of the federal welfare legislation of 1996, there were 1 million welfare recipients in New York City. By 2001, that number had dropped to 500,000.[22] In addition, college enrollment among welfare recipients declined by 80% during that same period, as the City's Human Resource Administration required all "able-bodied" welfare recipients to enroll in WEP assignments for a minimum of 35 hours a week to receive any benefits. In Carmina's case, it is ironic that her previous WEP assignment of picking up trash on an interstate highway would enable her to receive welfare benefits, yet taking care of her infant grandson would not. Rather, under the New York City welfare regime, unless Carmina wins the next legal battle, baby Matthew is destined to be one of the thousands of New York City's young children on a waiting list for subsidized care, most likely inferior and substandard, as his development is sacrificed on the altar of welfare "reform."

Carmina has been a central pillar of support for her daughter throughout this ordeal, enabling her to complete high school secure in the knowledge that Matthew is being cared for by his grandmother. Empowered by the low-income parents' advocacy coalition that has assisted her throughout the long family ordeal, Carmina continues to volunteer there several times a week, always accompanied by her grandson. Carmina recognizes the as-yet unmaterialized threats to Matthew's well-being, once her daughter completes high school. For now, however, he is secure as she prepares to mobilize for the impending battle over WEP and child care for Matthew.

LIFE UNDER THE WELFARE REGIME

For Annette, Francesca, and Michelle—three young mothers with infants—enormous amounts of physical and psychological energy, as well as hours and sometimes days of wasted time, have all been expended trying to secure child care, which, in many other societies, would be considered a basic human right. The unequal "human capabilities" that result severely circumscribe these young women's life chances, and their circumstances of poverty and inequality are directly related to the absence of social and economic rights and consequent lack of social care provisions in their lives. Running through the child care maze, desperately trying to make sense of welfare-to-work mandates that do not serve their interests, they have encountered escalating and often incorrigible demands, withheld benefits, harassment, and punitive sanctions that serve to disable them as citizens.[23] Their experiences under the current welfare regime conjure up images of the sinister and senseless world of Kafka's Joseph K, arrested for a nameless crime he did not commit and subjected to escalating and bizarre threats against his personhood and dignity, while he continues to believe that, as a citizen, he has recourse to the "Law." But as the priest tells him, "before the Law stands a door-keeper on guard. . . . From hall to hall, keepers stand at every door, one more powerful than the other," and the door never opens![24] Poor single mothers frequently inhabit a postmodern version of Joseph K's milieu. Critical support programs such as child care are weighted down with layers of obstructive red tape, practices of harassment and delay tactics are widespread,[25] and the National Campaign for Jobs and Income Support reports a pervasive problem of "endemic lawlessness" existing in states across the country, where a "culture of indifference, arbitrariness, and intimidation characterizes states' implementation of these programs."[26]

Frances Fox Piven argues that the Work First policies integral to welfare "reform" were part of a business-legislative compact destined to create a pool of captive and disciplined low-wage women workers forced to work at any job, no matter how bad the hours and how low the pay, in order to prevent their families from falling into destitution.[27] Under the guise of ending welfare dependency and promoting a "work ethic," poor single mothers are thus reduced to little more than indentured servitude, robbed of the power to make choices in their own and their children's best interests. Gwendolyn Mink characterizes the impact of welfare "reform" as transferring "poor single mothers from the welfare state to a police state," as they are forced to "purchase their families' short-term survival by sacrificing basic rights the rest of us take for granted."[28]

The resistance to sacrificing their basic rights and their persistence in seeking out child care and other support services is a thread that runs through all these mothers' lives. The active involvement and unwavering support of Carmina, and her determination to resist the threats and demands of New York City's WEP program, have been central to Michelle's capacity to complete high school, and both Francesca and Annette have doggedly persisted in their efforts to obtain child care, Medicaid, and other services. None of the mothers received child support or any other reliable or steady assistance from the fathers of their children, who had literally abandoned their sons. In both Michelle and Francesca's situations, it was the grandmothers of their children who stepped in to fill a gaping void.

It is also clear how quickly a fragile family unit can become destabilized. For Annette, gritty and determined, it was homelessness, third-shift jobs, and untrustworthy child care providers and the inexplicable failure of the welfare bureaucracy to respond to her acute needs. For Francesca, a competent student and able worker, loss of a job and no child care led to eviction and a move to her mother's cramped apartment, and the constant stress and regret of a wasted year as she was immobilized by a welfare regime that would not grant her the benefits to which she was entitled. For vulnerable young Michelle, a teen pregnancy led to dropping out of school and a welfare-induced move to a relative's abusive household, and a visceral fear of a welfare system out to "get her," generating fear, anxiety, and bleeding ulcers during a critical period in her adolescence. In all three cases senseless and harsh policy regulations threatened the well-being of both young mothers and their babies.

The encounters that all three young women had with the welfare system in both Michigan and New York resulted in a "damned if you do and damned if you don't" reality. With their rights violated by their respective state welfare agencies, it was only through the interventions of legal-aid attorneys and nonprofit community advocates that some redress was initiated. As U.S. citizens presumably growing up with the expectation of some measure of justice and equality before the law, their encounters instead led them around in endless circles, denied legal benefits to which they were entitled.

In all three families access to quality child care emerged as a critical factor in securing family viability. Yet, as we saw in Annette's situation (as well as Jasmine's in Chapter 1), low-income and less-educated mothers are typically concentrated in low-paying jobs with nonstandard hours,[29] and these jobs generate a growing crisis of unmet child care needs. Family and job characteristics are clear predictors of nonstandard-hours employment, and in the wake of welfare "reform," more and more poor women with young children move from welfare to these types of jobs, leading Presser and Cox to ask, "What does this imply for the care of children?"[30] Unfortunately the answer is most likely unstable, multiple, makeshift child care arrangements;[31] and in times of budget cuts and economic downturns, it is low-income families who bear the brunt.

What Annette, Francesca, and Michelle are able *to do and to be* as young mothers will hinge, in no small measure, on access to stable and high quality child care. Their opportunities to pursue higher education will be dependent on child care, and higher education, in turn, is critical to their capacity to secure family self-sufficiency and become autonomous persons with some control over their lives and their children's well-being.[32]

CHAPTER 3

Struggling and Juggling: School, Work, and Child Care

Melissa and Kim, two young single mothers in Iowa, have it better than most; they are in school pursuing college degrees and are receiving support from Iowa's Promise Jobs Program, which provides partial child care subsidies and permits two years of postsecondary education to count as work activities.[1] Yet despite Iowa's provision of time-limited opportunities for education and training, and its seemingly less harsh and somewhat more flexible welfare-to-work policies,[2] in comparison to those of New York and Michigan, these single student mothers are still poor and stretched, and they struggle to keep their young families afloat. Time demands for parenting, for studying, for working, are often overwhelming, and the ability to make it hinges on access to continued welfare benefits, child care subsidies, and supportive informal networks, as well as federal student loans. When child care is problematic, or when children get sick and a job is on the line, or worse, when Mom is ill, the tenuous balance tips, and family stability is threatened. Similarly, when Iowa's Promise Jobs 24-month time limits threaten one's capacity to stay in school, the most carefully crafted plan may be derailed. In the following two narratives of student mothers we see how difficult it is to complete a college education while living an uncertain day-to-day existence with young children.

MELISSA AND HER CHILDREN:
A DEFICIT OF TIME AND RESOURCES

> Sick children have been a real hindrance with my job . . . then my baby-sitter, you know, if my children are sick, she can't take them. . . . I wish I could quit my job so that I could just go to school and take care of my kids and be able to have time.

Thirty-one-year-old Melissa is the White mother of 6-year-old James and a baby daughter, Jenna. She has encountered continuing job problems because of work absences due to her baby's recurrent ear infections. She and the children are temporarily living with her elderly grandmother, as she has been unable to find affordable housing. Melissa is a third-year university student majoring in a technical arts program and is determined to complete her degree and graduate now that she has returned to school. But the past few years have been unstable and precarious. After the birth of James, Melissa experienced sudden health problems that required surgery, and on the advice of her faculty adviser, decided to take a year off from school because she "was just exhausted." She temporarily moved back with her son's father, who was unemployed and living in a small town in rural Iowa. Melissa found a job at a telephone company as a customer-service representative, starting out at $8 an hour and increasing to $10 an hour. However, she and her son were soon cut from welfare cash assistance and Medicaid as she "made too much money." Melissa was unable to find affordable child care or to qualify for child care subsidies, so her son's father became the caregiver while Melissa went to work. But they still could not make ends meet:

> It got so bad I was taking cans home . . . we were desperate, I was totally off welfare, and I had medical insurance for my son through my job, . . . so I was the breadwinner of the family—then my car broke down, luckily, my job was 10 minutes walking, so that was good. At work they had boxes for Goodwill written on, where people would throw bottles and cans, and I worked until like midnight or 10 o'clock, depending on what shift I was at. And before anybody would go, before they'd pick up the garbage and everything, I would literally, during my lunch and two 15-minute breaks for that 8- or 10-hour day, I would go and pick up cans on like at least two or three floors, whenever I had time, out of people's garbage. And then people caught on that I was doing it, they'd just come and bring bottles to my desk, you know, and it was funny, but we'd get like five to ten dollars a week just in cans, . . . a lot of it was for food!

After Melissa unexpectedly became pregnant, she took stock of her situation and decided, "I can't keep doing this. I'm going back to school," and she decided to leave the unstable relationship with her son's father, returning to the city with her young son and temporarily moving in with her grandmother. She was heavily in debt and worked out a payment arrangement at the university so she could once again receive financial aid. Now attending school part-time and working, Melissa's daily life is lived on the fly—rushing from work to school, taking care of her kids, and heavily dependent on her 79-year-old grandmother for housing and emergency child care. On the day of the interview, we arrange to meet at her workplace, a downtown fast-food chain, after Melissa finishes work, but Melissa's coworker does not show up for the late-afternoon shift, and, despite the fact that she has children to pick up, she is ordered by her boss to extend her day. As the only employee on the shift, she frantically makes calls to arrange for someone to pick up her children from child care, while hurrying to take orders from arriving customers, answer the telephone, replace the ice in the ice machine, mop up spills on the floor—the rushed conversations, the frenetic pace and multitasking all seem emblematic of her harried life.

Melissa's one-year-old daughter is currently with a temporary caregiver, the babysitter of a friend's child, while Melissa's regular in-home family day care provider takes a maternity leave. Melissa was satisfied with her daughter's child care provider, Mary, but is not happy with the current arrangement, and describes how her chronic lack of time necessitated a rushed decision in choosing a temporary caregiver for her daughter:

> I made a mistake because I just could not seem to make the time. . . .
> I found this girl 2 weeks before I was to transfer her [my daughter] . . .
> I didn't really go to great lengths. I did go through Child Care Service Resources, where they gave me a list of providers that would take her temporarily. I met her two weeks before she started taking care of Jenna, . . . but like I was saying, I made a mistake that I didn't gradually have my daughter get used to her. We only went to her house one time, and I stayed there with my daughter, and that was like four days before she actually started going there. I just could not find the time to be able to take her more than one time, so it was a big shock. And she cries every time I drop her off, but when she goes to Mary [the regular babysitter], she never cries. . . .

Mary, Melissa's regular child care provider, was unusual in that she provided care from 6:00 a.m. until midnight Monday through Saturday, and if Melissa had a night class or needed to work late or on Saturday, she could leave both her baby and 6-year-old son with Mary, whom she affectionately described as "a second mom." Trusting and liking her caregiver gave Melissa a deep sense of security, but the current temporary arrangement has created considerable stress for both Melissa and her baby. In addition, Melissa is frequently stuck when her children are sick, and reluctantly relies on her elderly grandmother for emergency child care.

My grandmother, I mean she's 79 years old . . . she's still mobile, but she gets tired easily, and my kids wear her out, you know how little kids are. So I have trouble with that . . . I mean I love her, and she does help me out a lot, but it's just, it's too crowded. My children take over the whole house, and I can tell she feels like, "I want my house back."

Melissa has had a particularly stressful time since her daughter was born, as Jenna has been sick frequently, with seven ear infections in her first year of life, and says Melissa, "her being sick that much has been a big problem for me." Each time Jenna gets sick, Melissa must take time off from school or work to take her to the doctor and often ends up depending on her frail grandmother or elderly aunt to care for a sick and cranky baby. While most of Melissa's instructors at school have been willing to work with her when she misses class and have been "understanding," her work situation is quite different and her manager has been neither understanding nor flexible. Melissa is the only employee who has children, and she describes her manager's behavior when she has to miss work: "My manager is really bad about letting me go when my kids are sick. . . . that's really stressful. I mean he gets really mad, he literally will yell at you. . . . And I'm really scared because he's threatened to fire me, and you know I don't think that's fair!"

Melissa is in constant fear of losing her job, particularly because the low-paid food-service job is the only one she was able to find. Despite the bad working conditions and disrespectful treatment by her boss, she stays, saying, "I'm very thankful to even have a job, because the economy, I know, is very bad right now." Melissa has worked at her present job for more than a year, starting at $6 an hour and now earning $7.15 an hour. Initially she worked full-time, at 38 hours a week, but since returning to school she has been working 20 hours a week. However, other than receiving free lunch or dinner, she has not received any work-related benefits: no medical insurance, no sick days, no vacation time. If she misses work, she loses pay, and her daughter's illnesses have been emotionally and financially costly as she must constantly weigh the needs of her sick baby against the loss of pay: "That's why a lot of times when my kids are sick it's so hard because I have to give up a day of pay, I mean, the kids need me, but. . . ."

Apart from the low-wage job, Melissa subsists on student loans, $300 a month in food stamps, and $100 a month in cash assistance from the Iowa Department of Human Services. Melissa describes herself "as just exhausted," as she juggles work, school, and parenting—always with a deficit of time. No time to take care of a sick baby, no time to do homework, sudden unplanned overtimes at work—all contribute to Melissa's stressed and harried existence. She describes a typical week:

> Tuesdays and Thursdays I'm here [at work] all day. But Mondays, Wednesdays, and Fridays, when my children are not sick, my son's in school by 8:30 in the morning. . . . I just drop him off at school and then I take the baby to the babysitter's, and then I go and do whatever I need to do for my Independent Study class . . . I'll do reading or research for either my photography class or my history lecture class. . . . And between 11 and 12:30 I'll go to work . . . and then I'm off at 1:30. . . . And then at 2:00 I have my history class. That's one hour. But I take the bus. I don't drive to class because it costs too much money. I take the bus from home, and then I take the bus from class, at 3 o'clock my class gets out. I'm home generally by 3:20, grab the car, pick my son up, go get my daughter, that takes about half hour, 5:30, 6:00 is dinner. Kids are in bed by 8; if I'm lucky they're asleep by 9. . . . From 9 if I'm not tired, from 9 to midnight I'll do readings for my history course. And I'm usually in bed by 11:30, midnight; I just can't stay awake. And then on Tuesdays and Thursdays, the kids go to day care, school, and then after dropping them off I come straight here to work, open this door around 8:30 or 9 in the morning, and I'm usually here until 4 or 5, working all day. . . . So, that's how it is!

Melissa is determined to complete her degree so she can exit poverty and find a decent-paying job with health insurance. Yet Melissa has limited time to achieve her goals because the welfare clock is ticking on the two-year postsecondary education work-requirement waiver. Melissa's Promise Jobs worker told her that in December 2004, all her public assistance would end, including child care and food stamps. That deadline leaves Melissa with just 12 months to complete her degree. If she were to give up her job and go to school full-time, she could possibly manage, but that leaves her with a huge income deficit, new debts, maximum student loans, and another year stuck at her grandmother's, which is stressful for all. If she does not complete her degree by December 2004, she will essentially be cut off child care subsidies and food stamps. She may be able to get a 50% reduction in child care costs if she can enroll her daughter in the university child care center, but that will still leave a large chunk of her monthly income ($250) to be paid out-of-pocket for child care—an unmanageable burden on a stretched budget, and even more so if she quits her job.

Yet, despite the looming obstacles, Melissa remains optimistic, appreciative of the educational and child care assistance she has received from the Iowa Promise Jobs program, with a caseworker who has encouraged her to complete her degree and has "even pulled strings for me," in contrast to the dearth of assistance and denial of child care subsidies in the rural Iowa county where she formerly lived. In addition, Melissa points to community and university assistance, her grandmother, and occasionally her children's father as sources of support at critical junctures in her life. What she most regrets is the lack of time for her children, saying, "I miss my kids and they miss me." As she looks to the uphill struggle ahead, she remarks, "I'm just very anxious to graduate . . . so I can find a good job that will make us able to be self-sufficient, where I don't have to worry so much all the time about scraping for money. I just take it day by day. That's my big thing, day by day."

If Melissa's children stay healthy, if she manages to keep her job, if she graduates within a year, and if she can find affordable child care and housing, her family may well exit poverty and be en-route to a decent and self-sufficient life. However, if Melissa's plans fall through because she or her children get sick and she loses her job, or because she cannot afford to pay the several hundred dollars in out-of-pocket monthly child care costs in 2005, her young family may be back where she began, stuck in poverty and scouring for cans.

KIM AND GENEVIEVE: DREAMS DERAILED

> Everybody loses . . . I mean the bottom line here is that you don't get adequate child care because you can't afford it—that's poverty—that's just a domino effect of poverty.

Kim, an articulate and determined young single mother, the child of Southeast Asian immigrants, is struggling to cope with motherhood, attend school, and forge an independent life for herself and her young daughter. Kim left California when her daughter Genevieve (now 3 years old) was a baby. Her family did not accept her biracial child, and Kim, who could not make ends meet on her own in California, did not want her daughter to grow up in a hostile environment. She describes the difficult decision:

> I wasn't making it . . . you know, it was like, what's the worst of two evils—homelessness or them? And I just couldn't imagine leaving my daughter, raising my daughter in that environment. Because it wouldn't

have been raising her, it would have been socially stunting her. . . . And she's a biracial child, so that was a problem for my family, and that marginalized her, and it's not fair to her, it's not her problem.

Without a high school diploma, lacking any resources or family support, she decided to make her way to Iowa to visit and take care of a friend, who was recovering from an illness. However, the arrangement soon fell apart, and Kim found herself without a place to live. "I was about a week away from being homeless . . . no one ever plans for anything like that, you know, all of a sudden you find yourself [there] and you're desperate."

After making contact with a nonprofit welfare advocacy rights organization, which helped her secure subsidized housing and a donated car, Kim enters the Promise Jobs welfare-to-work program in Iowa and begins to search for a job while receiving subsidized child care. As Kim faces multiple demands in a new and unfamiliar city, the stress of parenting begins to wear her down: "I mean, you know, there were days when, quite literally, I wanted to go out the window." She reluctantly places her baby daughter in a family day care home, describing her decision as a "trial and error." The caregiver seems "pleasant," but Kim is uneasy about leaving her baby in a small overcrowded apartment, where "the lady had a lot of kids, and her own kids were emotionally challenged . . . and my daughter was really miserable there." Kim wants to place her daughter in a child care center, but they are expensive, part-time care is difficult to locate, waiting lists are long, and there is little flexibility to accommodate her job-search needs:

> I wanted to get her into a structured, you know, classroom setting in a child care center; well they required her for a certain amount [full-time] and I only had so many hours to get jobs. I couldn't afford to pay anything else, . . . [I was] you know, just making it, so I just couldn't. So I wasn't able to put her into a center.

Kim at this point must settle for *less*–less than what she wants and less than what would be best for Genevieve–as she temporarily leaves her in the care of another low-income mother whom she has met through the support network of an advocacy organization. Good jobs are hard to come by in Iowa, as outsourcing has stripped the economy, with particular impact on rural areas. As Kim looks for a part-time job, she describes her difficulty finding a 20-hour-a-week job that will qualify her for child care subsidies:

There's no jobs. For every two companies coming into Iowa, we have five to eight that are leaving or going out of business or bankruptcy . . . if you do work, you have to work a minimum of 20 hours to be able to get any kind of [child care] subsidy to help . . . but there aren't even a lot of jobs that offer 20 hours a week—it's 15, that means that if they're not busy, they're going to send you home. So if I work 19½ hours I don't qualify for any subsidy, so that means that I'm stuck with that child care bill, which means that I'm actually paying out more than I'm making. Because after taxes, after what I pay for day care, that takes up my whole paycheck then. And probably more because with gas I put in, the food I have to take, everything costs me more to work, so I couldn't even work. You know I can't even pick up an odd job here or there to even just supplement, because I have to work a minimum of 20 hours, and they're looking to raise that minimum.[3]

With the help and encouragement of her newly developed support network that has formed through the welfare advocacy organization, Kim decides to complete her high school diploma and enroll in a community college. She finds out that Iowa's welfare-to-work plan permits full-time school in lieu of a work requirement for two years and that she is entitled to child care subsidies for school. Determined to take advantage of this opportunity, Kim develops a long-term plan to gain a liberal arts degree at a 4-year institution and then go on to law school so she can become an activist on issues of globalization and sweat-shop labor. Already she has joined together with other Iowa activists in opposing the Bush Welfare Reauthorization Proposal of 2003, which would severely restrict postsecondary educational options, currently still operating in Iowa and a handful of other states, and reduce child care funds. She describes how she testified in Washington, D.C., at a hearing on welfare and child care, saying:

I went to Capitol Hill to represent Iowa, and I just said to the lead person on the Finance Committee, "You know, I realize this is not meant to be a personal affront, but I have to be honest—the end result is the same. This tells me that I'm not worthy of postsecondary education, that I'm not worthy, and that my child should not, you know, be in adequate day care because I'm poor . . . that this is all I deserve. . . . And what does that tell my daughter?" And I just threw it out there, I said "I'm offended as a human being." People don't know how hard it is. So I said to them, "Don't speak for me if you've never asked me!"

When Kim enrolls at a community college full-time, she once again searches for a child care setting for her daughter. Determined to find a good placement this time, she visits 16 different settings, and finally settles on a licensed in-home family day care with 10 to 12 children, run by a retired businessman. Despite the fact that he has no education or training as a child care provider, Kim is pleased with the environment and likes the provider:

> My daughter loves it, which is just a wonderful feeling, after her saying, "No, I don't wanna go," [in her previous setting] to "Mommy, I wanna go to Mike's." It's a nice feeling . . . his whole front yard is a playground. But you don't see it from the street because there's trees, so he has privacy . . . his living room is all partitioned off for individual kids. He's got a whole room that's bright yellow and splattered with every color in the rainbow, and it's the play room. All the kids have individual cots for their naps . . . and he's a caterer. So they eat better there than they do at home probably. I walked in at lunch one time and my daughter has this huge, homemade mac and cheese baked from the oven and brownies and a whole fruit, and I'm thinking, "Yeah you better enjoy it because tonight it's just noodles."

However, while she receives a child care subsidy that covers the $115/ week cost of the child care, Kim runs up $230 in costs during a 2-week school vacation. During semester breaks there are no child care subsidies if Kim is not attending classes, and the day care provider must be paid even when classes are over or Kim will lose her slot. If she or her child becomes sick there is a 4-day-a-month sick allowance, but after that she is responsible for any out-of-pocket costs. With no subsidies for study time, Kim has to strategize in terms of scheduling her classes, so that there are segments of time in between her classes to study in order to use the maximum allocated child subsidy units of time to cover 10 hours a day of day care:

> They only pay for in-class hours now . . . you know, it's almost a double-edged sword, because here they say, "Oh, they're helping you," but they don't pay you, they don't help you with study hours . . . I mean, everybody knows it takes twice as many hours if not three times as many hours to study. And you've got to give people a chance. I mean you're not doing anybody any favors if you're paying them for the class hours but no study hours . . . there's no flexibility. I mean, we strategize, but if we need to go over to a study group on the weekends, what do we do? It goes

out of your own pocket. If I have an emergency, it comes out of my own pocket. . . . So, the thing about the poor person on assistance is you really do have to be quite ingenious about how you plan out your schedule!

Kim's tightly stretched resources create a great deal of stress. She struggles to pay her bills and subsists from month to month, receiving $361 per month in a welfare cash grant from Iowa's Family Independence Program (FIP) for herself and Genevieve, plus $245 in food stamps, and she pays an adjusted monthly rent in her subsidized housing apartment of $71 a month. She draws heavily on student loans and does not see any of the child support that the father of her daughter pays sporadically, as the state takes it all to recoup the public assistance spending on the family. Kim has considered working part-time to try and increase her monthly income while going to school full-time, but she will not be able to get any child care subsidies for work, unless she is employed for a minimum of 20 hours.[4] That seems an overwhelming burden for Kim whose time, as a single parent, is already stretched to the limit, and she comments:

I mean, I don't need a husband, I need a wife. I need a wife who will do my laundry and take care of my household and cook for me. I do everything on my own, so yeah, I don't even have 20 hours. I'd be able to spare about 10, maybe 15, but I couldn't do more than that.

Kim is overwhelmed as she tries to juggle scarce economic resources, the psychological demands of single motherhood, being a full-time student, and coping with the fears of not making it—and it all takes a toll on her health. She begins to experience "horrible migraines," there are times when she cannot drive home, and twice she has fallen down the steps. She has had to fight depression, and on some days, she cannot get out of bed. "I'm stuck all the time," says Kim, "that feeling of wanting to throw oneself out the window or the kid happens. It slips up on you." However, what enables her to go on during these periods is her strong support network provided by the welfare advocacy community, describing them as, "family to us here, but what about the people who don't have it. I mean, I don't know what I would do without my circle of support." While Kim is supported by a unique, activist, community-based organization that provides vital support to her and to Genevieve at critical moments, her life as a parenting college student in poverty is precarious. As she reflects on her current situation and educational choices she has made to try and secure a better life for herself and her child, she angrily remarks:

> I've done everything outside of thieving and prostitution; I think I've
> done everything demeaning. I try to make it work. This is just one more
> way—give it another shot. And I hope that it pays off. Is it a gamble?
> I don't know; I hope not. I think I've tried everything within my moral
> spectrum. . . . But no one's prepared for poverty. I never prepared for the
> fact that I could possibly be homeless one day, that I would struggle this
> hard, that it would be hard for me to get out of bed!

There is a daily toll that stretched time and a deficit of resources take on
young single parents, particularly when there is little respite from the demands of caring for a toddler. Kim describes never having an "emotional
break," as being "the hardest part . . . I mean it's daily . . . it's time. You
know, it's everything, just all bundled in one."

Although she has fortunately managed to secure a stable and decent
child care arrangement for Genevieve, Kim knows that her current situation is unusual, and through her recent political activism, has become
acutely aware of the many child care problems confronting other low-
income families in Iowa:

> Child care is such a drain on families, whether you're a two-unit family or
> not. It is just a major source. I mean, it takes almost a whole income . . .
> at the same time some of our lowest-paid people in the country are child
> care providers; why is that? You know there's something to be said about
> the fact that I leave the most important person in my life with the lowest-
> paid person in the country. I mean, there's something to be said about
> that paradox!

Through Kim's involvement in a child care advocacy network, her
awareness of social injustice has increased, "there's just so much need,"
she points out, as she articulates a developing critical social perspective
about the inequalities that filter down and impact those living on the
outer edges of the economy:

> I just want to be recognized as human, an equal—you know, in this
> world we unfortunately come in shades of green. How much money do
> you have to have to be considered equal? I don't have the right to sit
> back and not say anything. I think that people count on people not say-
> ing things. And the world's gotten by with a lot!

Kim recognizes that it is important that people like her speak up about
the need for affordable and quality child care as policymakers "don't talk

to the constituents who really need it." As she contemplates her future, intending to complete community college and transfer to a four-year university, she talks about her dreams for herself and her daughter:

> Well, I've got a dream. That's one thing, too, that I didn't even realize. I stopped dreaming for a long time. I didn't even realize I stopped dreaming. . . . I was like "Oh, God, where did it go?" So I guess that's a good thing. I got my dreams back, but it's still just a dream, because I want to write papers and letters and things that will really make a difference in the world. . . . I don't want to *just* prepare my daughter for the world; I want to help make the world better for her. . . . So, that's one thing that keeps me going. . . . I want the biggest thing for my daughter is to know that she can always say something. She never has to sit back and take it!

Not sitting back and not taking it is an integral part of Kim's identity and determination to fight the injustices of her life in poverty. But how long would she be able to juggle all the balls and catch them? How long will her daughter's child care remain stable? Six months later, Kim dropped out of school, when her college plans were derailed by a Promise Jobs caseworker who did not support her transfer to a four-year college. Her welfare grant was terminated, and her child care subsidies were cut.

Whereas Melissa had a sympathetic caseworker who encouraged her to complete her degree, despite the ticking welfare clock, Kim's experience was just the opposite, and hitting that wall was the final straw as, overwhelmed by competing demands, she chose to drop out of school. A change in status, as in Kim's case, means loss of child care subsidies and benefits with immediate consequences for her 3-year-old daughter, Genevieve. Children do not escape the instability in their mothers' lives, as welfare and child care subsidy cutoffs may result in displacement from a child care setting, or worse, from one's home.

The deficit of resources experienced by Kim and Melissa are not only financial but also involve the resources of time—time to study, time to think, time to sleep, time to parent one's children. Both Melissa and Kim suffered health repercussions, surgery for Melissa and continuing migraines for Kim, as emotional and physical exhaustion took their toll. This complicated balancing act, where a child's ear infection can tip the apple cart, is shadowed by the need for both stable and emergency backup child care. For Melissa and Kim, living on poverty's edges, life is just much harder than that experienced by most of their student peers, filled as it is with daily care uncertainties—child care for evening classes, for weekend study, for work overtime, for emergencies when children become sick; all become barriers to retention and successful completion of one's degree program.

Success in college depends for most students on adequate time to devote to one's studies, and the time and care deficit that student mothers cope with is clearly an added obstacle to success. Because child care subsidies pay only for in-class time, there is a chronic shortage of study time. To increase monthly resources, the federal work-study program on campus is often a preferred option for college students. Yet, to meet the Iowa Promise Jobs requirement, students must work at least 20 hours a week to receive child care subsidies for work; hence a full-time student and single parent would actually have to work *more* than the average, single, nonparenting student to receive any work-related child care subsidies. A more manageable college work-study assignment of 10–15 hours a week, for example, would not entitle a student mother to child care subsidies for those hours under Iowa's welfare-to-work policies.[5]

Leslie Bloom's case study of a community-based, welfare advocacy organization in Iowa documents the difficulties that low-income, single, student mothers encounter. As she points out, poverty shapes the priorities of student mothers; for "their lives are dominated first and foremost by care-taking responsibilities, and then classes, work, compliance with DHS and FIP regulations, and the daily grind of balancing those roles and making ends meet."[6] Like Melissa and Kim, the student mothers in Bloom's study encountered multiple obstacles that related to a deficit of resources, including food insecurity, temporal demands, sick children, and psychological barriers. Making it in college means succeeding above and beyond the myriad of obstacles that structure low-income, single mothers' lives–lives that are always intertwined with the care of their young children. The set of barriers that these mothers encounter as nontraditional students are rarely adequately addressed through traditional campus programs and services.

HIGHER EDUCATION,
LOW-INCOME STUDENT MOTHERS, AND CHILD CARE

Postsecondary education is a key social capital investment in low-income female-headed families, yet research on the access of the poor to higher education has neglected the distinctive dilemmas and burdens of low-income single mothers.[7] Heller and Bjorklund, reviewing the empirical research on the impact of financial aid on all low-income students, point out that the beneficial impacts of financial aid are greatest for the poorest students, and that there is strong evidence that aid, particularly scholarships and grants, facilitates college enrollment and retention. Financial aid assessments, however, usually disadvantage low-income student parents as they face greater amounts of "unmet need," which is calculated as " the difference between the cost of attending college and the resources available to meet those costs."[8] Low-income single mothers, a nontraditional student constituency, face the greatest financial obstacles as financial-aid packages do not adjust for dependent children nor do they generally take child rearing and child care costs into account, as they constitute "costs unrelated to the completion of a student's course of study"[9]—a deep irony, indeed, as unmet child care costs are one of the most significant barriers to retention and college completion. Federal student aid is also designed to support full-time students, or students taking at least six hours a semester, but many low-income single mothers must choose to go to school part-time and work; hence their opportunities to benefit from advantageous financial-aid packages are circumscribed.[10] In most of the states, under PRWORA legislation, mothers on welfare may *not* count postsecondary education as a work activity; hence, not only must they struggle to stay in school and succeed, but they are required to work 35–40 hours a week, and parent their children, alone, on tightly stretched budgets.

The passage of PRWORA has had a severe impact on the access of low-income, single mothers to postsecondary education, and, with its explicit Work First paradigm, constructs aspiring students as work averse, lacking a work ethic, and shirking personal responsibility to maintain their welfare dependency. Welfare "reform" thus presents a striking paradox: On the one hand, Work First policies and practice create increasing pressure on women to find jobs, any jobs, no matter how low the pay and how bad the working conditions, under threat of benefit termination and sanctions; on the other hand, these same policies and practices threaten their access to postsecondary education, which *could* ensure long-term economic self-sufficiency for their families.[11]

Women who leave welfare for work are generally employed in minimum-wage jobs with little opportunity for advancement or benefits. Such jobs offer few exits from poverty and little hope for family self-sufficiency. A recent study of a national sample of women who had left welfare found that among those employed, wages averaged $6.51 per hour, with only 23% of employers providing health insurance. Additional studies show that more than two-thirds of adults who are terminated from welfare are employed at jobs paying $7.50 an hour, with few if any benefits. These unstable jobs mean that those who transition off welfare frequently end up back on welfare, reporting housing and food insecurity as key hardships.[12]

Since the passage of welfare "reform" legislation, there has been a precipitous drop in the number of families receiving welfare–from 5 million in 1994, to 4 million in 1996, and down to just 2 million by 2002.[13] President Bush and the Republican Congress declared the 1996 welfare legislation "a resounding success," and under the reauthorization of PRWORA a 40-hour mandatory work requirement has been imposed, but no income and job supports, no investment in postsecondary education, and no additional child care subsidies. As Marian Wright Edelman of the Children's Defense Fund put it: "The President requires more hours of work, but not one dime more for child care. . . . Right now only one in seven children eligible for federal child care assistance gets it."[14]

The emphasis on Work First (recall Carmina, Chapter 2, in her WEP placement, sent to pick up trash in New York City), no matter how low the wage and how bad the working conditions, has severely circumscribed the educational aspirations and opportunities of low-income mothers, resulting in a precipitous drop in college enrollment. Approximately three-quarters of a million welfare recipients (mostly single mothers) were in college in 1996, the year in which welfare "reform" was passed. Post-1996 numbers point to drops in enrollments nationwide, ranging from 29% to 82%.[15] Most states permit only time-limited vocational education for up to a year, with little flexibility for two- and four-year degrees, and just a few–California, Illinois, Iowa, Kentucky, and Wyoming–permit postsecondary education as an allowable work activity for a two-year period. Maine's Parents as Scholars program is a notable exception, permitting welfare recipients to enroll in both two- and four-year degree programs, while providing wraparound services, including child care and up to four years of school.[16]

The importance of postsecondary education for women, particularly single mothers, has been documented in numerous studies during the past two decades. Higher education provides a buffer against job loss during economic downturns. Over half of the jobs lost during the 2001 recession occurred in those industries that had employed former welfare recipients. Job losses and dislocation disproportionately harm those with the lowest levels of education, and for women, increase the risks of living in poverty. Women who fail to complete high school are 43% more likely to live in poverty than men without a high school diploma.[17] On the other hand, women's earnings increase exponentially with each year of college, and completion of a four-year college degree reduces women's chances of being poor from 16.7% to 1.6% in comparison to those women who have only a high school education.[18] The advantages for college educated women over high school graduates are dramatic, particularly for women of color. White women with a four-year degree have a 77% earnings increase over White high school graduates; Latina women and African-American women see their earnings rise by 88% and 92%, respectively, in comparison with high school graduates of their own ethnic groups.[19]

Postsecondary education profoundly affects the whole family unit, particularly children's material and psychological well-being and educational achievement. The positive effects of college graduation on welfare recipients and their children point to higher standards of living, economic self-sufficiency, greater self-esteem, and aspirations to send their own children to college.[20] Haveman and Wolfe point out that one of the most important factors shaping children's academic success in school is the educational level of the mother, which "may proxy for a wide variety of maternal—and family—activities of an investment character," contributing to motivation and performance in school, and imparting to their children the value of learning.[21] Hence, college education is one of the most "powerful and dependable way[s] to interrupt the intergenerational transmission of poverty."[22]

Melissa and Kim recognize the promise of higher education, yet attempting to realize their dream has been an ordeal. From Kim's initial homelessness to Melissa's scouring for cans at her workplace, they have endured severe stress and emotional duress, and persevered in the face of many obstacles. Yet, of the two women, only Melissa now remains in college, and her capacity to pull it off as the welfare clock ticks on, is in doubt—despite her tenacity. With her time-limited postsecondary education period nearing an end, Iowa's marginally better state policy that has assisted her for 24 months is going to leave her in the cold, floundering to complete her final year with no supports and no child care subsidies. Kim, bright and articulate, has dropped out of school, her benefits and child care subsidies cut; she may or may not return to fulfill her dream of becoming a lawyer, fighting for the rights of poor mothers like herself.

Higher education is a pathway out of poverty for single mothers and their children; yet they cannot do it alone. Their engagement in a campus learning community is dependent on meeting their needs *and* the care needs of their children. Higher education institutions have a critical role to play in creating a family-friendly environment for parenting students and ensuring that they have access to high quality, affordable, subsidized child care on campus. Low-income student mothers have the right to an education that affirms their freedom to learn and develop their human capabilities, and so do their young children.

CHAPTER 4

On the Edges:
When Two Parents Can't Make It

> They are poor here and now, in the United States. They are
> dispossessed in terms of what the rest of the nation enjoys, in
> terms of what the society could provide if it had the will. They live
> on the fringe, the margin. They watch the movies and read the
> magazines of affluent America, and these tell them that they are
> internal exiles.
>
> —Michael Harrington, *The Other America*[1]

The working poor still reside in the "Other America" arguably worse off in the 21st century than they were when the War on Poverty was declared in the 1960s. Low-wage work in the United States comprises almost 30% of the economy, representing approximately 28 million workers.[2] Living in substandard housing, trailers, and doubled up with other families, often a paycheck away from homelessness, low-income families live and toil just beyond the edge of poverty. Officially classified as nonpoor but living below 200% of the federal poverty line, low-income parents and children are denied access to most public benefits, including Medicaid and child care subsidies.[3] Making "too much" is frequently their downfall, as they are deemed ineligible for the minimal services provided to welfare recipients; yet they lack the essentials for a decent human life. Single or married, they scrape by on a constant deficit of resources, learning the bitter way that hard work certainly does not pay if you are a parent in a low-wage job and do not have the means to sustain a basic social minimum for your family. Forty percent of children, more than 29 million, live in low-income families, and the majority (55%) have at least one parent who works year-round full-time.[4]

This chapter presents the diminished lives of two married couples with children. Hannah and Thomas live in California with their three children and cannot make ends meet. Despite two parents working odd-hours and low-wage jobs, they find themselves up against the wall, as they cannot pay for decent child care for their youngest child. Danielle and Ronald, homeless with two children in New York City, struggle to turn their life around as they confront a housing and child care crisis. Having a partner is not always a buffer against the ravages of poverty if jobs are marginal, unstable, and low-wage. It is simply not possible to afford stable housing and good quality child care at market costs, or to pay for health care, food, and other necessities. Even in two-parent families, "Work alone doesn't ensure a decent standard of living."[5]

HANNAH, THOMAS, AND SETH: SETTLING FOR LESS

It's the most frustrating thing in the world for me—I could yell and yell all day about day care. . . . You know, where people who have a lot of money can afford a beautiful day care environment—people like us get this ratty little building.

Hannah and Thomas are the parents of three children and live together in a blended family in a small rural area in San Diego County. Hannah, who is White, has a 16-year-old son from a previous marriage, and Thomas, who is Latino, has raised his 16-year-old daughter, alone, as a single father, since she was 2 years old. Together they also have a 6-year-old son, Seth. For years, Hannah and Thomas have struggled to manage by juggling work shifts and low-wage jobs, always unable to access any child care subsidies because their income as a working family has exceeded the eligibility cutoff for assistance.[6] During Seth's infancy, Hannah stayed home, and when she returned to work, Thomas worked a night shift as a security guard while Hannah worked days. With Thomas taking care of Seth during the day, stress and lack of sleep were chronic problems.

Hannah and Thomas's life has been complicated by the fact that they both have additional children to support, and neither Hannah nor Thomas has been able to find a job with good benefits, good hours, and decent pay. Hannah describes their child care needs as the "worst crisis," pitting rent and food against child care costs for Seth. Hannah has tried repeatedly to attend a community college but has been forced to drop out several times due to time demands, child care problems, and lack of money. There are few child care centers where they live, and transportation has been an ongoing problem.

When Seth turned 2, Hannah applied for child care subsidies but was turned down because Thomas made "too much," despite the fact that the family was barely making it on those earnings. Well aware of the importance of a good child care environment, Hannah applied for a publicly funded preschool and Head Start, but the waiting lists were over a year long, so she began the search for a private child care setting, but high quality child care was miles away and unaffordable. They reluctantly placed Seth with a family day care provider who charged $400 a month, but the provider was short-staffed, with too many infants to take care of, and "none of the kids really got much attention." Seth was not happy there, resisted going, and often regressed into wetting after he had been toilet trained. Frustrated, Hannah describes some of the problems:

> We had concerns . . . she actually lost him one time. So, I mean, there were some real problems we had with her. You know, we'd get him and he would be dirty, his diaper would be dirty. But because we couldn't afford to pay for a day care anywhere else in the world, it was pretty much we were stuck with it. . . . And I couldn't get help. I just couldn't.

Hannah's sense of "being stuck" with poor quality care because of limited options and no public support is a recurring pattern in the family's life, creating anxiety and ongoing anger and resentment at a "system [that] always beat us." Many times Hannah relates how they both worked "to pay the babysitter;" yet the care their son received in his early years was substandard, and Hannah regrets that it was "a really bad place to be." The poor quality of child care that Seth receives places great stress on the relationship between Hannah and Thomas and on the rest of the children. Hannah relates how:

> The day care was bad, and Seth didn't want to go there sometimes. And if he had a bad day, he would sometimes wet when he had—he has a tendency if he has a bad day or something goes wrong at day care, he'll wet at night time. . . . And we would argue. It affected us all together, we knew where we wanted to move him, but we couldn't pay . . . then we would argue about money, and you know, how were we going to do this? And it actually put a strain on our relationship because I knew we could not afford any more than we were paying

Hannah decides to take on a second job, and works 12-hour days "so that my day job would pay day care and my night job would give me money" and locates a nondenominational, faith-based licensed preschool center that she considers a world apart from Seth's previous setting, where "they had more staff, so he was much better taken care of . . . and they were actually teaching him . . . we were very happy with that center." Thomas corroborates the positive impressions of the center, saying, "It was more faith-based, but they were really pro-academic–they spent a lot of time on his alphabet and his numbers and his math and his reading . . . I mean, such a big difference between one child care facility and another one. It amazed me!"

Despite the fact that the center costs almost $80 more a month, both Hannah and Thomas feel it is well worth it, and they appreciate the fact that the teaching staff has early childhood training and certification. During this time, when Hannah and Thomas are working late afternoons and evenings, Hannah's teenage son picks Seth up from the child care center, takes care of his younger brother, cooks dinner, and baby-sits until Hannah arrives home from work at 9:00 p.m. However, Seth's year of "happy" child care experiences comes to an end when the family's subsidized housing application is approved, and they relocate to another community in metropolitan San Diego and can no longer afford the transportation costs and commuting time to his former child care center. Once more they are stuck. Fortunately the older children are home on vacation and take care of Seth while his parents are at work, and soon after he turns five he enters kindergarten. Hannah would like him to attend the before- and after-school program, but there are a limited number of slots and a long waiting list in their particular part of San Diego County. The subsidized, school-age 6-to-6 program in San Diego city is not offered in metropolitan San Diego, and as Seth only attends kindergarten half-day, Hannah must search for child care for the afternoons. She enrolls Seth part-time in a private child care center that costs $360 a month but is concerned about the lack of supervision and the fact that Seth is being bullied by older children:

> He'll say the kids are hitting him. He's a little chunky, and they make fun of him because of his weight. So one of the boys, when I went to pick him up—one of the boys ran after him with his head down and head-butted him in the stomach. You know and I got onto the boy, but I felt that the teacher should have been there . . . so it's not the same quality of care we got [at the other center] but, it's you know, *care.*

Thomas has also been disturbed by the general lack of attentiveness by the staff towards the younger children and describes an incident when 5-year-old Seth first began attending the center:

One time he actually soiled his pants, and I picked him up and went to the store. We were going to go to the store, and I smelled this odor, and I didn't know what it was. I thought that he had stepped on something or I had stepped on something. And then, when we got home, I realized what it was . . . you know it looked like it had been there for a while, and there was no attempt to change him . . . and I told the kids to take him up to the bath tub right away, you know, stripped off his clothes, and then I filed a complaint the next day.

Neither parent feels that Seth is well treated at the child care center, and Hannah angrily remarks, "It's so frustrating . . . some of the nicer day cares are just out of our range. All we can get is that kind of care." There are two after-school child care centers that Seth's public school refers parents to, and this poorly run center is one of them. The high quality center where Hannah wants to enroll Seth costs $600 a month for after-school care, but without any child care subsidies to help the family, that center is simply beyond reach: "It is just way too much for us," says Hannah, "the quality of care we would like to see him in is not in our world!"

Because Seth has frequently been sick with ear infections, pneumonia, and other ailments, Hannah and Thomas have found themselves caught between the needs of their young son and the threat of being fired from a job. Hannah describes the dilemma:

When Seth was sick, neither one of us could afford to take the day off, and then a lot of times we would split the day . . . Thomas would take four hours and I would take four hours with him, which was huge. One time Seth was in the hospital, you know, any time we take time off, especially during that time, we didn't have any benefits with our jobs, so, you know, to do anything like that was just devastating.

There were times when neither Hannah nor Thomas could stay home with Seth, because the loss of pay or the threat of being fired placed the whole family in jeopardy. So the older children would stay home from school:

We'd actually have to keep our older ones out to take care of him because we couldn't afford to. . . . You know, "Don't go to school today— take care of your brother so we can go to work." And that happened, you know, frequently, where the other children would have to suffer because we just had to go to work . . . I'm sure it hurt them, probably, educationally because they missed school, but they did it, you know. They did it, because we needed them.

Hannah has regrets and guilt about their ongoing dependence on their older children for Seth's care whenever illness or late work hours have required the older children to pitch in. Hannah relates how each time she has reapplied for some child care assistance, they have been denied, and she bitterly remarks, "One of the programs we went to . . . she [the caseworker] actually told me we made a dollar over!" For Hannah and Thomas, who constitute a "working poor" couple, with a family income of $35,000, there is no help forthcoming:

> All of our children suffer for it, because they have to take care of him, you know, and I know my son would always say, "Why do I have to take care of him, he's your son?" So, until he understood why, you know, at 13 that concept wasn't there for him. But now (at 16) he's like, "Oh, this is our family, and we have to take care of our own." But you know when he was little, all he wanted to think about was going out there and playing baseball. . . . She [Thomas's daughter] has also taken sick days from school to take care of Seth. So, it's been basically, we're trying to keep it even, so that not one child stays home all the time . . . so everybody takes a little bit you know.

Hannah has just recently quit her job and has decided to look for an evening position because she wants to pull Seth out of the current child care center, where he is clearly "not happy." Although Seth likes his public kindergarten (and according to Hannah, the benefits accrued from the one good year he had in an educationally enriching child care center are evident in his kindergarten class), he constantly complains about the after-school child care center and does not want to go. Hannah feels badly about the fact that "we have to fight him to go . . . I don't feel we should force him to, you know," as she is well aware of the inferior quality of care her son receives there. Hannah has continuing concerns about the lack of supervision, particularly the fighting that she feels is having a negative impact on Seth. While the center is licensed, according to Hannah: "It is not maintained. They're not monitored and the teachers don't pay attention . . . the quality of care is a lot lower, but it's what we have, you know, for now, and what we can barely afford . . . it's more than my car payment and that's huge!" Searching for an alternative, she figures that if she pulls Seth out of the center and finds an evening job, they could also save the much-needed $360 dollars per month, saying, "If I can get something in the evenings, I could hand Seth over to Thomas and then just go. Or hand him, you know, to his brother and sister. And then we wouldn't have to pay day care."

As Thomas and Hannah are still having difficulty making ends meet, saving the child care costs would help ease their budget deficit as they currently struggle to meet the monthly co-op association fee for their town house. Seth is due to start first grade in six months, in fall of 2004, and Hannah hopes that if they can find a six-month stop-gap solution, once he starts first grade, they will be able to look forward to an easier, less crisis-ridden mode of existence:

> We're almost done. We're almost done . . . but we're not sure about schedules (for the fall) if we can get the kids, somebody to go to his school to pick him up, then we'll be okay. So, I'm not sure how the schedule's going to work. It takes our high schoolers about an hour to get home. So I'm not sure if they have enough time to get to Seth, but we're hoping for that.

It is clear that child care is the tipping point in the family's household budget and that without older children to help, neither Hannah nor Michael could manage to keep the family afloat. There has been a considerable cost to the older children—school absences, missed extracurricular activities, the premature burdens of adult responsibilities. However, Seth has borne the biggest burden of all—forced, as a very young child, to endure cheap, low quality child care environments that, with one notable exception, have been harmful to his development. He has reacted to the stress by resisting, regressing, wetting himself, getting sick, and expressing his unhappiness in multiple ways. Hannah is filled with regrets, saying, "We just couldn't afford better. We just couldn't. And it wasn't fair to him, and it wasn't fair to us, but that's all we were given." From Hannah's perspective, working families like hers get the worst of all possible worlds as she compares her family's child care needs with those of families on welfare:

> I think the things that's most pressing to me, and I've always said this since I've had Seth—people who are not working are at home getting welfare, [and they] get day care. And I see it all the time . . . and they're getting free day care all day while they do whatever. And people like us who are a dollar over the minimum or maximum, get nothing. And, you know, there has to be a system where [it's] more flexible, where it's more based on the individual family.

Hannah concedes that single parents who are in welfare-to-work programs also need child care, just as she does: "I understand, you know, when they're going through all the welfare-to-work change, and people are getting day care to go look for a job. I understand that, but working people like us who want to work can't get day care."

Thomas, who is a veteran, and now works at a computer maintenance job for 32 hours a week, feels that it is impossible for working poor families such as theirs to make it on low-paying, no-benefit jobs, when good child care is out of reach for most families:

> I don't know, it's just ridiculous how much they charge, and then they expect, you know, with the job market the way it is, they expect people to, you know, be able to afford child care. But the pay rate that they're paying people in San Diego, the cost of living in San Diego is really truly difficult. . . . I don't know if the government can subsidize some of the payments, as a solution, but we need help. . . . Working families need help!

Yet, as Hannah points out, no government program has ever assisted them with child care because they were always "over the limit." Although Hannah was able to receive the WIC supplementary nutrition program for Seth when he was a baby, they have never had access to child care subsidies: "It seemed like every program we went to, we just couldn't get help. No matter how we tried, whether it is together, apart, it was always something . . . but we've suffered . . . and the system always beat us . . . so that's why we ended up just going on our own and trying to wing it."

So Hannah and Thomas continue on, "trying to do the best we can," resigned to day care "in a ratty little building" providing cheap and inferior child care for young Seth until his mother finds another job and he begins first grade. As Hannah looks back on their five-year struggle, she remarks, "You have to buy the quality of care, and it's not fair! . . . Our children are just as much valued and important as theirs!"

DANIELLE, RONALD, AND THEIR SONS: WORKING POOR AND HOMELESS

> You know, nowadays you've got to be real careful . . . just because someone on the block is watching kids, it doesn't mean I want them with *my kids* . . . and welfare don't care about that . . . as long as somebody's watching your kids and they got a welfare sign, you just have to go do it!

Danielle is a 30-year-old African-American intern at a community-based organizing and advocacy coalition in New York City. Married with two sons, ages 8 and 3, Danielle, her husband, and their children have all been living in a homeless shelter for the past year. Danielle and her husband, a Gulf War veteran, have fallen on hard times despite their attachment to the labor market, and are now in the city's welfare-to-work program, hoping that a subsidized apartment will open up soon. As shelter residents, they have priority on the waiting list, otherwise, according to Danielle "you could be waiting like 8, 9, 10 years to get in housing." Two years ago, unable to find affordable housing in New York, they moved to Virginia and tried to make it there. Danielle and Ronald both found low-wage jobs, working split shifts, and applied for child care subsidies, but they received nothing:

> The baby was like not even a year yet. And my oldest one, Andre, was about six. And they wouldn't provide us with child care, so I hardly seen my husband because he would work from in the morning until like four. And as soon as he came in he'd give me the car keys. I'd be waiting at the door for him and then I would go to work from like that time until 11, 12 at night. And when I got home, he was asleep to get up for work, so it was like because I didn't have child care, I had to do it like that.

Danielle and Ronald also did not qualify for food stamps or cash assistance as they were told they earned over the eligibility limit, despite their low-wage jobs, with Danielle bringing home $200 a week and her husband making "six and change" an hour in temporary work. They were barely making it, says Danielle, "when you broke down the bills and everything, what we were left with was barely, you know, what we had to eat." They stayed in Virginia for two years, never quite able to make ends meet, and because they were repeatedly denied child care subsidies and food stamps, they continued to work split shifts. But when Danielle was laid off from her job, the fragile household economy collapsed: "When I lost my job it became real stressful on us, and you know, it was like really hard. It was like we would have money, and it'd be either no food in the house, or the kid got to wear the shoes with the holes, you know."

After losing their apartment due to unpaid rent, they moved to a homeless shelter in Virginia, which Danielle describes as "more like a jail than a shelter." Demeaning treatment, a miserable and harsh environment, and then a lock-in curfew of 5:30 p.m. was the final straw for Danielle, who indignantly recalls, "I'm a grown woman, and I have to be in this place by 5:30!" They decided to return to New York City, where Danielle has family, and they went to the Emergency Assistance Unit (EAU). Initially refused assistance on the grounds that Danielle's mother and sister lived in the city (with six children and two adults in an overcrowded public housing unit), Danielle persisted and returned to the EAU, waiting there an entire day and night to be helped. When her baby son became horribly ill with food poisoning after eating the food provided by the EAU, an emergency room visit followed, and Danielle describes the practical distress of coping with an ill child when homeless: "My baby's sick for 14 days–I had a suitcase full of clothes; the whole suitcase was full of throw-up clothes. Everything I owned–everything–even my clothes was full of throw up. Everything."

Soon afterwards the family was allotted transitional shelter in one of the better family shelter units–a studio apartment with kitchen facilities. They have been there now for 13 months, waiting. Both Danielle and Ronald were ordered into New York's welfare-to-work program (WEP) when they entered the shelter system, requiring them each to work 35 hours a week in return for a meager $400-a-month cash assistance for the entire family. The WEP workfare program, which mandates that clients must work to pay off their benefits means that, in this case, two adults were each earning the equivalent of about $1.50 an hour, which Danielle angrily terms "legalized slavery . . . it's ridiculous. . . . I mean, if I'm going to work 35 hours a week, let me earn something, and let my husband work at what he wants!"

After receiving a WEP placement at a nursing home, Danielle attended a protest meeting in her neighborhood, led by an economic and social justice advocacy coalition, informing low-income parents of their rights and advocating for affordable child care and postsecondary education as an allowable work activity. Danielle began training at the coalition, and, empowered by her newly developed skills and knowledge about her rights, she left her WEP placement and began a paid internship at the coalition. Still homeless, however, after 13 months, frustrated by the lack of privacy in their studio shelter apartment, she has even considered "joining the service . . . (because) my basic thing right now is just being able to survive." Danielle is also angry that Ronald, a veteran, is eking out his days cleaning the streets in a dead-end and humiliating WEP placement:

> My husband, he's 42. He was in the air force for four years; he was military police. And you know, when we got in our situation where

we needed a place to live, I thought that it was really messed up that someone who protected our country has to go through the same things that a common person, you know someone off the streets, has to go through. . . . Like I don't feel we should have been in no shelter for a year, after my husband served his country, and watched the president's plane at that, you know?

Ronald would like to "clear up his license" and take care of the unpaid tickets from Virginia so he can get his commercial driver's license reinstated, as they both believe he could "earn good money driving if they're hiring right now." But there are no spare dollars to go around in the family, and until their housing crisis is resolved, Ronald is stuck.

Andre, Danielle's older son, attends elementary school, and 3-year-old Deron is cared for in the home of a family day care provider. Danielle describes how she was given a week to find a provider after she was initially approved for child care subsidies from the welfare office:

When they mailed me the letter, they just said you need child care, you know, and sent me the paper for a child care person to fill out, but they didn't send me a list that said these are the available ones (providers) within your area, call them! But you don't' know nothing about them. Then they didn't send me the list, and I was like, what the heck. I'm in the shelter down here, I had to go all the way to Harlem. . . . So everybody in shelters in Bronx, Queens, people were down there, so I had to go all the way . . . I had to wait half the day to see somebody to get the paper. . . . And it's bad because it's hard, I mean, they act like they're giving you this child care money, out of their own pockets half the time . . . and then I had to find my own child care, and I'm like, they could have, they might as well help you, you know! and it's like they say "You don't know anybody? You don't know nobody on your block who watches kids?"

Desperate to find a child care center, Danielle begins to walk the streets looking for places in the neighborhood where the shelter is located and close to her older son's elementary school. With less than a week to find a place and under constant pressure from the welfare center "to find someone on the block," Danielle sees the caseworker as completely indifferent to her concerns about quality and safety and her fears about locating child care in a dangerous neighborhood. "It's a shame," says Danielle, "it's like they don't care where your kids is, just as long as you do what they want you to do." After visiting centers and in-home providers with waiting lists, Danielle begins to despair of ever finding a suitable child care place for her toddler and third-grader:

> Before I found this lady, I didn't know what to do . . . I was like I was go-ing to all the little day cares, and it was like "Oh, the waiting list is three months." I'm like, well I gotta start this program on Monday, you know, and I've got a week to find a child provider . . . I want my child in a real place. . . . And so I was like going all over. . . . You know, [I saw] this house . . . and there was a sign that says "child care," I'm like I wanted a, you know, a *day care* day care, and finally I just said let me knock on this lady's door, and you know outside didn't look real great, but when she opened the door, there was the rug, she had the mat, she had all this play stuff, and I saw everything hanging from the ceiling, you know, like flowers and stuff like the kids, like at day care. So I went and I spoke to her and she said, "Yeah, I have two openings, so just bring him back to me." I went the same day, filled out the papers, I took it back, and then he was in there the next day.

Danielle, to her relief, likes the provider, whom she sees as warm and nurturing and as "really good with kids."

> She's pretty nice—you know, she feeds him [Deron] breakfast, she feeds him lunch, and a snack . . . she's really good with the kids. I mean, on his birthday, she was like, "don't buy a cake, I'm going to make the cake," you know. "I'm going to give him a party, don't bring nothing, just bring him and make sure he come that day so I can have a party," you know. She gave him a little present. You know she just loves kids.

The provider has eight foster children in the home and takes care of four or five children with help from some assistants. Although she is licensed, Danielle is unsure about any of the assistants' backgrounds, and as the provider has a night job, she takes naps every afternoon, leaving an assistant and her teenage daughters to take care of the children and foster children. Danielle appreciates the field trips to the park and the movies that the provider organizes for the children, as well as the arts and crafts activities, but she also confesses to feeling worried and always uneasy about the assistants, saying, "You're always going to have stuff in your head, like, wow, what if they hitting my child you know!" Andre goes there after school as well, and because the care is cheap, the cost is completely covered by her child care subsidies, so for now any nag-ging concerns she might have are overridden by her lack of choices, the convenient location, and the fact that she does not have any co-pays. Danielle also feels some peace of mind now that her 3-year-old son is talking, believing that he would be able to tell her if anything happens:

> He's at the age now where he like tells me everything, so I'm starting to feel comfortable. But when I first had to put him in child care when he was only 2 and he wasn't talking real good, I wasn't comfortable at all . . . also, my son's school is right across the street from the shelter, so it's like really convenient, and I mean she's, from what I see, you know, she's good. But I'm nervous about leaving my kids with anybody, period.

Danielle is not sure how long the present child care subsidies will last. Her internship will be over in one more month, and she would like to go back and complete her GED, obtain another internship, and go on to college. However, she is not sure whether that will be permitted under the WEP program, despite the New York City Access to Education and Training law that permits postsecondary educational hours to count as a work requirement.[7] Danielle almost completed her GED several months ago, but child care arrangements fell through at the last minute and, disappointed, she was forced to postpone the GED examination:

> I took the test to see if I was ready for my GED. And I passed the test with good marks. So they arranged for me to take my GED, and I was ready to take it. I had it set, you know, I had everything planned, and the day before the GED, 12:00 o'clock midnight, my friend who was supposed to be watching my kids called me and said she couldn't do it. And I didn't have nobody to watch my kids, so now I gotta re-apply for the GED and all that.

Danielle also worries that once Ronald's WEP assignment ends, her child care subsidies may be cut, disrupting both children's lives, until Ronald can find a job. Their marriage has been placed under strain while living in the shelter for "one long year" says Danielle, where "the only place you got for privacy is the bathroom." And Danielle, through her internship at the coalition, is ever mindful of the arbitrary sanctions resulting in cuts to welfare benefits and child care subsidies that have hit so many low-income parents:

> It's like a continuous cycle. So when you're sanctioned, they could put time lines on your sanction. You can be sanctioned for three months, six months, you know, and what am I supposed to do for those three months,

you know, or six months? And I think that's another thing that leads to homelessness too, because a lot of people on welfare . . . they can't pay their rent because the child care money didn't come through . . . and it's like a big vicious cycle you know!

Danielle recounts the multiple and intersecting crises that occur when low-income parents, such as herself, are caught in the punitive cycle of sanctions and how their rights to choose a job in the best interests of their own health, or their children's needs, are consistently violated:

> People who have babies, they can't go to WEP, but welfare don't care—if the welfare wants them to do a WEP assignment, which is going outside, cleaning the parks up and stuff . . . they don't care about them issues like health issues. So if you're not healthy enough to do it, and you say I'm not doing it . . . they cut your child care. But you may have something else in mind. Maybe I can't go out and pick up stuff in the park, but maybe I want to go to another training, you know. But they'll cut your child care off, and a lot of times they don't give you the information you need to find the proper child care, and you know, I've heard all kinds of stories—a lot of people are missing out, like losing jobs because they're not doing the work assignments, so welfare say, "I'm not going to pay this." I've just been pretty lucky as far as child care so far!

Danielle reflects on her life before "welfare reform" in 1996, when Andre, her older son, was a baby. Then, she was not forced into a WEP placement when he was an infant, and she had some choices when he was a toddler in terms of jobs. Now, all is far more punitive and frightening, and Danielle worries about the coming year:

> I mean the last time I had child care was like before they started the WEP and all that, where you didn't have to go to any assignments. And I would take my son to school and I did the work I wanted to do, and my child care was still paid for. So, I mean, I'm wondering how it's going to be when I leave the shelter system and how they're going to treat me. Am I gonna have the same problems that everyone else is having?

Poor parents such as Danielle, in need of assistance, now find themselves at the mercy of a welfare system that is in disarray. Arbitrary and often illegal cutoffs, constant threats of sanctions, active discouragement to clients seeking help, and a mismanaged child care system that fails dismally to meet a high and growing demand as more and more mothers (mostly single) are ordered into work placements when their infants are 12 weeks old. When child care subsidies are granted, payments are rarely received on time,[8] so parents often lose their child care slots. Danielle describes the chronic problem of late payments:

> They had my case for a month, and they [the provider] didn't get a check yet, so she told me we're not going to watch your kids anymore, and then they say they're going to sanction me because I'm not at the [WEP] program, You know, it's like a Catch-22. The child care providers stop providing services because they never received their checks. Because them hours they could be out doing something where they know they're going to have their money in their hand when they're supposed to. . . . And I've heard a lot of that, you know, doing outreach to the centers and stuff, you hear a lot of stories.

Danielle lives in two worlds. At the advocacy coalition she is perceived as a capable, resourceful, competent, and promising intern who efficiently runs the office and organizes action campaigns. In the New York welfare system she is just another homeless statistic, subject to arbitrary sanctions and cutoffs of child care subsidies. Without stable housing, reliable and continuing child care, and living-wage jobs, she and Ronald cannot make it up and out of poverty. Moreover, if they do find stable jobs, their child care subsidies will be cut, and they will need to find affordable child care in a city where full-time, good quality care runs between $8,000 and $15,000.[9] The odds are heavily stacked against Danielle and her family. Yet, she is not asking for much to succeed—she has drive, ambition, and determination—with public investments in her education, some help for Ronald to get back on his feet, and continuing support for housing and child care for their children, she and her family might face a very different future.

NOT GETTING BY IN AMERICA

> But the real question is not how well I did at work but how well I did at life in general, which includes eating and having a place to stay. The fact that these are two separate questions needs to be underscored right away. . . . Something is wrong, very wrong, when a single person in good health, a person who in addition possesses a working car, can barely support herself by the sweat of her brow.[10]

Barbara Ehrenreich, who embarked on a disturbing and eye-opening journey into the low-wage work world of America, vividly portrays her own difficulties making ends meet in Florida, Maine, and Minneapolis, Minnesota, as she took on an assortment of jobs as a waitress, maid, nursing-home aide, and Wal-Mart sales employee, earning on average $7 an hour. Finding a safe place to live entailed long commutes as she searched for cheaper rents in overpriced efficiencies off the highway, trailers, single-room rentals in dilapidated houses, and cheap motel chains. Lack of health insurance, lack of adequate nutrition, and chronic housing problems characterized the lives of Ehrenreich's coworkers, and most did not have young children to care for. As Ehrenreich reports on her "failure" to match income and expenses and construct a decent life as a low-wage employee, despite the wage gains at the end of the 1990s, she remarks, "There are no secret economies that nourish the poor; on the contrary, there are a host of special costs."[11] And special costs incurred by low-income households with children inevitably include child care, health care, transportation, and housing.

For Hannah and Thomas in San Diego, the special costs were Seth's child care, an unmanageable burden that had to be weighed against food, their co-op housing, and their older children's school attendance and academic achievement. For Danielle and Ronald in New York City, lack of affordable housing led them to relocate to Virginia, and even with both working round the clock, they could not make ends meet. Without access to public benefits they eventually became homeless when Danielle was laid off. With no cushion to support them, they returned to New York—fallen workers of the low-wage economy, consigned to the city's obdurate welfare-to-work regime to instill in its recipients a new and better work ethic! The special costs to their children and their marriage are yet to emerge.

It is clear that working low-income people are indeed living in poverty, even if federal income thresholds depict otherwise. The federal poverty threshold, developed by Mollie Orshansky of the Social Security Administration in the early 1960s was, as she herself pointed out, a crude criterion of income adequacy and assumed that poor families spent one-third of their income on food. That figure was multiplied by three (for housing and personal needs) and adjusted for family size; yet, as Orshansky has stated, this was designed to serve a temporary or emergency use and was certainly not indicative of an adequate living standard.[12] In the past four decades, the Census Bureau has continued to use this inadequate measure unchanged, and each year, using the Consumer Price

Index, sets the poverty threshold, adjusted for family size and number of children in the family. The poverty threshold fails to take account of urban/rural differences and the changing needs of families for child care, as well as transportation and increased housing and health costs; moreover, the threshold artificially depresses the number of people living in poverty. An updated alternative measure would most certainly increase the percentage of Americans living in poverty.[13] The poverty threshold has been severely criticized as outdated and inadequate, failing to conform to international comparative standards of measuring poverty. European and other affluent countries use a relative poverty line, defined as one-half of the national median household income.[14] This latter measure comes closer to the 200% threshold (twice the federal poverty line) that is used to categorize "nonpoor" low-income households in the United States.[15] With 13.5 million children (18%) living in poverty, and 29.2 million children (40%) living in low-income families,[16] the politics of numbers cannot hide the fact that the human capabilities of millions of children are impaired by shamefully negligent public policies that fail to address and prevent the lived realities of deprivation. Growing up in the United States is fraught with risks and instability for more than half the nation's children. The recent report, *Hardships in America*, documents that almost one-third of working families with incomes below 200% of the federal poverty line faced critical hardships such as food insecurity, eviction, homelessness, and lack of health care, and that 72% of these same families experienced serious hardships such as lack of child care.[17]

The Economic Policy Institute (EPI) has calculated basic family budget levels to assess the real cost of living in different communities, which include differences between rural and urban areas, and what it takes to maintain a safe and adequate life.[18] Basic family budgets include food, transportation, child care, health care, and other personal necessities and are individualized by region and family type to develop a realistic measure of how much income is needed "to secure safe and decent-yet-modest living standards" in a given geographic community. In contrast to the artificially low current poverty threshold, the family budget "offers a broader measure of economic welfare."[19] More than three times as many families fall below family budget levels compared with those who fall below the poverty line.[20] Using the EPI "Basic Family Budget Calculator," a family of four in New York City (two parents and two children) would need a monthly total of $4,888 and an annual income of $58,656, with housing costs assessed at $1,075, and quality child care for two children budgeted at $1,195 a month.[21] Yet, by way of comparison, the federal poverty line for a family of four is only $20,000.[22] In San Diego, California, a family of five (2 parents and three children) would need a monthly income of $5,905 and an annual income of $70,860 to afford monthly housing costs of $1,725 and child care costs of $1,300, whereas the federal poverty line for a family of five is $23,400! For Danielle and Ronald, scraping by on next to nothing in New York City, $58,000 a year is a far cry from their meager resources. Hannah and Thomas, whose combined income of $35,000 keeps them above the federal poverty line of $23,400, live far below a basic family budget for their family of five. Such economic deprivation is widespread among two-parent low-income families, leading to a diminished existence from which their children do not emerge unscathed.

It is also clear that marriage is no antidote to poverty when both partners are in the low-wage economy with few, if any, family supports available. So while President Bush's 2004 Marriage Promotion Initiative proposed $1.5 billion dollars to promote marriages for poor people as the latest Republican poverty-alleviation measure, it was, as the *New York Times* editorial declared, a "particularly cruel" one, for "to pour the money into marriage and relationship counseling for people without economic hope is a very expensive version of spitting into the wind."[23] Family-strengthening initiatives that are sorely needed in the lives of the parents and children portrayed in this chapter involve living wages, affordable housing, health care, and high quality child care provisions. As long as low-income families are left to sink or swim against the market tides, the geography of where one becomes poor and which limited resources are available will largely determine whose children stay afloat.

CHAPTER 5

"Difficult" Children: Disrupted Placements and Expulsions

June and Chiquila are two low-income single mothers who have struggled to find child care for their emotionally destabilized children—children whose behavior has marginalized them as unwanted troublemakers in their small daily child care worlds. These single mothers confront innumerable obstacles as child care arrangements break down time after time— many family day care providers, center teachers, and directors are simply unwilling to work with high-needs, demanding young children, whose perceived unmanageable behaviors make them pariahs in their child care settings. Their mothers must grapple with the fact that their children have become family hazards, threatening the viability of the family unit as disrupted child care most certainly means job absences and possible job loss. Five-year-old Joseph and 4-year-old Anita react to the continuing instability of their daily worlds with anger and aggression, experiencing a pattern of rejection, disrupted placements, and early expulsions from several child care settings. In June's family, a tragic outcome unfolds for Joseph; in Chiquila's family, a dramatic turnaround takes place in the life of Anita.

JUNE AND JOSEPH: A CHILD REJECTED

> I can't keep going on like this. The day care guy's getting to the point where he can't take Joseph anymore, and I gotta work to pay the bills.

June, a White single mother of five children ranging in age from 17 to an infant, is a survivor of domestic violence and a recovering alcoholic. Currently living in Iowa, she has endured fifteen years of violence, undergone treatment for substance abuse, and temporarily surrendered her children to the child welfare system while under treatment. Her children have suffered, but her 5-year-old biracial son, Joseph, bears the most visible emotional scars. A demanding, bright, and active child, Joseph is described by several adults as "unmanageable" and has fast become a young "persona non grata" as he has been expelled and bounced around from one child care setting to another, "demoted" from kindergarten, and recently placed on medication.

June left her abusive partner in 2001 and entered an emergency-shelter program for women and children in a college town in Iowa. Her story is layered with turmoil and struggle. When the substance abuse escalated, she sought help, but that presented new dangers in terms of finding child care or facing the risk of losing her children to foster care. One of her friends, who is present as June relates her experiences, describes the events:

> June's been sober just over a year now, and when she came back from treatment, she couldn't get her children, it got all messed up . . . she needed to go to these appointments, but there was no child care provided, and so that forced her to have to choose to have her kids in the child welfare system so she had the child care provided so she could continue to stay sober . . . so it just made this triangle.

Temporarily entering the child welfare system actually worked out in June's favor, as she was able to access counseling services for her children and, for a short period of time, received child-protective funds. Determined to stay sober, and with her children back at home, June began to look for a job while continuing to attend counseling sessions, as well as appointments with her children's therapists. However, as soon as June entered the Promise Jobs welfare-to-work program in Iowa, she encountered many hurdles accessing child care subsidy payments, as only the hours spent searching for a job are covered:

> Because of my kids' behavior issues, you know, as far as they have issues that they have to work on, so they'll have like different therapists and that kind of thing, so I had lots of appointments. So between the time that I was looking for a job and appointments, they would only pay for the time I was looking for a job. So then I was kind of in a Catch-22 because I had this other stuff to do and so it was hectic.

June needs time to search for a developmentally supportive child care setting for 5-year-old Joseph, but she cannot get any financial assistance from the welfare-to-work program for temporary child care, and now finds herself caught in the classic welfare paradox—no job without child care, but no child care without a job—as she struggles to balance all the other competing demands of her fragile and destabilized family:

> I found that difficult in the beginning, you know, if I didn't have a job I wouldn't even get the subsidy. I had to already have a job before I could get it . . . and I couldn't work at the time . . . it was like the hours I could put in for availability was very limited because of all the appointments.

With assistance from a local Iowa welfare rights advocacy coalition, June eventually finds a job in the kitchen of a local high school working from 9:00 a.m. to 3:00 p.m. every day, and with child care subsidies in place, she enrolls her baby and Joseph in a family day care setting. However, Joseph's placement soon becomes precarious. The provider does not want him there because of his disruptive behavior. June describes the list of behaviors that have created problems in the current child care setting, as well as in previous child care programs he has attended, "spitting, hitting, kicking, a lot of aggression kinds of things."

Through all Joseph's ordeals, the only center that seems to have accepted and welcomed him is a Head Start program that he attended the previous year in a neighboring city. June describes how Joseph "did very well there" and how the staff were supportive and were able to respond to Joseph's needs, but since he left Head Start and the family moved to their present location, Joseph has been bounced around from placement to placement because of his misbehavior:

> My child has behavior issues, so it's hard to get him to sit in time outs . . . so therefore it requires a little bit more attention, which would be taking away from the other kids. So his ratio needs to be lower as far as teacher-child ratios that they have in day care homes and centers. So because he requires extra, you know, time and attention, it's like basically he's three kids-in-one kind of thing!

Joseph was "demoted" from kindergarten and sent to a public prekindergarten during fall 2003, but he was considered a problem there as well because of his "aggressive behaviors . . . and a lot of talking and a lot of attention-seeking kind of behaviors." Marginalized in both his public prekindergarten and in the child care setting he currently attends, Joseph is a child under constant surveillance. His mother describes how, "because his behavior has been out of left field, so to speak, when he walks in the door everyday, they're watching him like a hawk."

June feels overwhelmed by Joseph's problems and has been unable to find a center that can handle him. She notes that many centers have quotas in terms of how many children they will accept on state-funded child care subsidies, which again limits a parent's choices, and this is exacerbated when a child has special needs. She wearily states what she would like:

> To find a child care center, preferably that would take more of the subsidies and not just have a certain amount that they'll take, and also be able to have, be equipped to handle children that have behavior issues, so they know how to deal with it without being so reactive—not reacting to every little thing!

In the previous city where June lived, she had the same problem—she could not find an affordable high quality center, and none of the family day care homes covered by the subsidies were willing to work with her or to help Joseph, then only a toddler, cope with the instability and trauma of his young life. With the notable exception of the Head Start experience, the norm has been exclusion and an unwillingness to deal with his special needs:

> They just aren't equipped to handle kids that have behavior issues. . . . They deal with it for a short time, but they get to the point where they can't handle it. And so, you know, the place that my child's currently in now, he [the provider] says he does crisis care, but he's getting to the point where he can't handle it either.

Joseph has been assessed by a psychologist at the mental health clinic, and June has been told that Joseph's issues need "more immediate attention." He has been placed on medication, and June is alarmed by the recommendation that he be sent away to a residential facility for treatment. While Joseph is clearly an emotionally destabilized and demanding child, some of his ascribed problem behaviors in prekindergarten and child care—aggression, not paying attention, not following directions—could just as likely be categorized as falling within the range of testy and challenging 5-year-old behaviors. The fact that Joseph was witness to, and victim of, an ongoing cycle of family violence during his earliest years, and that he, too, suffered emotional turmoil during his mother's struggles to cope with domestic violence and substance abuse, make it fairly predictable that he would exhibit some symptoms of post-traumatic stress disorder. However, because June is a single mother in poverty, overwhelmed by multiple responsibilities—Joseph's "unmanageable" behaviors, her older children's problems, the demands of a new baby, a constant deficit of economic resources and time, dread of another child care expulsion, and the fear of losing her job—5-year-old Joseph has become a threat to his fragile family's existence:

> I can't keep going on like this. The day care guy's getting to the point where he can't do it anymore, and I have to go to work to pay the bills, and so if I don't have no day care, then I can't work, you know. And the behaviors need to get under control. We've got to get it figured out now while he's young, rather than waiting until he's almost an adult to get it worked out.

It appears that the psychologist has convinced June that she would be acting in her son's best interests to send him away to a residential facility for up to a year. The facility under consideration is several hours' drive from their home, and June sighs as, visibly upset, she resigns herself to the psychologist's recommendation, saying, "It's just no other way around it, I guess. . . . It's just not going to be possible to have him [in day care] because of the magnitude of the behavior." The fact that no educational or child care setting can or will accommodate Joseph's special needs places June in an untenable position. The public kindergarten that "demoted" Joseph and the prekindergarten where he is not wanted has further increased Joseph's pariah status and leaves his mother feeling desperate for a solution that could help Joseph, but not jeopardize her job or the family:

> I don't know, the guy [psychologist] was telling me today it may take up to a year. And I thought, "Oh my God!" I'm real sad today, but I'm trying to hold it together you know, and try to think that, you know, it's for the best interest of him and try not to think about my own feelings so much. But I don't want anybody to feel sorry for me or whatever, if anybody feels sorry, it should be for him because he's the one that, you know, is going to have to be away, and it's just going to be hard.

Sending a little boy away from his mother for up to a year does indeed appear to be a drastic intervention borne of a mother's desperate need to maintain a low-wage job, while feeling stretched to a breaking point by the competing demands on her time and emotional energy. Neither the mental health system, nor the welfare system, nor the public kindergarten has invested adequate time and resources in providing ongoing and intensive therapeutic interventions for Joseph, a child coping with a traumatic early childhood. In addition, the glaring *absence* of affordable high quality child care that *could* offer developmentally supportive interventions only increases the mounting pressure on June.

As this family drama unfolds, several concerned community volunteers, in collaboration with the welfare advocacy coalition, meet to intervene and assist June, by doing some respite child care and contacting the mental health clinic about the pending dire recommendation and referral for Joseph. As June wrestles with her own guilt, she remarks how Joseph "has been through a lot of stuff . . . and it's not all his fault you know—he was in an environment where it wasn't good for the first four years of his life."

Clearly, for poor children like Joseph who have been through "a lot of stuff," there is minimal public support available; specifically, high quality professional child care settings where crisis interventions and appropriate developmental supports are provided. Joseph, at 5 years old, is a stigmatized, costly, and unwanted "public" child.

CHIQUILA AND ANITA: A CHILD TRANSFORMED

And they came to me at Christmas time, and they say, "We no longer want your daughter to return!". . . I felt like I was helpless . . . I had no options and I had to work . . . the teachers should have special skills to know how to handle a child who is a little different.

Chiquila, at 45, is a woman who is carefully and purposefully putting her life back together after years of drug addiction and alcohol abuse, a brief period of drug-related incarceration, and disrupted relationships with her two daughters. One of nine siblings, Chiquila grew up in a low-income African-American family in West Michigan. Her older daughter, 24, is now a mother with young children of her own, and she and Chiquila have only recently repaired a difficult past. Due to Chiquila's addiction problems, her older daughter lived with her father and did not see Chiquila during her formative years. Chiquila's "baby daughter," Anita, is now 4 years old, and for her first two years she lived with her aunt while Chiquila was in rehabilitation. Now "clean" and determined to stay that way, Chiquila has regained custody of Anita and moved to a new city in southeast Michigan, located within a 60-mile swath of hospitals, universities, community colleges, good schools, and a well-resourced community network. With a full-time job at Wendy's and assisted by a nonprofit family unification agency, Chiquila moved into a two-bedroom subsidized apartment in a public housing site, located near a shopping mall, a bus system, and an elementary school. Chiquila is very grateful for the support she has received from AA and NA (Narcotics Anonymous), as well as from the community organizations that have helped her "get back on my feet." Chiquila describes how, once she regained custody of Anita, "that's when my child care problems began!"

Anita, in her young life, has endured many early traumas related to separation and abandonment from her mother. When she was released back into Chiquila's custody at age two, finding good child care was extremely difficult. Working both day and odd-hour shifts at Wendy's gave Chiquila little time flexibility, and with no car her choices were limited to the bus routes to and from Wendy's and the apartment. Eligible to receive partial child care subsidies from Michigan's Department of Human Services FIP program, Chiquila finds a licensed family day care provider with early and late hours midway between work and home. Shirin, the provider, is a recent immigrant from the Middle East and speaks only limited English, and Anita does not adjust to the setting:

> And my daughter struggled, my little daughter, because she didn't speak very much English. . . . two other little girls would come that was from the same country as Shirin, but they didn't speak that much English. So I guess my daughter kinda like, looking through her eyes, was like in a foreign country with foreign people, but feeling like she, you know, didn't belong. . . . And I knew that I needed to keep my job, and I did the best that I could, and I was like "Oh my God," I really don't want to leave my daughter because she cried every morning. That just tore me up so bad!

As Chiquila must be at work by 7:30 a.m., she has to drop Anita off at the provider's at 6:30. With no car, she uses a combination of taxis and buses, and in winter that proves difficult:

> So, you know, I would take the cab to Shirin's, drop my daughter at 6:30—She'd take her in the house screaming, and me, I'd have to go out and wait from 6:30 until 7:00 for the bus. So that's a 30 minute wait in the cold . . . then I had to get a bus from where I work, and I would get off and I would walk to get Anita. Then we would wait for the bus and get back on. . . . It was a lot of bus transport, and it was very stressful.

Afraid of losing her job and possibly custody of her daughter if she fails to fulfill all the court-ordered mandates to provide a stable and suitable home, Chiquila feels that she has few options. Everything hinges on her maintaining a job and staying "clean" and sober. Earning $8.50 an hour at Wendy's, with food supplements from WIC and food stamps, she faces a deficit of resources and a deficit of time to attend to her daughter's needs:

> I said, I gotta do this, you know, I gotta hope that everything'll be okay. And I would go get her. I would try get off work early. I'd tell my boss, "Look, I can't handle this. My daughter's at a place where she's not comfortable. I'm not comfortable, you know, being here at work trying to perform my job."

Chiquila becomes increasingly anxious about her daughter's distraught reactions when she leaves her at the child care provider every morning, and she decides she has to find another child care setting, saying:

> Oh my God, it was such a struggle . . . she would just cry and scream, and hold onto me. . . . I felt helpless, and I've had no knowledge and I just felt trapped you know. . . . Why am I putting my daughter in this lady's care, you know . . . and I'm like, "Okay, I gotta do something else."

With the help of the regional child care agency of the Michigan 4C, Chiquila locates a licensed family day care provider in a trailer park on a bus route. The provider, Mary, cares for four other children and charges $125 a week. Because Chiquila was on public assistance when her adult daughter was a young child, the FIP program now deducts from her meager monthly earnings to pay back her "debt" from more than twenty years ago, which lowers the amount of the child care subsidy, and Chiquila ends up making a $30 co-pay each week. In addition, the transportation problems are even worse:

> I would get up at 5:30. And me and Anita would get on the bus at 6:45, and I would have to take another bus to get to Mary's house. . . . And I had to take [Number] 22 and get off at Mary's house, drop Anita off, run back to the bus stop and make sure I got on the bus. . . . It would take us two hours to get there, and two hours back every night. And every night Anita would cry. She would, Oh my God! She would cry getting up, getting on the bus. We've had to stand in the rain, in the sleet, in the snow—Oh, goodness. And I was like, I can't do this no more. I can't take it. And I would go to my [AA and NA] meetings, and I would share that, and I would say, you know, I never knew parenthood was this tough. You know, after I've screwed my life around, and I

wanted to be a parent, because I didn't want to lose my parental rights for my daughter. . . . I had not a clue that it would be this difficult. It wouldn't have if I was at home, but I chose not to go back home. I chose to try to start a new life here!

But her new life is filled with daunting challenges that focus on her young daughter's distress in the new child care setting. Anita cries inconsolably, and Mary the provider, complains that she aggressively pushes the other children and snatches toys from them. She is also not fully potty-trained, which irritates Mary, who already has labeled Anita a "problem child." Chiquila reluctantly keeps Anita at the provider while she searches for other child care options. The situation continues to deteriorate, and Chiquila feels that Mary is indifferent to her daughter's needs. After three months of searching she finds a place at a child care center within walking distance of her job, so she informs Mary that she is pulling Anita out immediately. Mary becomes very angry with her and calls Child Protective Services and reports her for "abuse." Angered by the provider's "vindictive" behavior and shocked when she hears about the "false accusations"–that Anita's crying was a sign that she was afraid to go home with her mother and that she was performing "adult acts" on little children, "like pulling their pants down and laying on top of them"–Chiquila tells the child protective services caseworker about her ongoing problems with Mary, and her fears that Mary's report could place her custody in jeopardy. However, after the abuse report is investigated, the case is closed and Chiquila, angry but very relieved, describes how the caseworker "went back with all the information to her boss, and the next day she called me and she said, 'You're fine.' So that was an ugly experience!"

Chiquila enrolls Anita at Lollipop Learning Center, her third child care setting in four months. Lollipop is a large center with over 200 children at two locations, and it is expensive at $800 a month. As Michigan child care subsidies do not pay the market costs of child care, Chiquila is left with a co-pay of $168 a month.[1] Although the location is very convenient, the quality of care is poor, and the teacher–child ratio does not meet minimum required standards on many days.[2] Anita, now potty-trained, begins to regress. Chiquila describes how, "Each time I went there she had accidents." Oftentimes, there would be 25 children with one teacher and one teacher aide, and Anita's screaming and behavior "problems" worsen. Chiquila describes how, "there was a setback in her. And I wasn't sure if it was just because there was so many children, or she needed more attention, or whatever the case may be."

Stressed and anxious about her daughter's worsening behavior problems, Chiquila pulls her out of Lollipop and returns for help to the 4C child care agency. They assist Chiquila in finding a spot for Anita at a child care center for low-income parents with sliding scale fees. Chiquila is very relieved, and with a promotion to manager at Wendy's and earning almost double her previous wage–$13.68 an hour–she begins to look towards better times. She purchases an old car, which cuts down on transportation problems. However, increased earnings at her job result in a total cutoff of child care subsidies from FIP,[3] and while the new center has a sliding scale fee, Chiquila is still charged $440 a month. The 4C agency gives Chiquila a child care scholarship, which pays part of the cost, and Anita, at 3 years old, begins her fourth day care experience. The first weeks go well and Chiquila is hopeful. However, Chiquila is trying to cope with the escalating demands of her new position, which requires several night shifts that create additional child care problems. Commenting that Wendy's was not "a job that had any compassion," Chiquila applies for a transfer to an hourly wage manager; that way she figures she will be able to design an easier hourly schedule and spend more time with her daughter.

However, the new schedule is even worse as Chiquila must work until closing on weekends to keep her pay rate. Her new schedule–Tuesdays, Wednesdays, and Thursdays from 8:00 a.m. to 4:30 p.m. and Fridays and Saturdays from 4:00 p.m. to 1:00 a.m.–means that as before, Chiquila has to rely on girlfriends to take care of Anita on two weekend nights, resulting in unstable and makeshift arrangements. Chiquila has little choice in the matter–having no job threatens her court-adjudicated custody, and yet the job she has, which pays almost a living wage, has impossible hours that places her own mothering at risk.

Anita reacts to the constant instability of arrangements at home and in her various child care placements by lashing out at other children. Soon the teacher is sending home incident reports, and Chiquila feels at her wits' end: "Anita was having confrontations all the time. . . . Like she was spitting. She was pushing the kids. She was jumping off tables. She had a meltdown. She scratched a little boy, or, you know, there was constantly negative reports–Never nothing positive." Chiquila's hope that the "professional" teachers at her daughter's new center will be understanding and extra-sensitive to her daughter's plight is short-lived:

> So we got together and we all sat down. . . . And, you know, I felt at the
> time in my spirit and my heart, this was the goodest and the best thing

> to do was to inform them, you know, that Anita was having difficulties as a kid growing up, you know, due to the lack of me. . . . And I said, a lot of it could be because she's just a child that needs to be taught in a different way.

Anita is moved to a different classroom and an early intervention specialist from the 4C agency consults with the teachers and suggests ways of helping Anita adjust and of creating a more accommodating classroom environment. But Chiquila sees no change or sensitivity on the part of the teachers:

> No matter what Anita did, they looked at it as, "Oh, she just had a meltdown.". . . And suddenly then they put my child out of school . . . they come to me at Christmas time, and they say, we no longer want your daughter to return . . . so, when they told me that, I got on the phone and I called [the 4C agency]. And I was devastated and I explained to them, you know, the difficulties that I was having at the center because, you know, they were paying the money for Anita to go there.

The agency responds to the growing crisis for Chiquila and Anita, and once again the early intervention specialist consults with the child care staff, suggesting that Anita be allowed to return for a transition period, while they assist Chiquila in finding another placement and arrange for clinical assessments. Anita, now 4, is diagnosed with Attention Deficit Hyperactivity Disorder (ADHD), and becomes eligible for special education early intervention services at a public preschool in the county. Meanwhile, as the search for an alternative child care placement is underway, Anita is permitted to temporarily return after Christmas to the center that has "expelled" her. However, one day later, Chiquila reports that "they said it was over. Meanwhile, I had her in no kind of nothing and I was working." Desperate to find a good place for Anita and to keep custody of her daughter, Chiquila applies for a one-month leave at her job: "I told them I won't be able to return back to work until some time in February. So I'm going to need all this time off because they put my daughter out of school and I don't know how or what I'm gonna do."

With a month's leave of absence, Chiquila begins an urgent search once again for quality child care. Assisted by the early intervention specialist and the agency, which has been a godsend for Chiquila, she locates a special education teacher who runs a small family day care program for children with special needs. After the clinical assessments are completed, Anita is accepted at the county's intermediate school district special education program in the afternoon. Whereas the afternoon program is public and free, the child care program is expensive, at $180 a week ($720 a month) for only half-time care. Chiquila receives a partial child care scholarship from the agency, and she pays $110 a week with the scholarship making up the difference.

Chiquila returns to work and to her odd-hours schedule, but management is unresponsive when she requests a change of hours. Disaffected and extremely anxious about the impact of her weekend absences on her daughter, Chiquila begins an active job search. The GED and culinary courses she completed while in prison and her experience as a prison cook prove useful; she finds a job as a cook at a nearby hospital. There is a slight pay cut to $12 an hour, but the promise of a union job with good benefits and day hours is clearly worth the drop in pay, and Chiquila hands in her notice at Wendy's. After such a difficult two-year struggle, trying to locate a good child care setting for her daughter, Chiquila's life changes dramatically. Suddenly and unexpectedly her 4-year-old daughter starts to thrive, and Chiquila describes the child care provider Ellen, a certified special education teacher, in glowing terms:

> She's been in day care for fifteen years . . . and she has helped me so much with Anita. Now Anita tells me how she feels. She tells me what she doesn't like. She didn't used to be able to tell me that. She learned that through being at Ellen's. All the things that the other place labeled her as, she's not like that at Ellen's. Ellen gives her space and tells her when she's ready to talk, then they'll talk.

Anita bonds with Ellen, forms friendships with the other children, and is stimulated by the variety of activities every day and adjusts well to the small group size of six children:

> She loves being there . . . and all the little kids just love Anita. Oh my God, they just love her to death. I bring her in the morning; they are like "Hi, Anita.". . . And then she has a little friend, his name is Charles, and they get along just like marvelous. They're out riding bikes, Ellen takes them swimming, they go to do gymnastics, you know, they eat at McDonald's on Fridays. They go to the library on Wednesdays, which she likes. The new library is right behind Ellen's house, and they walk and they work on the computers, it's totally different. And I don't know if it's because it's a smaller group. I don't know if it's because Ellen shows Anita a lot of care and concern. I'm not real sure what it is, because she's so different!

Chiquila is also very pleased with the early childhood intervention program that Anita is bussed to every afternoon and regrets that she could not send Anita there earlier. As the summer approaches, Anita will attend Ellen's full-time, once again benefiting from the continuing agency scholarship support. Chiquila, in training for her new job, feels optimistic about the future. She has successfully won a child-support order from Anita's father, and her first checks with back-dated child support are coming in at $500 a month. Because she is no longer receiving any FIP subsidies, there are no debt deductions and she is receiving the full amount.

In the fall Anita will attend a full-day kindergarten program at the public school, where she will receive special education services. She will need early morning and one hour of after-school care until Chiquila gets off work to pick her up. The cost of the before- and after-school program is $400 a month, and Chiquila plans to apply for a partial scholarship from the public schools. Of course Chiquila's hopes for a "normal life" hinge on her daughter's continued progress and a successful adjustment to kindergarten. Chiquila, planning for the future, wants to attend community college and enroll in medical transcription courses in the hope of finding a different job with better pay and better hours. As Chiquila looks back on the past four years, fraught with her own personal struggle and constant child care crises, she comments, "Sometimes I sit here and when I'm here by myself and Anita's out playing, I'm like, you know, in space thinking, Wow! She's came a long way!"

Chiquila's life and that of her young daughter have stabilized, for now. With the extraordinary support of the 4C agency staff and other caring and committed community partners, Anita has finally come into her own with early intervention services and top quality child care that she—and every child—deserves.

EVERYTHING ON THE LINE:
DISRUPTED FAMILIES, DESTABILIZED CHILDREN

June and Chiquila, women who suffered the ravages of substance abuse and addiction, both lost custody of their children temporarily and fought successfully to regain custody after they completed substance-abuse treatment programs. In June's situation, her children not only experienced the trauma of their mother's addictive behavior, but also were witnesses to, and victims of, the ongoing domestic violence perpetrated by June's partner and father of one of her children. Chiquila lost her older daughter as she sank into a world of drug addiction and prison, emerging years later determined to repair the damage and do better with her second child, born when she was 40 years old. For both mothers, coping with an emotionally scarred and difficult-to-manage child placed everything on the line: parenting, a job, mental health, family stability, and ultimately family survival.

In Chiquila's case, maintaining her job while a single mother entailed balancing the higher wages of a promotion against the emotional costs to her child. Working evening and weekend hours meant long absences from her daughter, resulting in unstable, unreliable child care arrangements. For single mothers like Chiquila, who lack education, jobs with nonstandard hours are often the only ones available. Such mothers are disproportionately represented in the low-wage, odd-hours sector, and, Presser and Cox's research confirms that they "appear drawn into working nonstandard hours by a lack of options."[4]

For Anita, who had endured so much in her earliest years, her sense of security and stability was repeatedly disrupted by Chiquila's inflexible work schedule, as well as indifferent and poor quality child care placements, where scant attention was paid to her special needs. Chiquila's capacity to maintain her job forced her to rely on friends and acquaintances to take care of her child, while she worked nights and weekends. With little time or resources left to cope with Anita's escalating emotional problems, the disrupted placements and the child care expulsion incident created ever-ready threats to the tenuous family life that Chiquila had struggled to construct for herself and Anita. If not for the persistent interventions and support from the regional 4C agency, Anita would have been just another one of hundreds of thousands of publicly discarded poor children, a "misfit" child with no place to go—as her desperate mother searched for some affordable setting that would accept her child. In such situations, supportive early childhood interventions provided by trained, sensitive, and caring early childhood professionals *can* and *did* make a world of difference for mother and child.

The absence of such supportive interventions in Joseph's life created a situation of forced abandonment where a young boy was on the brink of being sent away from home to a residential facility, because his desperate mother could see no other way out. The clinic psychologist, in evaluating Joseph's failure to adapt and adjust to the inflexible routines of cheap, inferior quality child care settings, failed to consider how a negative and harsh child care environment may have actually exacerbated Joseph's problems; instead he persuaded June that there was no other viable solution. Yet, only one year earlier, Joseph had done well in a high quality Head Start center, where his special needs were acknowledged and he was given individualized attention and developmentally supportive interventions. However, having aged out of Head Start, and in the absence of available and affordable high quality child care programs, Joseph was marked for expulsion and exile—where, no doubt, his earlier trauma of abandonment would only be compounded by the removal from his home. Rejection, as Garbarino points out "corrodes and damages the sense of self-worth in much the same way that cancer damages the body; it twists a child's outlook and makes every action painful."[5] In Joseph's situation, poverty, family violence, and the accumulation of other risk factors overwhelmed his capacity to cope.[6]

Garbarino's emphasis on the importance of understanding children's development from an ecological framework, in the context of the *macrosystem* that shapes the early years,[7] is particularly relevant when we consider vulnerable families and children. Poverty, stressed parents, emotionally destabilized children, inadequate and inferior child care settings—all increase psychosocial risks, where powerlessness is a key factor leading to "impaired development."[8] Negative experiences of a child in the *microsystem*—in this case, the child care setting—"color his or her whole view of the world,"[9] and rejection, social isolation, and punishment that often precede the expulsion event may well damage the child's developing sense of self. Clearly Joseph and Anita were difficult children to handle, particularly in group settings. Both emerged scarred from early crises that undermined their trust. Yet it is important to note that both children were responsive and began to flourish when placed in developmentally supportive environments, where interventions by trained early childhood professionals produced positive results. Unfortunately for Joseph, his successful period was short-lived, but it was a time his mother remembers as the only one in which Joseph seemed to do "very well."

The experiences of Joseph and Anita mirror a widespread and disturbing phenomenon in the United States, where, in the absence of a national child care system—no federal child care licensing requirements and no national child care quality controls—high quality child care is neither accessible nor affordable for the majority of low-income children with special needs. Publicly funded early interventions for troubled and traumatized young children do exist in select preprimary, special education programs, but those programs require referrals and assessments, and many poor parents are simply unable to access them. Some states pay higher subsidy rates for special-needs care,[10] but there is a great variation

CHAPTER 6

Immigrant Mothers: Child Care in the Shadows

Low-income immigrant mothers face distinctive obstacles in locating good quality child care when they possess neither English proficiency nor the resources to pay the market costs of high quality child care. Currently one in every five children in the United States has a foreign-born parent, with the majority of immigrant families experiencing high levels of poverty and restricted access to public benefits. Among immigrant families, more than 25% of young children live in poverty, and well over 50% live below 200% of the poverty threshold.[1] As the fastest growing segment of the nation's young child population, low-income immigrant children are far less likely to gain access to quality child care, and are underrepresented in public prekindergarten and Head Start programs.[2]

The five Latina immigrant women whose difficulties are chronicled here[3] share a desire for child care that is "educational," professional, and center based, but despite their best efforts, their children end up in the informal and/or cheapest care sector, where their child care experiences have been particularly bad, and, in two cases, damaging and dangerous. Often socially isolated, fearful of getting "in trouble" with immigration or agency authorities, and lacking knowledge of their rights as well as the necessary cultural competence to navigate the maze of child care subsidies, the women turn to neighborhood providers, who are typically unlicensed and, as more than one mother put it, "only in it for the money."

ANA AND LUCIA AND THEIR CHILDREN: STUCK WITH BAD OPTIONS

I haven't been able to work, because I don't have anyone I can trust to take care of my kids (Ana)

> I have been without day care for four years . . . I tried to get day care, but I haven't got anything. I've applied, but I had no response (Lucia)

Ana and Lucia are good friends and recent immigrants, living in the same low-income neighborhood in New York City. Lucia, from Ecuador, is married with two children, ages 10 and 5; Ana is a single mother from the Dominican Republic, with a 12-year-old son and a 3-year-old daughter. Both women attend ESL classes at an adult literacy center and are enrolled in a job-training program. As low-income immigrant mothers with legal residency status, they are eligible to receive child care subsidies, but they have experienced continuing problems locating subsidies, as well as safe and affordable child care. Neither mother has ever heard of Head Start or other public preschool programs operating in their school district, and with limited English proficiency, they have not yet become system-savvy in terms of locating resources.

Lucia describes her many futile attempts to obtain child care subsidies from the city over the past three years:

> I have always worked, and I have tried many times to get day care [subsidies]. . . . I went twice to the office this year, and I filled out the application; they told me they would call. Then they called me at home telling me that they needed more papers from me, but I haven't heard anything from them. . . . It's a big problem for myself.

Consequently, when trying to locate before- and after-school care for her 10-year-old, and child care for her 5-year-old, Lucia looked only in her immediate neighborhood, in the informal unregulated day care sector, where several women run small family day care businesses, offering cheap child care to their neighbors and others in the community. Lucia has had a string of negative experiences with such providers, creating chronic disruptions for her children as she has pulled them out of successive "bad" environments. She describes the most recent experience, where her son (then 9 years old) was able to tell her what was happening to him and his younger sister:

> I took my children to this lady's apartment . . . she wasn't part of any day care program. . . . She also had three kids more, but they were her grandchildren. One day my child told me that they didn't want to stay with that babysitter because she was treating them bad. So then I took them away. . . . She would scream at them, and she wouldn't give them

the food that I would take for them . . . I had to take them out of there
because I wouldn't allow a babysitter to mistreat my children!

Ana, listening to Lucia's account, concurs. She too reports a set of disturbing incidents that she encountered with her 3-year-old daughter:

Yes, I agree because I have experienced the same thing. I have a youngest child, 3 years old, and the lady that was taking care of my child; she
would tell my child to wash dishes. . . . And the other babysitter that I
had, she would make the oldest child in the group take care of the rest of
the children and she would leave! I've had many bad experiences. Thank
God now, my oldest child is older now!

Ana describes how, as a single mother earning $30 a day, $10 would
go to child care costs, consuming a third of her take-home pay. As a
single parent she just could not make it with such high child care costs,
and she left her job to go on welfare, return to ESL classes, and begin
job-training in the hope that she could increase her earnings. The Adult
Literacy program that she attends does offer child care for students who
are taking classes. However, the program does not provide on-site child
care, which Ana would prefer as she feels it would be safer because "during breaks I can stop in and see if everything is OK." Instead the program contracts with cheap informal providers in the area. Ana describes
her anxiety and concerns about the provider her 3-year-old daughter
was assigned to:

My worry though, is that they have this lady come and pick her up.
I don't know who she is and how she will be with my daughter. The
lady's house is so far and out of sight. I don't know what could happen.
When my child was taken to this person's house, and when I was in my
classroom I wasn't really concentrating on the things my teacher was
telling me because I was thinking about my child. Right now I'm not
bringing my child there anymore, because she doesn't want to go to
that lady. She cries and cries, and she said she wouldn't give her anything to eat.

In order to continue attending her ESL classes, Ana pulls together a
makeshift arrangement for part of the morning with a neighbor, but she
is caught between the needs of her daughter and the time schedule of the
program:

> Right now I'm leaving her at home [with the neighbor] until 11 to 11:30. I'm supposed to be here [at the program] until 12. The person can't stay with her later than that. Because my child doesn't want to go with that day care lady [at the ESL program], I can't force her. . . . I can't leave my child with just anyone. . . . I have talked to my teacher, and I asked him if I could leave early because I need to go take care of my daughter, but he doesn't agree. And I know that they're going to remove me from the program because I'm not supposed to be leaving early.

Faced with an inflexible instructor and being dropped from the program, which also means welfare sanctions and possible benefit cutoffs, Ana feels stuck with no good options, saying:

> I'm very depressed, because I don't know who I'm going to leave my child with, and I am very dependent on child care help. It's very stressed for me right now. I feel really desperate, and I have tried to go out and find a job. But then again it's very hard because I don't know where I'm going to leave my child. Even to go out looking for a job, I need someone to be watching my kids.

Ana and Lucia have developed a profound mistrust of the child care providers operating in their immediate neighborhood, and their concerns are confirmed by other mothers in the ESL program, who express similar concerns about "bad day care." With no other support from family or their partners, the women are trapped in a child care maze that keeps them from pursuing any permanent job opportunities. Lucia, who lost a job in a factory because she could not find dependable child care, remarks that now she, too, is "stuck," as her husband's income is too low to support the family. Lucia yearns for some independence and wants to work again, saying:

> The money that my husband brings home, it's not a lot. What he gives me is very little . . . and because of this economic situation, I have had a lot of problems with my husband . . . I was about to divorce from all the stress that I have. When I was offered a job, I couldn't accept it because I couldn't find a person I trust to take care of my kids. . . . I want to be able to count on this person's help. I want to find a person I can trust . . . I want to be very independent. I want to buy my own things, I want to buy things for my children, and I feel very bad because I'm not really able to do the things that I want. I also feel really bad because when you work you feel useful!

Work for Lucia represents not only a measure of economic independence but, also, a sense of autonomy and dignity that she feels is lost when she is stuck at home playing the traditional "housewife" role: "And when you don't have a job, your husband will order you and will pressure you, and you're doing the cooking and doing all the chores, and your husband doesn't see that. And he's putting pressure on you all the time. And he insults us!"

All Lucia's attempts to secure child care subsidies have met with agency indifference. She has never actually been denied, but neither has she ever actually been approved by the New York City Daycare Administration. Lucia feels frustrated and powerless and wishes that information about obtaining child care subsidies and locating the centers that accept them were more readily available. On the occasions that she herself located such a center, she lost the slot because her subsidies were never approved.

> I have never received anything. . . . They should open more centers and provide more information, so someone can find a good educational day care center. There are many kids that need day care and not enough spots. The centers need to open up near the mother's workplace, too. Sometimes we don't get the information that we need . . . when I tried to put my kids in a day care center they [New York City Day Care Administration] never called me so I lost the places.

Ana's experiences are similar to Lucia's. She too has experienced indifference from the city, inexplicable delays, and ultimately dropping of her child care case:

> I think there should be more attention to ones needing the services they supply. The people that attend us are impatient. Sometimes I don't know if I have to wait, and I don't know if they're going to call me or not . . . how do we know if there is a day care slot available and if we can get the subsidies? No one ever tells you!

Lucia also points out that of the jobs she was recently offered, most were odd hours or third-shift jobs, which means that finding child care becomes more difficult and more expensive:

> The job that I was offered was very difficult. I didn't want to work late or on a Saturday or Sunday. . . . And if I did want her to stay later, then

> I had to pay her more money. . . . A lot of providers didn't want to take care of children during those evenings and weekends . . . like for a grocery store, where most of the business comes out of the weekends, and those are days that providers don't want to work.

For Lucia and Maria, child care that is dependable, "educational," safe, and with flexible hours represents a pathway to independence and autonomy from controlling husbands and partners. Neither woman expresses an interest in college; their aspirations center on mastery of English and current job training (focused on computers and data entry) as offering them a way up and out of poverty. Both express a strong desire to work but are stopped in their tracks because they cannot make the child care system work for them. Although many of the child care providers are immigrants like themselves, running small in-home child care enterprises, they see them as negligent and, at worst, abusive and only "in it for the money." They express strong preferences for an actual licensed child care center; in Ana's case, for her 3-year-old daughter, and in Lucia's case, a child care center and school-age program for her 5- and 10-year-old children. Ana describes a center as "more educational" and Lucia agrees, adding that "it is safer too, and you can trust the teachers." However, because neither mother has been able to access child care subsidies, such centers are far too expensive, and at a minimum of $200 a week, well beyond their price range; they must settle for *less, much less.* Settling for less is a common fate for low-income immigrant parents like Lucia and Ana, who inhabit a zone of constant anxiety, guilt, and fear about the netherworld of unregulated child care for their children.

In New York City, the vast, unregulated sector is often the choice of last resort because the city has such a fragmented program, which fails most low-income families, citizens and immigrants alike. As we saw earlier in Chapter 2, Francesca, Carmina, and her teenage daughter, Michelle, all struggled with intransigent welfare-to-work regulations and the failure of the city to come through with child care subsidies. And Ana and Lucia are *legal* immigrants. What happens when low-income mothers are undocumented and living a life of concealment?

CRISTINA AND MATEO: AN INVISIBLE AND TENUOUS EXISTENCE

> The problem is I cannot find anyone to take care of my son. I haven't been able to work for four years because of this.

Cristina is an undocumented immigrant from Ecuador, currently living in New York City with her husband and 4-year-old son. Cristina came to the United States in 1997 and has been trying unsuccessfully to obtain legal status ever since. Because Cristina and her husband do not have "legal papers," they are not eligible to receive Medicaid health care services or food stamps; nor are they able to obtain "legal" jobs. Mateo, their 4-year-old son, was born in New York, and as an American citizen he is eligible for Medicaid and other services. As one of an estimated 9.3 million undocumented immigrants in the United States, Cristina must carefully tread a dangerous path, since seeking services for her son may also expose her own illegal status.[4] Both she and her husband live in the shadows of an underground economy, working low-wage under-the-table jobs, vulnerable to exploitation and ever fearful of deportation. The fact that Cristina is not proficient in English has compounded her difficulties, and she has recently enrolled in an adult literacy program in one of the poorest neighborhoods of the city, where she is taking ESL classes:

> For me, I've been living here in this country for about seven to eight years, and I haven't been able to obtain my [legal] residence. It's very difficult because the jobs that I apply to, they require me to be legal and have my residence—for the type of places that I go to look for jobs, sometimes they don't allow me to speak Spanish, and they tell me, "well, you have to learn to speak English," and it's very hard. With having to take care of my child, I hadn't been able to take English classes before now.

When Mateo was 2 years old, Cristina became very concerned about his behavior problems. Afraid to disclose her own status, yet concerned about her son, Cristina attempts unsuccessfully to obtain a referral for early intervention from a clinic physician. During that same period, with the family in economic distress, Cristina begins to search for a job to supplement her husband's meager earnings. Suddenly a new crisis looms—finding child care for Mateo.

With limited resources and no eligibility for child care subsidies due to her "illegal" status, Cristina begins to search for child care in the unregulated child care sector. Because her son is difficult to manage, and her choices are limited to her own poor New York City neighborhood, where unlicensed immigrant child care providers are the norm, Cristina has few good options open to her. She dreads leaving her son at the home of an unknown provider; however, with little choice but to work, she reluctantly places her child at the home of a neighborhood provider, who appears harsh and insensitive to Mateo's needs. Cristina tearfully describes the harmful consequences to her son: "I left my child in her care for three months, but then I had to leave my job because my child was having so many problems. He fell into a deep depression. He stopped speaking!"

Cristina does not know what happened to her son during that period. He became more and more withdrawn, began to develop severe behavior problems, and then became mute. She does not know if he was abused, but when he stopped speaking she panicked, left her job as an undocumented worker in the garment industry, and stayed home to take care of him. She was afraid to report the day care provider because an investigation might bring unwanted exposure to their status as undocumented workers. However, her husband's earnings were not adequate to keep the family afloat, and, desperate, she applied for food stamps by concealing both her marital status and the fact that she is "an illegal." Somehow she managed to slip through the cracks, "I tried and I got it, but I had to lie. I told them that I was a single mother, and that's how I got it. Now I am receiving coupons, I am getting food stamps." Alarmed by what has happened to her son, who suddenly changed from a talkative and active boy to a child who is mute, she seeks medical help once again:

> I was very depressed because I couldn't find the person that would be able to take care of my child and help me . . . I took him to a therapist, and they told me that he was delayed up to a year and a half. They would do some evaluations. And then they sent my child to a program, a Head Start program, and that's where they gave me the help that I needed.

After the therapist's evaluation and referral, Mateo begins attending a part-day Head Start program, where he receives speech therapy, occupational therapy, and physical therapy. Cristina is very pleased with the early intervention program and feels that she receives "very good help from his teachers." She begins to see a gradual improvement in Mateo's condition, as he slowly starts to speak again. Mateo attends the program part-day, and each week there is a home visit, for which Cristina must be present. However, during this period, Cristina's husband is barely making enough to support the family and pay the high rental costs of their basement apartment. Once again, Cristina begins to search, much more carefully this time, looking for a child care setting where she could leave

Mateo and take up a part-time job, but she cannot find a provider whom she feels she can trust and who is willing to care for a child with special needs: "I need to find someone who can understand my son. . . . The people that I have found, don't have experience with this. . . . Right now he is starting to talk again . . . but certain things that he doesn't know how to say. . . . You have to know how to understand him."

Cristina has few other support networks to help her in New York. She does have family members in the city, but says, "I had to separate from my family" because she feels their treatment of Mateo only exacerbates his problems, and her husband has not been supportive, nor was he of any help through the child care abuse crisis. As a result, Cristina feels "very much alone" in trying to help Mateo: "Right now, my priority is my child, and his advancement. I want him to learn language and to learn." Cristina would like to find a good child care center that her son can attend part-day following the Head Start morning program. With that in place, she would be able to continue ESL classes with the goal of obtaining a job that would stabilize the family. "I want to continue working and get my residency," she says with determination, as she struggles to piece together good child care, with no family support, no health care for herself or her husband, high rental costs, unsafe housing, and no legal rights—all played out in a shadow world of invisibility in New York City.

Like New York, California is also a key immigration state, home to a large community of Mexican immigrants with young children. Do low-income, immigrant women fare any better there? The following two narratives from Mexican mothers (who are legal immigrants) portray their child care experiences.

MARIA AND HER CHILDREN: A STRUGGLE FOR INDEPENDENCE

I called about child care and they told me that if I had welfare in the last two years, they could have helped me, but they couldn't because I hadn't received welfare . . . or I had to earn $28,000 or less, but my husband right now makes a little more over that. So I don't qualify, so I don't have child care.

Maria came to the United States from Mexico 15 years ago, pregnant with her oldest daughter, who is now a sophomore in high school. At that time, Maria, who was a single mother, worked part-time as a home health-care aide, while receiving public assistance and child care subsidies for her young daughter. Seven years after arriving in the U.S., Maria married her current husband, who is from Guatemala, and they have two children, a daughter aged 5 and a son of 18 months. The family of five lives in the San Diego metropolitan area, and Maria's husband is self-employed, running a small business. Maria helps him with the billing and other bookkeeping tasks and attends ESL classes at a local community agency.

Maria currently feels trapped and overwhelmed by the barriers she has encountered: a controlling, emotionally abusive husband, lack of system knowledge about how to negotiate the various bureaucracies that she must deal with, limited English, and child care she cannot afford for her two young children. She frequently weeps as she relates her experiences and says she "feels like a nobody." Her overriding desire is to become proficient in English, enroll in educational training, and obtain a job so she can become less dependent on her husband and make some choices about her life:

> Sometimes, when I argue or fight with my husband and think about separating, I realize what would I do? I don't know how to do anything. I have to train to be able to be someone so that if I am left alone, then I can get ahead with my kids. . . . I don't know how to do anything right now.

Maria knows that in order to become self-sufficient, she needs "to get ahead in life . . . to stand on my own two feet," but she feels defeated by her situation and regrets that she never learned English sufficiently well when she first came to the country. Living a life isolated from the mainstream, in a self-contained community of Mexican immigrants, Maria has had neither the incentive nor much opportunity to interact with many native English speakers, and the English she learned years ago has faded. Returning to ESL classes with the goal of entering computer training has been an important decision for her; yet she has been thwarted in her progress. She attends ESL classes twice a week because on those days there is free on-site child care, and she has no one to take care of her children on the other days. However, even this arrangement is unsatisfactory. The women who bring their children to the ESL program complain that they cannot concentrate, because the poorly supervised, informal on-site child care means constant disruptions. Maria describes the setting:

> The class is chaos. We are in one room and the kids in the other, but if the
> kids need something it causes an interruption in the class. . . . If one of
> the children happen to go to the bathroom on themselves or hurt them-
> selves, somebody comes in class and calls you out to change the child.
> One of the assistants out there watching the kids, will come in and say,
> "Hey, your baby's crying," and then here goes one mother outside, and
> as soon as the mother comes back, then there's another one, "Hey, your
> baby's crying.". . . And because the room is right next door sometimes
> you can hear when it is your kid's crying. . . . Do you go to take care of
> them or stay? It just totally distracts me and makes me so unfocused!

Maria feels that to master English, she needs to attend classes five days
a week, but without child care she cannot do it. Her husband consistently
belittles her attempts to improve herself and refuses to pay for child care,
now or in the future. "He will not help me with the kids. The other day I
told him that maybe I will go to school, and he said, 'Well, you'll just die
of hunger.' But I have to do something."

Maria's young daughter attends a late-afternoon Head Start program,
and while Maria appreciates the early educational enrichment her daughter receives, the hours are a problem, coming as they do at the end of the
day. Every night Maria has to prepare her husband's dinner and cannot
use those hours to search for a job or attend classes—particularly as she
has a toddler son to take care of. Her search for subsidized child care has
been a frustrating one, and she feels intimidated by the various social
service agencies she must interact with in order to access help. Although
the family has a sufficiently low income to obtain federally subsidized
Section 8 housing, that is apparently not the case for child care subsidies.
Maria has made successive attempts to access some child care assistance
but to no avail.[5] She relates the most recent denial of child care subsidies
from a caseworker:

> One of my husband's clients who dedicates herself full-time to take care
> of kids said that there is a program where the government can pay for
> your child care, the woman told me there isn't a need for me to be pay-
> ing. . . . I called them, but because I didn't receive welfare, they said
> they could not help me, and my husband needs to make less money, so
> I didn't fit into the category. . . . You have to know how to look and find,
> but I don't know where to look!

Unable to access child care subsidies, Maria has resigned herself to waiting until her children are a little older because the cheapest care she

can find for her son (full-time) and daughter (part-time) would be $600 a month. Her husband will not allow Maria to use "his" money for child care and is indifferent to her needs:

> But even if my husband makes enough money by their standards to have child care, he is very cheap. I ask him for money, but he's too tight. He doesn't think helping to pay for ESL is worth while. . . . At no time am I free to have my own money. If I had my own money, I could put it where I needed. I could put my little boy in child care, but as it is now, I will have to wait until he is older. I have to wait until then to get ahead.

In the fall, Maria's daughter will start kindergarten, and she hopes that her son would then become eligible for Head Start. However, she has been told that the poorest and most at-risk families will receive first priority and that there is already a long waiting list. Disappointed, Maria relates how, when she was pregnant with her son, she was able to enroll her daughter in Head Start without any problem, and so she "figured when I was pregnant the same would happen with the little one. But it turned out not to be so."

Depressed about the lack of control she has over her life, discouraged by her slow progress in her ESL classes, Maria briefly considered doing hairstyling as a way to make some money, but she remembers bitterly what her husband told her: "Well, you're going to end up starving because nobody's going to want you to do it!" Although she does all the housework and helps her husband with the bookkeeping for his small business, he continues to demean her and to take her work for granted. For Maria, the way out of a marriage in which she feels exploited and abused is economic independence, and for that she needs affordable child care:

> Right now, it's hard. Either I go out to work and pay all the money I make in child care costs or I stay home and watch the kids. . . . But I need to get to have a career so I can get, you know, on top of things and start working at a good job. And I need help with the child care in order for me to do that. . . .

Maria regrets that she has no immediate family in the area who are able to help her with the children. Maria's mother and other relatives live in Mexico, and the lack of an extended family is hard on Maria, as she sadly comments, "If my mother was here, I would leave the kids with her during the day, I would go to school or to work, and that's it, it would be much easier. I would help them and they help me." Maria's oldest daughter gets home from school at 5:15 p.m. and helps her in the evenings, but she has homework to do. Maria is reluctant to take any time away from her daughter's school responsibilities, as she is determined that her daughter will graduate from high school and have the opportunity for a different future.

Interestingly, as she discusses her child care needs, Maria does not expect a fully subsidized child care program. What she would like is an affordable center, or one where she pays partial costs and receives a partial subsidy:

> I hope for some type of child care facility or some work place where I could take my kids and it would be like a reasonable rate to help parents like myself. . . . You know when Governor Schwarzenegger was running, I told my [older] daughter, I would like her to help me write a letter to tell him that we need some type of programs that would help mothers like me, that have to struggle with child care, get ahead.

Maria's dreams are not unusual: to get ahead, find a well-paid computer job, "make my own money and be happy," and find good child care for her two youngest children. Child care for Maria represents not only an exit from an emotionally abusive marriage, but also the opportunity to become economically self-sufficient, affording her a new sense of dignity and self-respect: "So that mothers like me don't have to marry men that will make us feel stupid and dependent. Like we are worth nothing. . . . Just because I am poor and a woman does not mean I can't make it!"

MARABEL AND HER DAUGHTERS:
A MOTHER'S WORST NIGHTMARE

> They should have day care centers that the kids can be safe in . . . the day care providers are just in it for the money. . . . You don't know these people, and you leave your child there with all your trust and come back to hear something happened to your daughter.

Marabel is a 40-year-old Mexican single mother of four children, ages 13, 11, 6, and 5, living in San Diego. A domestic violence survivor–both fathers of her children were violent and abusive–she recently relocated from the New York area to California, hoping to make a new start. Marabel is currently enrolled in a CalWORKs adult education program, studying for her GED.[6] With four children in need of child care, two of whom have disabilities, Marabel cannot marshal the necessary resources to find good child care placements for all four of her children. Fortunately her 11-year-old son is accepted into San Diego's 6-to-6 free, public school-age child care program, but finding after-school care for Alejandra, her 13-year-old daughter with disabilities, and Carlos, her 6-year-old son with special needs, proves daunting. The CalWORKs child care subsidies do not cover the full costs of higher quality center-based care, and unable to afford the co-pays, Marabel settles on a subsidized, "licensed" family child care home, recommended by her church, that will provide after-school care for her two children with special needs and full-day child care for her 5-year-old daughter, Isabella.

Marabel feels uneasy from the start as there are several young teenage boys who arrive at the home for after-school care, which appears, during her one and only visit, to be understaffed and poorly supervised. Caught by the inflexible demands of the CalWORKs program and the lack of any resources of her own to pay for higher quality care, she promises herself that "it would only be for a short time," until she can find a better place. However, the time constraints and work requirements of the CalWORKs program, which does not permit any time off for attending to children's child care needs, place Marabel in an untenable position. Fearful of being sanctioned and cut from benefits, she really does not have any "mothering" time to look for a satisfactory place. Instead she lives each day filled with anxiety and tries to monitor the program by persistent calls to check up on what is happening. Despite these efforts, her worst fears are realized: 5-year-old Isabella is molested, and 13-year-old Alejandra is assaulted. Marabel relates what happened:

> She [the provider] had older boys there as well, like 13, 15. My 5-year-old daughter is like a type of child that's quiet. She's shy . . . but she's a very smart girl. Then one day she was coming home sick, she was too quiet . . . she would cry and cry and point at a rock and touch her privacy.

Marabel describes how, before this happened, she had become increasingly concerned about the presence of the adolescent boys at the provider's home and the general lack of supervision. The provider was frequently absent, leaving her young, adult daughter in charge:

> I said, you know, what is going on? The child care lady was never there, she always left it to her daughter. And I say, "Wait a minute." I called it to

her attention, I said, "You know, I don't feel right.". . . Oh she was getting
tired of me calling her. But I had like—you know—a mother has an instinct
. . . so I would call her constantly, "Hello, can I speak to Bianca." They
would go, "Oh, well she's not here." I said, "Where is my daughter, you
know, tell them Mommy's on the phone." "Oh, she's sleeping right now,"
and then again I'll call her back again. "Has your mother gone back, is
Bianca there?" She'll go, "No, she's not here. She went to the store. Why
are you constantly calling me?" I said, "because I'm a concerned parent
and I feel that I have rights to call to see how my daughter is doing."

Marabel subsequently finds out that when the children were "supposed to be watching TV or playing games," they were left entirely unsupervised; and in a room where no adult was present, the older boys,
ages 13 and 15, had been tying Alejandra down and beating her in the
presence of the other children. Then 5-year-old Isabella, whose behavior
has been of most concern to Marabel, suddenly starts urinating blood,
and Marabel takes her to the emergency room:

We took her to the emergency room at the hospital; they say I should have
took her to children's hospital. I don't know nothing around here. . . . So I
don't know what kind of laws they have here. So I just took her, and they
tested her . . . my daughter described to me, [she said] they was like putting a rock up in her privacy . . . saying, "I'm going to put a rock in you if
you tell your mother," and, you know, touching her.

Marabel pulls all three children out of the provider's home and reports the molestation incident to Child Protective Services. A caseworker
visits Marabel at home and investigates the abuse allegations against the
child care provider. The investigation is inconclusive, and the provider
continues to operate:

They did an investigation. I don't know what ever happened to that
lady. . . . She was saying that I'm going to jeopardize her job. I said, "No,
that's not my concern, I don't care, you jeopardized it. If you are tending
to children, you should be focused on them, and that's your job, taking
care of these children. It's not no one else, you know. I'm not going to
trust the people you have there. You have 13-year-olds, you have 15-
year-olds. I mean, boys, you know, doing all kinds of crazy stuff."

Marabel is not certain what really happened to her youngest daughter—whether she was actually molested or whether she was threatened

but not touched. At times she is convinced the boys did molest Isabella, saying "I will definitely believe my kids through anything," and Isabella told her "they was trying to put rocks up in my privacy." The fact that the little girl was urinating blood after the incident was never satisfactorily explained by the doctor who examined her. Yet, at other times, Marabel views what happened as a warning light that alerted her to act before her daughter could be sexually assaulted:

> I thank God that nothing happened to my daughter, but it was attention to something that would have happened to her, when they were saying "Oh, I'm going to put a rock in your privacy," you know. It was about to start. But luckily, me, calling there every day, and I took her out right away, it didn't happen. . . . But it was starting to.

Forgotten in the crisis over the reported sexual molestation, is the assault on Alejandra—an incident that was *not* reported to the police. After Marabel pulls all her children from the child care provider's home, she misses CalWORKs training for several days as she tries to cope with Isabella's reactions and insecurities and locate alternative safe child care. Marabel angrily describes the punitive sanctions that operate in the Cal-WORKs program: "You know, we can't even take out a day just to deal with our kids because we gotta be here." For Marabel, whose family of five depends on a monthly welfare cash grant of $839 and $300–$400 in monthly food stamps, sanctions means a reduction in monthly benefits, which Marabel can hardly afford. She points out how difficult it is to ensure her children are well cared for if she cannot take time off to visit child care providers' homes:

> They should, you know, allow for that. There's a lot of things going on, even with the child care providers with licenses. Sometimes those child care providers are not there. You know, they have somebody else there while they're doing their errands, when actually they should be doing their errands at night, not when the kids are there. So that's one of the reasons parents need to check, you know who's there, who's watching the kids, what are they doing. . . .

Marabel finds another provider who is licensed and who appears to be trustworthy, but she still suffers constant anxiety about the children's safety, even though she describes the new provider as "good with my kids . . . but you don't know, you don't know these people." Marabel would prefer to place her children in the San Diego after-school 6-to-6 program run by the public schools. Her oldest daughter has just aged out of the program, and her 11-year-old son currently attends. There is a waiting list for the younger children, and Marabel hopes to find slots for Isabella, who starts kindergarten soon, and Carlos, her son with special needs. Based on her older son's experience, Marabel describes it as "a great program" and far "more educational." Because it is run by the public school system, she views it as more transparent and accountable. She believes, as do many of her friends, that a child care center "is more trustworthy" than a private family day care provider, which she says "is not an educational environment, you know, it's not. They're not there for the kids—they're just in it for the money."

Frustrated by the time constraints of the welfare-to-work program, Marabel feels her mothering has been constantly undermined by her lack of choices and lack of time. She cannot attend parent-teacher conferences at her older daughters' school, nor deal adequately with her 6-year-old son's special educational needs. He has had seizures since he was two and his speech is delayed:

> I love to get involved with my kids. There are times I would like to have a day off just to go to the teachers, go to the child care . . . see what my kids are doing, what are they eating, what are they playing, you know, who are there, who are the people come and go . . . talk to the principal, talk to the counselor. . . . You know, I can't do that, because I'm scared I might get sanctioned.

With a disabled adolescent daughter traumatized by bullying and assaults, a 5-year-old daughter traumatized by an actual or threatened sexual molestation incident, a 6-year-old son with seizures, and the family's past history of domestic violence, it is clear that Marabel's children need intensive attention. For Marabel, trying to forge a new future for herself and her children in California, after escaping the terrors of domestic violence, life has not been easy and her children have suffered. Marabel describes her ongoing mothering dilemma, which is rooted in her poverty, her immigrant status, and her inability to make child care choices that are in the best interests of her children, saying, "I'm a single parent. I'm not from here. . . . I'm alone, it's very hard, you want to trust these people, but you don't know these people."

Largely because of her own experiences with bad child care, Marabel has decided that she would like to pursue an associate's degree in child development at a community college after she obtains her GED.

She is currently volunteering at a Head Start program as part of her required community service in the CalWORKs program and she describes herself as one who "loves working with children." Yet, ironically, she cannot stay home and care for her own children at critical points in their young lives, nor does the CalWORKs program, which provides "guaranteed child care" for former and current welfare recipients enrolled in vocational and postsecondary educational activities, protect her children from the damaging consequences of cheap, unsafe child care. Over half of California's low-income children whose families receive subsidies (vouchers) are in "license-exempt" care, where neither monitoring nor accountability is required. In the licensed sector, two-thirds of low-income children, like Marabel's, attend Title 22 family child care homes (FCCH), where fiscal incentives are weighted towards the lowest quality care, with no educational requirements for providers who must merely pass a fingerprint check and adhere to minimal health and safety regulations.[7] In general, for all low-income families, demand far outstrips the supply of quality, affordable child care slots, and the Children's Defense Fund estimates that in 2004 there were 280,000 children in California on waiting lists for child care assistance.[8] Unfortunately, provision of child care assistance in a largely unregulated, private child care market means the luck of the draw. And poor children usually do not draw the lucky straw.

IMMIGRANT FAMILIES WITH YOUNG CHILDREN

Immigrant families constitute almost 12% (34 million) of the U.S. population, with their children comprising 22% of all young children under 6. Yet, more than half of the young children of immigrants and almost two-thirds of foreign-born children live in low-income families, where poverty, lack of education, and lack of access to public benefits are significant obstacles to family viability.[9] The 1996 PRWORA federal welfare legislation restricted noncitizen access to food stamps, health care, cash grants, and child care subsidies,[10] causing severe hardships and exacerbating the existing high levels of poverty. A high percentage of young children live in two-parent immigrant families (86%), where gender-traditional roles are more normative, with one parent (usually the father) in the labor market. Immigrant women have lower rates of employment, and as the vast majority of immigrants are working in the low-wage labor market, a two-parent family is no buffer against poverty.[11]

The Urban Institute reports that over 90% of young immigrant children under six are citizens, yet they live in mixed-status families, with one or both of their parents noncitizens, and 29% of young children actually live in families with undocumented parents, who have neither legal rights nor access to any public benefits.[12] In cases where the child as citizen is entitled to benefits, parents such as Cristina, profiled in this chapter, are afraid to claim the benefits for their children since their own undocumented status may be endangered. With over nine million undocumented immigrants living below the radar—fearful of exposure and deportation, working under-the-table jobs with odd hours and low pay— their children's access to early intervention services, child care, health care, and food stamps is severely restricted.[13]

Clearly low-income immigrant children stand to benefit from early intervention programs such as Head Start and high quality child care, but as a group, the children of legal immigrants are also underenrolled. Parents' educational levels, income, and language barriers are frequently cited as key factors affecting children's participation in early care and education, particularly among families from Mexico, Central America, the Dominican Republic, and Indochina.[14] Latin American and Caribbean immigrants constitute the largest immigrant group (64%), and within that group 39% are Mexicans.[15] Hence, lack of English proficiency and lack of education—58% of immigrant children have a parent with limited English proficiency and 29% of immigrant children live in families in which one or more parents has not completed a high school education—are impediments to access.[16] Immigrant parents must struggle to navigate their way through various bureaucratic mazes in order to obtain public benefits such as early intervention, special education, and child care assistance.

LIVING BELOW A MINIMUM SOCIAL THRESHOLD: IMMIGRANT MOTHERS AND CHILD CARE

The five mothers profiled in this chapter, Ana, Lucia, Cristina, Maria, and Marabel, are determined and persistent women, yet they have suffered in relationships with husbands and partners. From family violence and emotional abuse, to lack of support and indifference to their needs as individuals, these mothers have not been recognized as having "a life to live, deserving of both respect and resources."[17] The care and education of children falls fully and completely on their shoulders, and as immigrant women, they experience a double oppression—from their husbands and partners and from the state. They aspire to decent paying jobs that will enable them to become economically self-sufficient and (with the exception of Marabel who is proficient in English) see mastery of English and job training as key to developing independence and autonomy from controlling men. Yet none has been able to achieve her aspirations because child care is too costly, too unstable, too inaccessible, or fraught with the terrors of injury and molestation.

Language proficiency is an added obstacle to finding a job and navigating the child care maze, but even language proficiency and citizenship do not shield a low-income mother from the exigencies of a welfare-to-work program that places little value on ensuring that young children receive quality care. In New York City, the children of Ana, Lucia, and Cristina fell victim to the unregulated informal care sector—a black hole into which immigrant children routinely fall and where child care subsidies (when received) only cover the costs of the cheapest care. In California, Maria was unable to access child care subsidies, and Marabel's children were harmed irreparably by abusive care at a family day care home.

All five mothers desired educational care at licensed child care centers and expressed strong mistrust of in-home family day care providers (both licensed and nonlicensed), intuitively confirming numerous research studies that have documented the links between low quality care and the lack of standards and accountability. Such problems are pervasive in the informal sector, as well as in family day care homes, leading to bad early outcomes, particularly for the disproportionate numbers of poor children in these settings, and the substandard and dangerous care for infants and toddlers.[18] In their eyes, center-based care that focused on their children's early learning and development was seen as a guarantor of quality, together with the education and training of the staff.

Although current research findings about early education and child care show that low-income immigrant parents are less likely to use center-based care, these arrangements *do not* necessarily indicate free choices. Cultural preferences, family characteristics, and family socialization[19] certainly play some role in parents' decisions about child care, but often forgotten in the surveys and statistical counts is the stark reality that low-income mothers frequently have no choice or, at best, few good choices. As with so many women whose struggles are presented in this book, they *settle for less* against their intuition and their maternal judgment, and sometimes they settle for far worse than *less*.

Information, resources, opportunities for language learning, education, and access to good quality child care are all essential ingredients for making it as an immigrant mother. Yet few immigrant women are aware of their rights, and undocumented women have no rights. Stuck at home, isolated in poor communities, struggling in marginal and often illegal jobs, victims and survivors of family violence, lacking autonomy and opportunity, they and their young children subsist below a minimum social threshold. Threatened benefit cutoffs, sanctions, and loss of a low-wage job that serves as a lifeline for family survival create desperate decisions—decisions that no mother and no parent should ever have to make. However, as with housing, health care, and education in a shrinking public space, the poorer you are, the less you get. And so too with child care. Add to that social isolation, language disadvantage, gender inequality, and current anti-immigrant fervor, and the result is a toxic mix of social injustice and discrimination. Poor children are expendable and cheap; poor immigrant children even more so.

CHAPTER 7

"It Was a Wonderful and Different Change": When Child Care Works

What does it take to make it as a low-income mother? What is it that really makes possible the transformation of a mother's life? Of her children's lives? Here, the lives of five women and their children are profiled, each with a distinctive story to tell. All are stories of resilience and success—stories where investments in child care, after-school care, and educational supports were available and accessible. For these women, child care was the engine, driving desire, determination, and resilience into achievement. Clearly networks of support, resources, and public infrastructure services are critical, but the crucial stabilizing factor for these mothers and their children was high quality reliable child care—not just *any* care—that made all the difference.

TANYA AND HER CHILDREN:
AN ENDURING BELIEF IN EDUCATION

> Education is something you will always have. No one can take that away from you, and it is education that will help you succeed.

Originally from Michigan, Tanya moved to Iowa in the mid-1990s with her two young sons after her marriage broke up. Juggling single parenting, work, and school, she put herself through community college, transferred to a four-year university, and completed her degree after giving birth to her third child. Given the odds stacked against her, as a low-income African-American single mother with young children to support, 34-year-old Tanya's story is one of ambition and determination, with an enduring belief in the power of education to transform her life and that of her children. Aided by a network of child care supports when her two sons were small children, including her mother and a community of friends, and with access to exemplary child care for her baby daughter, now attending a university child care center, Tanya and her children have blossomed. But it was not always easy. Soon after her second son was born, she separated from her husband and decided, "In order for me to take care of my family, I need to finish my education." After moving to an urban area of Iowa where her cousin was attending school, Tanya temporarily postponed her college plans and began working full-time at a nursing home.

Child care in the city was unaffordable, and Tanya applied for child care subsidies for her two boys, aged 2 and 4, but she was denied because there was such a long waiting list. Determined, however, to make it, Tanya decides, "I'll just take care of this on my own," and begins to search for a family day care provider:

> I really didn't know anyone except for my cousin, and she had a friend from church that she knew. So, like a friend of a friend of a friend! I met this lady who provided day care in her home. So she was willing to work with me as far as when I got paid and how I got paid—and she knew I'd just moved there—so she watched the boys.

The day care provider, Gwen, is also African-American, and Tanya immediately bonds with her, seeing her as a grandmother figure for the boys. She agrees to give Tanya a discount; yet, even with a discount, child care costs $600 a month for the two boys for full-time care, which consumes "a huge portion . . . more than half" of her monthly budget. Despite the high costs, Tanya sees the stable nurturing care her two boys receive as well worth it: "They were basically with her all day, and she fed them. I mean, she potty trained Justin. . . . It wasn't really like they were in day care. She was like an extended family. . . . She really took care of them, so, I felt very fortunate."

Tanya enrolls part-time in school to complete her associate's degree, while continuing to work full-time, and Gwen encourages her to pursue her degree and offers to keep the boys until late in the evening, so Tanya can attend classes. Her flexibility enables Tanya to maintain her job and attend school: "She was always willing to work with me. And when I was going to school, she also let them stay over, and she didn't charge me for [the extra hours], and I would get out of class like at 9:00 or 9:30 at night." During this time, Tanya is laid off from her nursing home job, and she immediately applies for temporary positions at a Manpower agency. One of her long-term assignments turns into a "real job," and with increased earnings and the temporal demands of the new job, Tanya again puts school on hold. When Tanya's older son, Christopher, enters kindergarten, her mother, who has retired, moves out to Iowa to help take care of the children. Because of her mother's support and willingness to care for the children, Tanya plans to cut back on her work hours and enroll in school full-time, but at that point she is offered a promotion at her job from secretary to an administrative assistant, with a raise of several thousand dollars. "So I came home and talked to my mom. It's like 'Well, what should I do? I mean this job, or go to school?' I really wanted [to] go back to school, but she asks, 'Well, do you think you can do both?' I said, 'I don't know. We'll try it!'"

Working full-time and enrolled in school full-time, with her mother taking care of her children, Tanya describes their family situation as "doing okay . . . it's not like we were living in the lap of luxury, but we were all doing okay." However, Tanya's mother becomes ill and is hospitalized, and when she returns from the hospital, she can no longer watch the boys. At this point Tanya faces a very difficult situation: she is now the sole caregiver for her mother, and in urgent need of child care for her younger son, Justin. After a frantic search Tanya locates a child care center near her apartment and describes her relief:

> Actually, we were blessed again, I found a day care not too far from where I lived, and where I worked, I was paying $400 a month for him, $100 a week. . . . We could walk. I could drop Justin off at day care, and then walk like a block and go around the corner to work. . . . It was convenient. It really worked out.

Determined to complete her degree and priding herself on managing on her own, Tanya decides not to apply again for the waiting list for child care subsidies, "I was like, I have a job now. I can manage myself, thank you!" She turns instead to friends and her kindly work supervisor, who generously offer to help out with child care in the evenings as she juggles her hectic work and school schedule:

> Oh, people at work chipped in, and the nights that I had class, they would watch the boys. They would keep them overnight. . . . And then one family I met while I was working there, we became friends, and they would take the boys, the nights the supervisor couldn't watch them, they

would take them, and then they would take them to school and to day care. . . . So it all worked out and I was able to finish school.

After Tanya completes her associate's degree, she enrolls at an Iowa public university for a bachelor's degree and moves with her boys to a college town. She finds a job working on campus, joins a church, and makes contact with a nonprofit advocacy coalition, where she meets other single mothers and receives "emotional support." During this period, her mother dies, and she becomes pregnant with her daughter. With both her sons now in elementary school, Tanya continues to work and attend school, right up until Maya's birth. She makes special arrangements to take her finals: "So I was able to come home from the hospital, get on my computer, do what I had to do . . . they actually set it up where I could take my finals, in their office or somewhere on campus . . . because I had to tend to Maya. Yeah, it worked out. It worked out!"

For the first months of her baby's life, Tanya is reluctant to leave her infant daughter "with just anyone." After an arrangement with her pastor's wife falls through, Tanya's extensive network of friends, mainly single mothers with older children, rally around her, and they take turns watching Maya as Tanya attends classes and goes to work. Most of her friends attend her church and are also students, and Tanya describes how "they would have Maya in between our classes, and it worked for a while . . . I mean she was like just a couple months, and they really helped me."

Tanya begins to search for a good infant day care center that she can afford. She is still working, going to school, and nursing her baby, and she is very particular about what she wants for her daughter: "She had to be close enough to me so that I could go in between classes, nurse her, go to class, come back and nurse her again, go to class, go to work, come back and nurse her and take her home." Fortunately for Tanya, the university child care center has infant openings, and the university partially subsidizes child care for student parents through a federal CCAMPIS grant.[1] Maya qualifies for a 50% child care scholarship, and Tanya pays about $250 a month for full-time infant care. She expresses her initial misgivings about placing her baby in a predominantly White environment and worries about how the teachers would treat Maya:

> That was one of my concerns putting my baby in day care. Because her caretakers are not of African-American descent. They just, they're basically Caucasian or Asian, so my concern was, are they going to be, you know, feeling a little funny towards my baby? Are they going to treat

her any differently than the other kids? You never know who's watching your kids. I prayed about that a lot, but it just worked out. Her caretakers, and usually they have one primary caretaker—they have just been phenomenal! They have given her extraordinary care and love, so it just all worked out.

Tanya's initial misgivings about her daughter's "fit" with the center, and whether she would experience racialized treatment as one of the few African-American babies at the center, are allayed by the dedicated and committed care she observes from the staff: "They really love the kids . . . I feel very comfortable in leaving her there. It's hard, she's my baby. . . . It was hard, you know, it was hard going to class and wondering, are they going to take care of my baby? But I'm very happy with the child care."

Maya is now almost 2 years old and has been attending the center full-time since she was 4 months old. Tanya appreciates the rich early childhood learning environment and describes with pride how much her daughter is learning, "she knows her ABC's and she's learning to count." Tanya also points to the low turnover and the long-term stability of the trained staff at the center that has enabled Maya to form strong attachments to her teachers, remarking, "it's been pretty steady in there."

In spring 2003, Tanya graduates with her bachelor's degree and continues to work full-time on campus, while applying to graduate school. Maya is still enrolled in the campus child care center, although Tanya now pays the full cost of toddler care at $460 a month, as she is no longer a student. Life has become easier for Tanya as Christopher, who is 12, is old enough to watch 9-year-old Justin for an hour until Tanya returns from work at 5:30 p.m. When needed, her girlfriend picks up Maya from the child care center.

During the past eight years, while Tanya was struggling to work and go to school and provide for her children, she never received child support from her ex-husband and he has not seen or contacted his sons. Maya's father "helps out every now and then," but Tanya has no expectations that either of the fathers of her children will take their parenting responsibilities seriously, despite the court orders for support:

I know my children deserve their support, but I'm not holding my breath . . . and if we never get a dime, I'm going to do what I have to do to make sure my family is taken care of! God has given me the ability to work. I have a little intelligence. They're going to be taken care of, whether they help or not. If I have to work three jobs, I'll do it!

Tanya's dedication to her children, her emphasis on the importance of education, and her own strong presence and positive role modeling that she has presented to her children have clearly reaped dividends. Christopher is an excellent student and is in the gifted and talented program at his new middle school. Justin has followed in his brother's footsteps and is also an academically successful student and attends the gifted and talented program in his elementary school. Tanya describes the teachers at her children's schools as "wonderful," and she feels they are getting a sound education at good schools, which will prepare them for a college future, saying her sons know "how serious I am about their education." If Tanya has any regrets, they relate to lack of time with her children, saying,

> Of course I'd like to have spent more time with my kids, but you know, I had to go to class, I had to study, and I had to do projects. You only have so many hours in a day . . . but I told them, like my mother said, "Education is something you will always have. No one can take that away from you, and it is education that will help you succeed."

Tanya credits her own success to finding a good and flexible child care provider when her boys were younger, the child care scholarship program at her university, which enabled her to send Maya to a high quality campus child care center, the scholarship she received for her studies, and the strong network of support that helped her take care of her children—the first family day care provider, her late mother, her work supervisor, and her circle of girlfriends, whom she describes "as an extended family for each other," and who continue to help her when needed with child care. As Tanya looks back on the challenging years since she first moved to Iowa with two small children, she remarks:

> Women have been doing this for years, and you do what you have to do to take care of your family. And like I said, it was by much prayer and I was tired. Yes, I get tired, but I need to do what I need to do for my kids to have a better life. . . . You can't do it alone. There are times when you're at your lowest and you just can't go on. You need someone to encourage you. Yeah, there were some times I wanted to quit. But I was so close and people were like, "Oh no, you're not quitting. No, you're too close.". . . It was my mother and finding good child care and my friends . . . that's how I made it!

She also appreciatively describes how her kids have helped her: "I couldn't ask for another thing that made it easier and made it work than my kids. They made it possible for me to go to school . . . I couldn't ask for better kids!" Tanya also emphasizes the role that her faith has played in the life of her family, and as she reflects on all the successes—her own as well as those of her children—she reiterates, "I did not get through school and work by my own strength. It was God that brought me through. We've been blessed."

Several months later, Tanya receives an acceptance letter from a prestigious, out-of-state graduate program, admitting her for the fall of 2004. Tanya's extraordinary determination to succeed, her years of hard work and dedication to her children, her capacity to strategically marshal resources and develop networks of support—are all invested in the dream of creating a better life and a viable future for her children. As she contemplates her past and makes plans for the future, Tanya remarks, "I didn't do anything special. I wasn't extraordinary . . . I haven't done anything that hasn't been done before!"

CLARA AND ANTHONY: A DETERMINED PURSUIT OF EDUCATION

> It was very difficult because I would have to take him to class with me . . . when the after-school program opened it was a wonderful and different change!

Clara is a single mother of a 12-year-old son. Clara's parents immigrated to New York City when Clara was 14, while Clara stayed with her extended family in Barbados until she completed high school. At 18, she rejoined her parents and sisters and has been living in the city now for 13 years. At 31, Clara has accomplished a great deal. She is the first in her family to go to college and has succeeded in obtaining associate's and bachelor's degrees and is currently enrolled in a master's program. As a newly certified special education teacher, she has climbed out of poverty through the determined pursuit of education, which she says her parents and her extended family in Barbados always impressed upon her, emphasizing, "'you're going to finish high school' and it was just set out that's how it was going to be done." When she arrived in New York, it was Clara's mother who pushed her to attend college. Although she had never completed any formal education herself, she nevertheless dreamed of a different life for her daughter, and the importance of going to college "was instilled in me from the time I came to this country," says Clara.

Since she was 18, Clara has worked almost continuously—first at low-wage jobs, and then on college campuses, using work-study earnings and a combination of maximum financial-aid grants and loans to put herself through school. At 19 she became pregnant with her son, Anthony, and while she and her son's father were together, she stayed home during Anthony's infancy. However, the relationship ended when Anthony was 2 years old. Since that time, Anthony's father has not paid child support nor has he shared any responsibility for Anthony's care. Clara is adamant that she never wanted to endure the humiliations of the welfare system. "I mean, I really have no tolerance for it," so, as she puts it, "I chose not to go down that road, I really did!"

When Anthony was a toddler, Clara relied on her family to help take care of him while she worked, and when he entered a Head Start early intervention program, she went back to school. With the help of her father, who picked up Anthony from Head Start each day, Clara managed to juggle child care until he entered elementary school.

At this point, mindful of choosing a good school for her son, she moved away to a different area of the city and could no longer rely on the close-by help of her father and sister. Clara describes the discomfort and anxiety she experiences when Anthony begins kindergarten and she searches for after-school child care for him: "I mean, you have programs where you are paying a lot of money and then you have people that are yelling at your kids and the environment is just not, it's not good. It's not good, and it's amazing how expensive child care is!"

Clara enrolls Anthony in an after-school program at his elementary school, which she finds poorly run and understaffed:

> And so you have a big open space with 30 children, one person that's taking care, that is responsible for them. . . . and it really scared me. Like, okay, this is really not the environment for my son . . . and so you're yanking him from one place to the other place because you're not comfortable there.

After Clara pulls Anthony out of the after-school program at his public school, she enrolls him at a child care center, but this one fares no better:

> I didn't think it was safe, you know, there are a lot of issues. And so I'm like, you know what? Anthony, you'll go with me for the time being. If I have not to go to school for one semester, then I'll do that. But I'd rather that than have him somewhere where I'm really not comfortable.

In addition, the inflexible times of the center added to Clara's dissatisfaction. She describes how she tried to juggle work, school, costly child care, and an almost impossible time schedule:

> It was very expensive, and not only that, it was only available up to 6:00 o'clock. I remember I used to get out of class at like five minutes to 6:00, and I would have to run. . . . Every single day I'd have to run. I'm like panting, running to get him, because if you get there late, they start to charge you. Five after 6:00, you're going to start paying every minute after that. You know, it's frightening for a child when they see that all the other kids are gone, and they're the only person there . . . also, they used to take the kids to the precinct, after some time, they would take the kids to the police station. . . . Oh my! . . . I had enough of that, and I think my body couldn't take it anymore . . . so I was like "he's going to class with me."

For the next three years, Clara and Anthony spend their afternoons and evenings together attending college classes. Clara carefully and meticulously arranges her college work and class schedule and, using maximum college aid and loans, manages to support herself and her son, saying, "I owe $85,000 in loans, but you know what, it really did give me a peace of mind. I'm in debt for the rest of my life, but it gave me peace of mind!"

Anthony, a bright, enthusiastic, and well-behaved child, adapts to accompanying his mother to college. To Clara's relief, many of her professors are very accommodating, which facilitates her ability to take a full load of classes. For the most part the arrangement works, although there are tense periods of anxiety for both Clara and Anthony:

> Every day I had class, he went to class. There were some problems I encountered—where at one point I had a lab, and he couldn't go to lab. And so one of my professors was very good because he would let him sit outside of the lab. I can say that I have encountered good professors where they allowed him to come to class with me, and he would sit there, do his homework and whatever. He wasn't disruptive, so they didn't have a problem with it. When I had a group dynamics class, actually, he had to stay in the library, and it was very nerve-wracking. . . . Every 20 minutes I would run out of class and run into the library. At one point it also became nerve-wracking for him because one evening he was waiting for me, and I think that he thought I was a little later and he became very frightened!

During Clara's junior year, the janitors in the School of Education building, where most of her classes are located, befriend Anthony, and he spends his time with them in the early evenings. Clara appreciatively remembers the support from both men: "And Ben, I mean, he was so good to Anthony, and Chris, he used to work here before, so I used to get to bring him here. And they were fine. Anthony would help Ben and help Chris around the place."

When Anthony is 10 years old, the School of Education at Clara's university opens an after-school program supported by a federal CCAMPIS grant to accommodate the growing child care needs of their students. The program is run by a professional educator and support staff and enrolls children 5 to 12 years old from 3:30 to 9:00 p.m. Educationally enriching, well run, and with dinner provided by a gourmet deli around the corner, the program is spoken about in glowing accolades by Clara and her fellow student parents. Not only does the program provide free child care services to student parents, but its progressive and child-centered approach creates an educationally engaging, nurturing environment for the children. Anthony was the first child to enroll, and Clara laughingly refers to him as the "veteran" of the program:

> It was a wonderful and different change because now I didn't have to lug him to class and do all that stuff. He could come here at 3:30. He can do his homework. He can get a hot meal. He has better dinner than I do! I mean, you see the art work. You don't have a room with children who are just doing their own things. They're always engaging in something . . . it's either computers, it's the artwork, they're putting together their portfolios or whatever—you don't know how at ease I am. It's unbelievable!

Anthony has been attending the program for over two years now and will soon age out. He loves the program and does not want to leave once the school year is over. Clara says she has never encountered such an excellent program in all her forays into the world of child care and after-school care, describing it as "so different, it's just totally different, even when Anthony has no school, he wants to go to the after-school program!"

The older children in the program also receive help with their homework, and the focus on expressive activities, geared to children's different interests and age levels, creates an environment brimming with artwork, stories, poetry, music, and an extensive array of multiage projects.[2] For

Clara, who reflects back on her years of child care problems, the program has been an immense help to her:

> I was surprised when they first started. I think people were like "Oh, no, it's probably not believable, you know, a program like that!" I think a lot of people also don't attempt to go back to school because of the lack of child care. You have to really think about it. There are a lot of sacrifices that you have to make and, you know, your children have to take first priority before you do anything. And child care, I mean, you have to be so careful who you leave your children with and if the neighborhood's safe. And this is just so, so wonderful, a wonderful program. . . . When I pick him up, he's had dinner and the homework is done. I can relax, and he can go to bed!

Education has been the driving force in Clara's life—college has significantly transformed her world view, and her determined pursuit of a fulfilling career that would bring her economic security has been shaped by her dreams for her own son:

> It has a lot to do with my son, and the ability to give him that life, you know. . . . I needed to educate myself so that I can better raise him. I mean, I needed to expose him to things that I wasn't exposed to. And I got that; actually I got all of that in college myself. You know, coming to school and talking to other parents, and hearing what they're saying and what they're doing with their children . . . I want for him to be able to go to college right after high school, and, you know, succeed at something!

Clara's own success, achieved despite the obstacles centered around the lack of child care for her son, has given her a unique and empathic perspective that she now brings to her own students and their parents in her position as a special education teacher. Clara has become an advocate for poor parents and their children, particularly for single mothers struggling in New York City's welfare-to-work program, unable to find good child care. Many of the young children she teaches have been bounced around in makeshift arrangements, with "desperate parents leaving their children in the care of others they do not trust. . . . This opens the door for so many things, like sexual and physical abuse, because good child care is not there." And says Clara, "when it's available, it's not financially possible for a lot of people. . . . It's a chunk out of a budget if you don't have the money!"

Clara's awareness of the child care crisis also extends to student parents, who like herself have struggled to find child care while attending classes. There are not many after-school programs like the one Clara has for Anthony—programs that are both free and of high quality. Clara questions why all colleges and universities don't make such services available to their student parents:

> I was driving in the city the other day, where my community college used to be, and I sit in the car, and I'm looking at all the people that are going to classes, and they're all women. I'm telling you, throngs walking to classes. . . . And probably most have children, and I'm sure that not all of them are in an after-school program!

While Clara succeeded in taking Anthony with her to school for three years, she is well aware that not all faculty are as flexible and tolerant as her professors were, and that with a very young child, or a child who may be disruptive, such an arrangement is not an option. Thus, many single mothers must drop out of school. The solution that Clara envisions is to fund child care at all levels for all in need—for welfare recipients, for low-income parents, for college student parents. Speaking from years of her own experiences and now as a teacher on the other side, Clara emphatically states, "Child care! Child care! Child care! I truly believe that more money should be spent on child care. It is a huge, huge problem."

Clara and Anthony have benefited enormously during the past two and a half years since Anthony began attending his after-school program. Clara's life has also changed dramatically as she has entered the ranks of professional teaching. However, she recognizes the crucial role that high quality child care has played in her life and that of her son, remarking, "It was a wonderful and different change!"

KATHY AND HER SONS: STRATEGIC MOTHER WIT

> It's very hard when you're trying to start off in the world—You really have to search for good child care, and the problem is always the expense.

Forty-one year old Kathy is the mother of two teenage boys living in San Diego, California. As an African-American single mother, Kathy has struggled alone to raise her sons while working continuously in low-wage jobs. Currently she is enrolled in a vocational-training program to upgrade her skills and earn an administrative-assistant certificate so that she can work in a hospital setting, interacting with patients and assisting them. She enthusiastically describes herself as "always wanting to be there for people. I love, *love* people, and I like helping them."

When Kathy's sons, Brendon and Devon, were young, she moved to San Diego to try and "make it on my own" and found a job at a hospital cafeteria. However, with an odd-hours job paying $7 an hour, and a toddler and a baby in need of child care, she soon found herself facing a looming crisis and turned to a good friend for help: "This job was just handed to me so fast . . . I had a friend that I could trust, and I left them there . . . from 5:00 in the morning until 2:00 in the afternoon." While her friend kindly steps in as instant caregiver for a baby and toddler, Kathy begins to search for a permanent child care setting for her young sons. She is very particular about the kind of placement and concerned that it be "comfortable" for her and the babies:

> I had to search for child care real quick, but I took my time . . . I knew that it's important to have a licensed child care. Then, when I found the child care that I wanted to take the children to, that was $180 a week . . . and then I found like, Oh man! I'm spilling this amount of money taking the bus to work, you know, and basically all I had out of my check left was maybe forty or fifty dollars. But after I did that, I was left with nothing.

While the licensed family day care home has early morning hours, Kathy finds herself paying almost two-thirds of her income on child care–$720 out of total of $1,120 in monthly earnings. For six months Kathy struggles and juggles finances, but she cannot sustain her young family with such high child care costs, "I'm working for nothing, you know, and I'm leaving my children, and I'm not really making anything. So I kinda started feeling like I'm working for the child care!" Kathy describes how, "It became too hard on me" as she struggles to even afford the costs of keeping two babies in diapers, and she makes a decision to quit her job and stay home with her young sons, although she says, "I really wanted to work" and regretfully, she applies for welfare saying:

> If you have the expense of child care, a lot of times it's what stumps you. If you're low income and trying to make it—it's what stops us from being able to get work—as a single parent, paying, you know, all bills, I didn't have any type of subsidized program. I didn't get any help, so what I had to do is try it on my own. But then you find yourself working for the babysitter. So it's like, you weren't getting anywhere because you have to

pay for your child care, you have to pay for your transportation and then also maintain your life. . . . You know, when you can't see any future, and you're out there working, and you're just working, it's not a very nice feeling.

Kathy briefly returns home to the Bay area, where she has family and tries to make it there. But maintaining a job, while dependent on family members for child care, means that child care arrangements frequently fall apart:

I went back to the Bay Area . . . but I found that it doesn't work, when you depend on family members because that's not their job . . . I mean, it needs to be a dependable family member to help you. . . . I'd rather go out there and put my children in a licensed program. That way they'd also be learning their ABC's.

Kathy returns to San Diego determined to find a better-paying job and to solve her recurring child care problems, but she realizes that in order to afford high quality child care, she needs access to child care subsidies and reapplies. She reflects on what it takes to find quality child care and her own feelings about leaving her children in child care:

You have to really search for good child care and make yourself comfort-able in dropping your children off . . . you know your child better than any one . . . you have to tell your children . . . you have to let them know you're confident in leaving them, [and] . . . that you're doing this for them, too, because it's a different feeling for them also. So, what I'm say-ing is that the biggest obstacle is making sure you can first find out infor-mation on these child care providers . . . where you can kind of like *invest*, you know, like being able to go and see their backgrounds . . . you have to go in and make sure how long they've been in the business, you know. Are you able to come in there and drop off, drop-in at any time and see how your kid's doing? That's important to me—to be able to come by . . . I want to be able to drop in at any time and make sure, not only my child is safe, but others too . . . because it can be crazy out there!

Kathy describes the changes in her life once she begins receiving child care subsidies that, to her relief, cover the costs of a good, licensed fam-ily day care setting that she chooses for her two sons. For Kathy, the subsidies are a godsend, enabling her to obtain a better job as a customer service representative:

> And then, when the subsidized programs came about, they helped [me]
> to have reliable child care, affordable child care, you know, where you
> can be comfortable, and just say, okay, I can go here and take my chil-
> dren here, and don't have to worry about the cost, you know. . . . It re-
> ally helps you achieve your goals until you're able to take care of things
> yourself.

Kathy is now able to afford her rent on a $400 apartment and, with care-
ful budgeting of her low-wage earnings, she successfully manages to keep
her family afloat.

The child care subsidies essentially sustain the family until the boys
begin public school. When the boys begin school, Kathy strategically
dovetails her work with her young sons' school hours and obtains a job
in the school cafeteria: "That way I worked the school hours . . . and then
I [could] be there when they're home. I'd just bring the children to work
with me and they went to school. And that way I didn't have to worry
about no one watching them before school and afterwards." Kathy, ever
mindful of her children's comfort and stability, emphasizes how she always wanted to be there for her sons so they "could tell me how their day
went" and, in retrospect, sums up the arrangement during their elementary school years as one that "came out pretty good for us."

Once her children are older, Kathy switches jobs, and begins to work
full-time as a customer service representative for a large corporation. Still
a low-wage earner, her sons, in upper elementary and middle school, are
able to attend San Diego's fully subsidized, popular 6-to-6 public school-
age child care program, which Kathy regards as a boon:

> That's what made it even nicer for me. The programs were attached to
> the schools . . . and they were able to go in the morning before school—
> 6:00 o'clock is the earliest you can bring them. And then they were able
> to go after-school—6:00 o'clock is the latest. So that gave me time to get
> to work and time to get back to get them. So that was real helpful
> . . . and the important part about it was . . . [that] the subsidized pro-
> gram helped me to make an adjustment where I could advance myself.

Throughout these years in her family's life, the after-school program
for her sons fulfills a crucial function, providing stable, dependable, be-
fore- and after-school care and educational enrichment. Kathy enthusiastically touts the benefits she sees for her sons, who are both academically
successful students, engaged in their school activities, many of which are
offshoots of the after-school program:

It's *so* important . . . it was so helpful, and it helped you help your children, to become responsible, because my boys are very responsible now.
And it helps them too, from them going to day care early, it helps them
to get up and go to school early. . . . They set their own alarm clocks.
They get up and they get prepared, and they're on time. And that's what
I tell them. It's important that you be on time, because if you're on time,
you're on time for work and you're on time for life. . . . So they're really
good with that. They're doing really good in school.

Kathy describes how the homework and tutoring components of the
after-school program have provided invaluable resources and a comfort
level for the children, which, she believes, made her own sons confident
in seeking out help and resources and negotiating their way through the
school system: "If they need any help with their homework, they're there
to help you. They know that there's help there for them. So, that's why I
know that having the program, they really learned, it made them learn a
lot, and they always know that they can go after school for help."

Kathy's sons have just recently aged out of the after-school program,
which serves children through age 13, but she credits their knowledge of
school resources, their comfort level in school, and their confident expectations about their education as due in no small measure to the impact
of their years in the 6-to-6 public after-school programs. Kathy describes
how her older son, Brendon, who has just entered high school, has inde-
pendently taken the initiative to seek math tutoring after school:

They know, they're aware. . . . Because of them going to before- and
after-school [programs], they know to go, if they need some help on
their homework. So my son takes advantage of that, he'll stay after
school, and he'll go get help with his math if he needs it.

While Kathy struggled under often desperate conditions when her
sons were very young, once she obtained child care subsidies, her life
took a different turn. Her children benefited from good child care during
their preschool years, and particularly from the educationally enriching
school-age child care programs. Her sons, now 13 and 14, continue to
blossom in school and the family has remained stable and, for a period
of time, self-sufficient.

Recently Kathy was laid off from her company because of downsizing, and after a period of unemployment, she decides to take advantage
of the CalWORKs job training program to upgrade her skills, hoping
that the program will help her land a better job and higher earnings.

With a strong work ethic and a continuous work history of low-wage jobs, Kathy is anxious to find a job with prospects of advancement:

> I always love to work, you know, I love to be around people. And I think it's good to work because working helps you to achieve and make you more responsible with your life. . . . I want to get into a setting that you can advance and move on. . . . That's my goal.

Kathy enjoys her computer and technical-training classes and appreciatively describes the CalWORKs program as, "help[ing] me to make changes, get back on my feet . . . and they help you get everything you need for school. They help you with your books. . . . They really are here for you." Kathy's long-term goal of a stable well-paying job, of wanting "to advance . . . to stay . . . to be able to grow with the company" has been elusive, not because of any lack of her own strong work ethic and dedication, but rather because of her vulnerable status as a low-wage worker subject to arbitrary layoffs and downsizing by the corporations she has worked for over the years. During Kathy's latest period of unemployment she realized with fear that "you never know what's going to happen in the future"; hence her resolve to retrain as an administrative assistant so that she can obtain a higher-paying job with benefits. She currently looks towards the future with optimism, anticipating prospective earnings in the range of $40,000 once she completes her one-year certificate program. In Kathy's case, CalWORKs appears to have been a successful experience, confirming Mathur's study of the positive outcomes of CalWORKs community college programs, where those who complete certificates or associate's degrees show the most gains in earnings over time, relative to other welfare participants.[3]

In many ways, the experiences of Kathy and her sons are glowing testimony to the success of public investment in good quality child care and school-age care. Kathy's boys are healthy adolescents, actively engaged in school and successful students who are college bound. As their mother, she has single-handedly fought for their future, consistently seeking out public funds, and effectively strategizing so that her sons were able to receive good quality child care. But Kathy's story is also emblematic of the battle to make it as a female head-of-household and low-wage worker, with no buffer against the ravages of the market economy. Kathy is still struggling; she is persistent and determined to find a job where she can "move on, move up . . . I want to advance. I want to stay." Yet for most of her adult life the statistical odds have been stacked against her. As a female without a college degree, she has always been most vulnerable to economic downturns in the market, for those with the least education suffer disproportionate impact. Kathy's fervent hope is that the additional training for her one-year administrative-assistant certificate may enable her to move up and out of poverty with her two sons.

NETWORKS OF SUPPORT

Kathy, a dedicated and able low-wage worker pursuing a vocational certificate, struggled to succeed in an era of layoffs and downsizing. Tanya and Clara, two successful student mothers, demonstrated how determination and drive and academic prowess in combination with hard work still was not enough to ensure their families' well-being. All three mothers used a considerable degree of "maternal invention"[4] to cope with the child care deficits in their overburdened families, and informal and formal networks of support were vital for their success at critical junctures in their lives and those of their children.

Grandparents

Tanya's mother and Clara's father invested substantial time and effort in caring for their grandchildren when very young. Tanya's mother actually relocated to Iowa after she retired, caring for Tanya's two sons until her untimely death a few years later. Clara's father played an important role in grandson Anthony's early childhood, as he picked him up regularly from the half-day Head Start program and took care of him while Clara attended school and worked. Michelle's mother, Carmina (Chapter 2), not only cared for her baby grandson but also fought the New York City welfare-to-work program for the right to work as a care provider while her daughter completed high school. Francesca's mother (Chapter 2) supported her daughter and baby grandson, Tameron, while she worked full-time and attended school full-time. Even Melissa's elderly and frail grandmother in Iowa (Chapter 3) helped with child care when her great-grandchildren were sick, and for more than a year, Melissa and her children lived in her household.

The U.S. Census Bureau's most recent report on "Who's Minding the Kids?" indicates that for employed mothers, grandparents are a significant source of care, with 29.1% of preschool children cared for by their grandparents.[5] Single, never-married mothers rely more heavily on grandparents for child care, as do separated, divorced, and widowed mothers, with 37.8% and 31.9% of their preschool children, respectively, cared for by grandparents. For low-income mothers, who use relative care at far higher rates than do their nonpoor counterparts, grandparent care is also seen as far preferable, safer, and more trustworthy;[6] particularly because their children are likely to end up in the lowest quality of care in the cheap informal care sector. While reliance on grandparents (usually grandmothers) is often precipitated by a child care crisis, or the lack of good quality and affordable care, it is also a reflection of strong intergenerational ties and family cohesiveness.[7] Tanya's mother relocated to Iowa because she wanted her daughter to fulfill her dream of obtaining a college education and actively encouraged her to go to school full-time and work full-time, while she devoted her retirement to her two grandsons. When she unexpectedly became ill, Tanya, in turn, took care of her mother, as well as her own children.

For grandparents who live with their children and grandchildren, as well as those who provide child care from their own homes, there is a significant investment of time and emotional commitment to their children's families. Alterations in routines, lack of time for their own needs and social networks, as well as lifestyle changes characterize the experiences of many grandparents as they accommodate to the needs of their young grandchildren.[8] The grandmothers (and grandfather) in this book, who supported their daughters with child care and other resources, were also strong advocates for their pursuit of postsecondary education and instilled in their daughters a drive and determination that was often quite remarkable, given the odds stacked against their success. Clara's mother and father left Barbados and worked to bring their daughter over to join them in the United States. Clara's mother instilled in her from the outset the expectation that she would be the first to go to college; and it was Tanya's mother who always told her, "Education is something you will always have. No one can take that away from you and it is education that will help you succeed."

Friends and Community

Friends and community members also played a crucial role in supporting and encouraging Tanya in her pursuit of education, pushing her the extra mile when she came perilously close to quitting. During her years in Iowa, Tanya forged lasting friendships with other single mothers, built social relationships at her church and university, and, through her membership in a community-based advocacy organization, created an interlocking web of social connections that formed her community. For Kathy, relatively isolated, who chose to relocate away from her family to San Diego, it was a close friend who generously helped her through the nightmarish early months of working an odd-hours job with two babies. For Clara, the informal network she established at the university she attended in New York, and her friendship with two janitors in her college building, provided a sense of safety and reassurance as she attended classes accompanied by her young son, Anthony. Flexible college professors eased mothering responsibilities for both Clara and Tanya, as they made accommodations for their student-parent status, particularly after Tanya gave birth before her final exams. In addition, the infant care center that Tanya's daughter attended on a tuition scholarship and the free school-age child care offered at Clara's university were both funded by federal CCAMPIS grants that made high quality child care affordable and conveniently accessible for students. School-age child care programs were also a formative experience for Kathy's sons in elementary and middle school, creating a safe and enriching educational space for development.

School-Age Child Care

The majority of school-age children currently live in households in which both their parents work. As the number of women in the labor force has increased (see Introduction), there have been rapid changes to the traditional family structure, with over 77.5% of all mothers with children 6–17 years old, and 81.9% of single mothers with children 6–17 years old, currently in the labor force.[9] In addition, changes in welfare legislation have resulted in an increasing number of poor children living with a single, working parent. The expanding low-wage labor market, which Jared Bernstein terms "an integral part of our macroeconomy and our lives,"[10] means that low-wage parents frequently confront working conditions that are inimical to participation in their children's school lives and to the supervision of their children after school.[11] With jobs that lack paid leave, permit little time flexibility, and often require odd hours, after-school care becomes a critical factor in stabilizing school-age children's lives.

With half of elementary school-age programs funded by tuition fees that average $3,000–$3,500 a year, low-income children are shut out and denied opportunities to participate; demand far outstrips the supply, and most states have long waiting lists for after-school slots. Estimates from the Children's Defense Fund indicate that two-fifths of low-income working parents encounter "significant problems" accessing school-age care.[12] Over 7 million children between the ages of 5 and 14 years old care for themselves during part of each week, and of those, 5.8 million are elementary age children living with their mothers.[13] Many of these same children are in self-care for significant amounts of time during the summer months when school is out and they have no access to supervised activities. Unsupervised school children are most at risk between the hours of 3:00 and 7:00 p.m., when juvenile crime peaks, and in dangerous neighborhoods juveniles are far more likely to be the victim of violence in the immediate hours after school lets out.[14] As Maeroff points out, poor children "who live in the worst neighborhoods pursue their out-of-school life at some peril."[15]

While low-income children are least likely to be enrolled in after-school programs, research studies point to significant positive outcomes for those who do attend formal after-school programs. The positive outcomes observed in low-income school-age children are similar to those for preschoolers: positive peer relationships, improved emotional well-being, and overall academic achievement.[16] Children enrolled in structured and well-run after-school programs are exposed to academic enrichment activities, including art, music, drama, and individual tutoring–activities from which they, in contrast to their more affluent peers, are usually excluded due to tight household budgets, lack of available opportunities in their neighborhoods, as well as transportation difficulties. Such enrichment activities expand their learning opportunities, build positive adult-child relationships, and broaden their horizons–building social capital through social connectedness, enhanced academic initiatives, a sense of well-being, and community engagement.[17] The experiences of Anthony, Clara's son, and Brendon and Devon, Kathy's two sons, confirm what research findings tell us: high quality after-school programs make a significant difference in children's lives; and too, in the lives of their mothers. Clara credits the after-school program with her successful graduation as a special education teacher and her current opportunity to enroll in a master's program. Kathy attributes her capacity to hold down a full-time job and keep her family afloat to San Diego's 6-to-6 before- and after-school program. Most important, the benefits accrued to the whole family unit result in an overall sense of family well-being.

In the following section, two Native-American single mothers are profiled, where family, community, child care and after-school care exist in a distinctively different milieu.

AN OJIBWE OASIS

A small Indian reservation in the upper peninsula of Michigan[18] provides a unique window into a working model of community investment
in housing, health care, and child care—a testament to what can be done
in terms of poverty alleviation when a strong infrastructure of social support services is developed to promote and sustain family and child well-
being. As one of the original tribal reservations established in Michigan
after the Indian Reorganization Act of 1934, the tribe's fortunes have
dramatically changed since the advent of casino gambling in the mid-
1980s. Tribally owned and operated, the casino has become an engine for
community revitalization and development, with the tribe strategically
reinvesting casino profits in the economic and educational development
of its members. From a reservation once mired in poverty to a flourishing
community, the transformation is most visible in the lives of women and
children who benefit from the available opportunities for land and home
ownership, tribal employment, and child care, creating a unique milieu
for Native-American single mothers and their children. With an acre of
free land for all its members, along with low-cost HUD-funded home
mortgages negotiated by the tribe, there are additional family supports
that are of particular benefit to single mothers and their children: a well-
run, high quality child care center, after-school care, a newly opened Indian charter school, a medical clinic, and an extensive tribal social safety
net that includes comprehensive Indian health services that supplement
traditional health insurance and Medicaid, as well as provide free services for the uninsured. A children's clothing supplement and commodity
food program are also available to tribal members.

The tribe's generous educational policy promotes postsecondary
education through financial incentives, including 6 hours of paid educational leave a week and an educational incentive that pays $150 for
every earned credit hour towards an associate's or bachelor's degree, and
double the amount for a master's degree. This has resulted in a diverse array of educational opportunities, particularly for Native-American single
mothers, who are able to strategically marshal their educational and child
care resources to maximum benefit for themselves and their children.

The well-designed and attractive child care center,[19] located in the
woods overlooking a scenic lake, offers both Head Start and Early Head
Start services and uses a High/Scope Curriculum, serving infants through
5-year-olds.[20] All but two of the 72 children are Indian, and the majority
of teachers and teacher assistants are drawn from the immediate tribal

community. The center director has a bachelor's degree in child development, and the teachers have Child Development Associate (CDA) credentials from the tribal community college or are working towards completion. The center operates from 8:00 a.m. to 2:00 p.m. and offers high quality wraparound child care for working parents from 2:00 to 5:00 p.m. Although the wraparound care was free for the first few years, it is now only partially subsidized by the Tribal Council, with parents paying $2 an hour for the hours from 2:00 to 5:00 p.m. This change caused difficulties for some parents who have more than one child at the center.[21] The popular after-school program was discontinued at the same time, despite parental protests, and folded into the Boys and Girls Club, which targets "at-risk" school-age children and offers an array of educational and recreational after-school activities.[22] Initially serving only children from 8 years and up, the Tribal Council, responding to the protests by mothers about the cuts in after-school child care services for kindergarten and early elementary children, recently lowered the age of eligibility, and the Boys and Girls Club now serves children 5 years and up. It, too, is a well-run program, staffed by educational professionals providing educational and cultural enrichment, tutoring, and recreational activities. The parents' only fee is an annual $12 registration for the program, which runs all year. As children may only enroll after their kindergarten year, there is a potential one year gap in the otherwise seamless child care services provided from birth through adolescence. However, the newly opened charter school on the reservation offers a full-day kindergarten program that will resolve the former gap in child care services.

Corinne and Kiara, two Indian single mothers living on the reservation, describe their lives and that of their children.

CORINNE AND MATT: NESTED IN THE COMMUNITY

My son has been going to the center since he's a month old and the tribe picked up the cost of day care.

Corinne is the 29-year-old divorced mother of a 5-year-old son and lives on the reservation in a comfortable three-bedroom home on land provided by the tribe. Corinne's monthly mortgage payments are based on a sliding scale, and she proudly predicts that "I'll own my own home in about 15 or 16 years," while paying only $226 a month. The tribe's investment in education has certainly borne fruit for Corinne, who calls herself "a professional student." With an associate's degree in computer information and a second associate's in business–both earned from the community college on the reservation, Corinne currently holds a job in the accounting department of the tribal administration.

Corinne divorced her husband when her son, Matthew, was a toddler, as she was not willing to put up with her husband's aggression and violence. Having grown up in a family where her own father had beaten her mother, Corinne was determined not to expose her son to a childhood of violence, saying, "My mom finally left him when I was 16 years old, but I had experienced the violence. I knew I didn't want my son to experience that. . . . It all goes back to my grandfather and his drinking and beating up my grandmother. It goes back generations!"

Corinne's mother, who is White, was permitted to stay on the reservation and in the family home after her divorce from Corinne's father until Corinne reached 18; at that time she moved off the reservation into a nearby town. Corinne admires her mother's strength and credits her own sense of who she is to her mother's continuing support, saying, "And if it wasn't for my mother, I wouldn't be the person that I am. She's the one that raised me." When Corinne's husband, whose own family was dysfunctional and violent, first assaulted her, Corinne made a swift decision:

> We got into one fight and he pushed me, this was when Matt was just young, and I thought I'm just not going to let him go through that, so I divorced him. I just knew I didn't want Matt to experience that. He'd be better off with just me. . . . And I'm a strong person anyway, as everybody says. It must be from my mother!

Matt's father has not seen his son since the divorce, which, says Corinne, "is his choice, not mine. He chooses his drugs over his children." With three other children from a previous marriage, Matt's father, according to Corinne, "chooses not to work, because all of his money gets applied to me and her for our kids, so he doesn't work, he just does drugs." There is a warrant out for his arrest, but he has left the reservation and not shown up for any tribal court hearings, and Corinne has had all visitation suspended. Shortly, the tribal court will move to terminate his parental rights.

With the help of the tribe's extensive infrastructure of supports, Corinne manages to live a comfortable and independent life with her son. She receives an array of benefits from her job, including health insurance with no co-pays, and there are full prescription drug benefits from a well-run clinic on the reservation that provides quality health services. Corinne has also been able to use the free Head Start[23] tribal child care center for Matt since he was an infant. Corinne describes how she placed Matt there soon after he was born:

> I got a really good job opportunity offered to me, and they wanted somebody right now in accounting. So I had to put him in day care after he was only a month old, but the tribe is really good about that, because they would let me go up there whenever I needed to, and I was still breastfeeding, so I breastfed—I pumped there, and I'd find myself my own little room for the time that I needed, and everybody would understand when I went down to the center.

Because the center is located close to where Corinne works at the tribal office, she was able to juggle breastfeeding and full-time work in a flexible environment. She describes how mothers of very young infants are permitted to bring their babies to work, or, in situations when they encounter child care problems:

> People used to always bring their kids to work . . . if they're very young, they let you bring them to work still. . . . I took Matt a couple of times. You can't do it for too long, because then they start running around, and, you know, you just can't get anything accomplished. Then you have to have day care, but if it's an infant or if you need care for a day . . . or if they [the day care] close down for a day, you could take him with you to work and it's a flexible environment. . . . I've had Matt with me a couple hours there every once in a while.

Matt has attended the center for five years now, and Corinne comments that in such a close-knit tribal community, teachers are more likely to take special care of the children:

> There's a couple of things that I had to fight over with them, but in general I would say that it's a really good setting. Because I know its different in the cities—here, being on a reservation, and everybody knows everybody, and everybody's related, they take more consideration in taking care of your child because everybody knows you.

Corinne describes her satisfaction with the quality of care and, in particular, comments on Matt's social development:

We went to my cousins in Wisconsin, and she keeps her kids at home and she was surprised at how polite and how social Matt was. And we attributed it to the good day care, because I don't think that those people [child care staff] are just earning their dollar, where at some day cares you know, they don't care how your child turns out. But *here*, at Matt's place, it's kind of very different.

What makes it different, in Corinne's eyes, is her sense of trust and security rooted in the personal connections, the positive attitudes, the stable staffing levels, and low turnover of the teachers at the center, and her feeling that Matt has spent his early years in a place where the teachers genuinely care about him:

As a matter of fact, all his teachers really, really, like him. And the woman down the road had him in the infant room as an infant, and she still wants to take him, you know, every once in awhile—I don't have to pay or anything—she loves him. . . . He goes over to her house. He plays with her kids and stuff.

Corinne describes how she and other single mothers went to the Tribal Council meeting and protested when the tribe recently began to charge parents $2 an hour for the remaining three hours of wraparound child care at the center from 2:00 to 5:00 p.m.

And so anyways, it got brought to the Council, and a bunch of us mothers were against it. There was two issues being brought to the Council. One was that they were, they were getting rid of the 5-year-old program, which was also part of that. When you're 5, you're not Head Start, and that was part of the day care, and they were moving that to a separate location, and there was paying for the after-school program. Of course, we all thought it was a bad idea, but they said that the expense, $400,000 over [the budget for child care]—they couldn't afford. We argued with them, but they made their decision. And once we got there I found tribal politics is a problem—people don't want to rock the boat too much. Because, I don't know, they always feel that their job is on the line, since they work so closely. And the people that had something to say didn't have too much to say afterwards, you know, except for me. I don't care. I argued! I argued long! But they had their minds made up!

To Corinne's and other parents' disappointment, they did not succeed in convincing the predominantly male Tribal Council to continue funding an all-day program, and the relocated after-school program closed temporarily, restricting options for the youngest school-age children, until the Boys and Girls Club lowered age eligibility. Besides the center, there are few options available for child care on the reservation. One tribal member has an informal and unlicensed in-home day care, but as Corinne points out, most parents prefer to send their child to the tribal child care center, which has a good reputation and is free for six hours a day from 8:00 a.m. to 2:00 p.m. For those single mothers in need of child care subsidies for late afternoon hours, they need to travel off the reservation to the nearest city and apply for FIA child care subsidies. As Corinne is not income-eligible for FIA subsidies, she must pay the extra $30 a week in child care costs. With affordable housing and health insurance, Corinne strategically budgets her educational incentives that she has accumulated with two degrees and manages to pay for the three hours of after-school care every day. But, she points out, it has been a blow to other parents, some of whom have several children under the age of 5, saying, "There's been problems . . . and I know there's some people that have outstanding child care bills." Although parents who have delinquent child care bills typically have money deducted out of their pay checks, or in some cases have been taken to tribal court, the children are still permitted to remain at the center, as, says Corinne, "I don't think anybody would get kicked out of day care because they weren't paying!"

During vacations and holidays Corinne relies on her neighbors' teen daughters, her mother, who visits every summer, and her network of friends and relatives on the reservation. When the center closed down last year because of a contagious illness, all the parents were stuck, and many took their children to work or traded care with relatives and friends, which was difficult for all because the center literally functions as the work engine of the reservation. Without it, everything grinds to a halt: "When it's closed, there's nowhere else to go—so you have to find a family member or friend, so somebody is always off work!"

In other communities, low-income parents, particularly single mothers, may find themselves in desperate straits when there is no child care for periods of time, or when suddenly faced with a $120 a month child care co-pay; but in this case the generous tribal benefits do serve to mitigate and avert such crises, even the unfortunate subsidy cuts that were made to the wraparound child care program. Corinne, like many of her friends who are single mothers, enjoys housing security, a living-wage job with extensive benefits, easy access to low-cost loans from the tribe, and a flexible workplace that allows her to integrate parenting and work. Because of the emphasis on higher education and the educational incentives, going to school pays in multiple ways. Successful completion of just one 3-credit course brings in $450. As tuition is free, the educational incentive payment is a boon for parents *and* young children; as parents strategically recycle it from higher education to their children's early education.

Corinne has plans to continue her education–she has already enrolled in a bachelor's degree in paralegal studies at a regional university in the area, and from there, on and up to law school, hoping to become a lawyer working for her tribe. As she prepares for the new academic year, her son is enrolled in the all-day kindergarten at a charter school run by the tribe. She is excited and upbeat about the coming year, and at twenty-nine years old, she and her son face a promising future, made possible by Corinne's resourcefulness, hard work, and the strong infrastructure of tribal support services that promote family stability. As Corinne points out, "You know, without Matt's day care and all this assistance, there's no way I would manage!"

KIARA AND HER SONS: "A PLACE TO ALWAYS COME BACK TO"

> As a single mother with two kids, two different dads, Native-American, under 30—I'm probably on every statistic list there is!

Kiara is a 28-year-old single mother of two sons, aged 7 and 5. Kiara spent her early years with her mother and brother on the reservation, and after her mother married her stepfather, the family moved to a nearby town. After more than two decades away, Kiara moved back to the reservation three years ago and now works in one of the tribal offices. She describes how the opportunity to own her own piece of land with a low-cost mortgage influenced her decision to return:

> One acre is free to all tribal members, and so I got the land and then I was holding on to the land. I was OK, well I got it; if I ever need it, it'll be there. And then the tribe got a grant about three years ago which offered housing through HUD, and you could mortgage homes at a very low cost . . . the most I'd have to pay ever is $213 a month!

For Kiara, who has struggled alone to raise her two sons on limited resources, the chance to move back to her family's tribal lands, achieve some economic security, and *buy* an affordable home for the children was an opportunity to be seized:

That's more than good! It's the best thing that I've ever heard in my life! I was living in apartments [in the town], going to school, and working two jobs, paying $400 for merely decent living quarters. And that would be per month without utilities and everything else, so when I got the opportunity to come out here, and I was single with my kids, I said I have to take it. It's the best thing I can do for my children. . . . In most ways, it's the best thing because we do have a beautiful home. We do live on nice land. We are close to family.

However, Kiara is also ambivalent about the move; she has not lived on the reservation since she was 8 years old, and there are drawbacks to living in an isolated tight-knit rural community, but such drawbacks are clearly part of the price she is willing to pay for a measure of stability and comfort for her children:

I really had not ever dreamed of raising my children here, just because it is a closed-in community. . . . It's very hard to come back to such a small community . . . a few of my friends ended up dead or in jail—There's not much to do here. . . . There's more bars than churches, but my kids come first, and I would never have come back home but for my kids . . . I pretty much lived in a town all my life, except for when I was very young. I never lived a country type of lifestyle. But to have to buy in bulk and to have to travel so far to a good store, you know, a lot of times I've had car problems and things like that, and I had no way to get to [the town]. It's hard to live so far away from so many resources.

Kiara remembers life on the reservation 20 years ago, where, despite the grinding poverty, her mother, whom she describes as "full-blooded Indian," was always ingeniously resourceful and, she says, taught her that "mothers can pull miracles out of nowhere because they have no choice!":

I can remember so many times. . . . We didn't have any water, living on the reservation. That was way back when. We lived in an A-frame with no electricity, no water, wood heat, you know, you know, you had a porta potty for the bathroom. And none of that mattered to me. I will never forget how much love was in our house!

Kiara was 21 and living off the reservation, attending community college, when her oldest son, Aden, was born. She reluctantly dropped out of community college to take care of her baby and soon split up with Aden's father, realizing, "I felt very stagnant in our relationship." While he made "good money," Kiara did not want to be "just a mom and a housewife" and thought "there was a lot more" she wanted out of her life. However, two years later she became pregnant with her second son by a man she was dating. He turned out to be violent with a bipolar disorder, so at 24 years old, with a baby and a toddler, Kiara found herself at a critical juncture:

> I thought there's no way I can do this. There's no way I can do this, and there's no way I can do this to my children. I can do it better on my own. And the way I figured it, is that I was happier and safer and so were my children alone than with him. If I had to start from scratch without anything, I could do it, and I did. And you know, it wasn't easy. But I did. And I made sure after I had Alex, I told the doctor I was having no more children, and I've had the operation, and I'm not having any more children. Because I know how much I can handle and how much I can't. And I know what's fair to my children and what's not!

Kiara maintains a good relationship with Aden's father and his family, and he pays regular child support of $50 a week when he's working, "but when he's not working, he falls behind." The situation with Alex's father, however, has been traumatic. When Alex was three, Kiara endured repeated threats from him—and once, she describes "freaking out" because he did not return Alex for 15 hours after a weekend visit. However, it was an incident that took place when Alex was visiting Kiara's parents that led Kiara to report Alex's father to the police and seek protection for her son. As Kiara recollects, Alex began to cry when her parents tried to change him into his pajamas and "he brought up that his dad had done something to him, and he demonstrated it. . . . When I heard this it just completely devastated me." During the police investigation Alex's father denied he had sexually abused his son, and there was no physical proof, but Kiara successfully petitioned the tribal court to end visitation. Because of subsequent threats, Kiara, her parents, and her best friend all filed for protection orders so that "if he is in any house or property on the reservation, he will be arrested." Alex has had no contact with his father since the incident, and although Kiara still worries about the impact of the abuse, she is outraged that Alex's father went unpunished. The case was dismissed because of lack of evidence, and a toddler's word against an adult's is always fraught with problems. Kiara comments, "My son was very hard to understand at 3 years old, but 3-year-olds don't lie!" Kiara describes the aftermath of the incident:

> For about a year, I killed myself thinking, how can I prove that he did this? How can I make him pay? And then I came to my senses, and I thought, you know, I've got this beautiful boy, and it's punishment. He can't see him. He can't come around him. By his own guilt, he will not know this child, and that, to me, is punishment enough. Because for me, how could I ever live without my child?

Two years have since passed, and Alex has developed into a seemingly healthy 5-year-old. Kiara has enrolled at the community college, benefiting from free tuition and the educational incentive. Working full-time in one of the tribal offices, Kiara sends Alex to the child care center, but since the recently instituted charge for wraparound child care, Kiara has encountered unexpected child care costs and finds herself "in that bracket where I make enough money but not enough money." She decides to apply for state child care subsidies and, to do so, must travel off the reservation to the FIP office that serves the whole county. She describes her feelings of humiliation going to the FIP agency, a dramatic change from her dealings at the tribal community office, where, says Kiara, "they help you and make you feel good as a person, they say, 'this is available, do you need it?'" However, going to the FIP office is a different matter:

> You know, it doesn't make me feel very good. I'm not very proud to go into those places. . . . And it does make me feel like I've been knocked down a little . . . I know that there's resources available. I believe they're there for people who need them. I would like to not need them. When I do need them, I sure would like not to have to feel that it is very degrading to go in there, and I wish the tribe would understand that. Because there are times when bills will add up or things like that, and they'll say "first go to the state." And I say, I'll just pay myself . . . I would rather struggle to get it paid on my own than to go through that kind of humiliation.

With the tribe no longer paying the full cost of after-school care, Kiara must figure the child care costs into her budget. While paying for the wraparound child care is an extra expense and a hardship, Kiara still sees the child care center as providing "the cheapest and best day care you could find. . . . I've had my ups and downs there, but financially it's the best thing for me."

As the boys are now 7 and 5, both currently attend the summer program run by the tribe for children 5 and older, but this summer will be the last one before the Tribal Council closes it down. Aden, who will soon turn 8, will attend the Boys and Girls club next summer when school is out, but Kiara worries about plans for Alex[24]:

> This summer is the last summer for the 5+ kids, so there goes one of my options. I've heard that there's some people opening day cares, but, like I said, I don't really trust a whole lot of people with my kids. . . . I have to find something every day from 8:00 to 4:30 during the summer, because he won't have anywhere to go.

Kiara will consider taking Alex to work with her part of the time, as she has done with both boys in the past, when she has had child care problems, remarking that the tribe "is pretty good about it–if I need to bring my children to work I can." Taking Alex to work, or finding a family member or trusted friend will mean piecing together makeshift arrangements until the Boys and Girls Club accepts younger children. Kiara has also thought about taking on another job (to pay for more expensive child care) or figuring out an arrangement with other single mothers in order to make things work: "I'll find a way. Pretty much as I have in the past. I've had to work more than one job, do extra things for the people, find a way. I do have a select group of girlfriends who have children, and they are in the same situation that I am."

Kiara, and many other working parents, are very dependent on the popular program, which has been such a vital support and an educationally enriching experience for the children of the reservation. For this year, Kiara must find an alternative, saying, "I'm stuck. I'm stuck with the child care thing." Fortunately, her mother and stepfather live about 40 miles away, and "Grandma's house" is a safety net, available for emergency child care.

Most important to Kiara is that her children have a taste of the "outside"–the world beyond the reservation. "I want my kids to go places and do things . . . I've brought my kids to plays, I've taken my kids on trips. Last year I took my sons all the way to Massachusetts on the train!" As a tribal government employee Kiara also benefits from the small loan program to employees:

> I'm going on a trip next month to Colorado with my kids on a plane. So, I'm going to take out a $500 loan. And you don't have to tell them why. You don't have to tell them, you have up to $500 that you can take, and then you just pay it off in six months. And once that's paid off, they

tell you it's paid off, and they ask you, would you like another one, or would you like to wait? It's always available to you as long as you're an employee here.

For the immediate future Kiara plans to stay on the reservation, recognizing that as a low-income single mother, the reservation offers unmatched stability for herself and the children and "is the best place to be, a place to always come back to." Kiara's sons have benefited from their years at the Head Start child care center and after-school programs, services that are vital for single parents. Fortunately, with the new charter school offering all-day kindergarten, and with the age limit of the Boys and Girls Club reduced to 5 within the year, most of the child care needs of reservation parents will be met. The paid educational leave and the educational incentive program have enabled Kiara to return to school while working full-time and "get on my feet again." She anticipates a future when her children are older and no longer in need of child care, and sees a landscape of possibilities opening up "so I can be a single mom—taking on the world!"

CHILD CARE AS A FAMILY INVESTMENT

For Kiara and Corinne, single mothers living on the reservation, child care is a vital service and fundamental component of their children's development. Child care has enabled both mothers to pursue higher education, and, with living wage jobs, health care, and home ownership, they are on the pathway to successful lives. Their children have benefited from stable, nurturing, and high quality child care and are embedded in a network of social relationships in school, child care, and after-school care contributing to their tightly knit cohesive community that Kiara acknowledges "is great for my kids;" although oftentimes constricting of her own vision of becoming part of the wider world beyond. However, without the tribe's investment in high quality child care and postsecondary education, both women would be living far more precarious lives with their young children.

For Tanya, Clara, and Kathy, life was very different. They struggled against the odds when their children were very young, yet they succeeded in strategically marshalling all possible networks and resources—Tanya's mother; Clara's father, sister, sympathetic college professors, and even the building janitors; Kathy's friend who watched her sons during a critical work transition—until they were able to access affordable and good child care. When their children were enrolled in high quality child care and after-school care programs, the snowball effects on their mothers were quite remarkable, enabling Tanya and Clara to graduate and pursue master's degrees, and assisting Kathy in a certification program for an administrative assistant position. Interestingly, all three mothers speak in glowing terms of the positive impact that good child care has had on their children's social and intellectual development. Tanya's toddler daughter is blossoming at the university child care center, and her two older brothers are academically gifted students. Clara's son has, according to his mother, "learned so much—he's always engaging in something, in artwork, in computers" in the exemplary after-school care program he has attended for nearly three years, and Kathy remarks how her sons have, as a result of their positive educational experiences in San Diego's 6-to-6 program, "learned a lot—they are so responsible and they see school in such a good light because of the program."

An investment in child care is a two-generational investment in development and education at all levels. As we see in these five mothers' lives, the stability of good quality child care lays the foundation for a sustainable family life, enhances children's learning and development and, in turn, enables mothers to complete their education and become autonomous and self-sufficient. While child care is often the tipping point that causes a family to fall over the edges, it is also transformative, creating a profound shift in the existential promise and meaning of a life constrained by a chronic lack of resources. The transformative capacity of good child care is such that, in Merleau-Ponty's words, it "makes a fresh structure of social space possible . . . room for a new project in relation to living."[25] In short, a decent life, engendering the human capabilities of both women and their children. Why then, is child care not a fundamental human right in the United States?

CHAPTER 8

The Right to Child Care

but her words live, they issue from this life.
She scatters clews. She speaks from all these faces
and from the center of a system of lives
who speak the desire of worlds moving unmade
saying, "Who owns the world?" and waiting for the cry.

—Muriel Rukeyser, *Ann Burlak*[1]

The women of this book have spoken. From the center of their system of lives, they also speak for a world yet unmade. Their words are tethered to daily realities that reflect the harsh injustices that they face as women, as mothers, as individuals who lack ownership of their small piece of the world. They speak truth to power in order to articulate the wrongs that have been done that surely should produce rights, paramount among them the right to care and to receive care for one's children. Such rights are embedded in a notion of public care and public responsibility that supports their human capabilities and makes possible the "fundamental functions of a human life"[2]: caring, learning, earning, and participating in the civic, cultural, and political life of a democracy.

That a deep and serious crisis of child care exists in the United States is only in doubt *if* we fail to accord to poor children the same expectations of concern and care that are meted out to their middle- and upper-income peers: the expectation that their lives are deserving of attentiveness, care, enrichment, and developmentally appropriate early education. That millions of children are denied basic rights the rest of the populace takes for granted is an outrage that requires urgent redress–for as Steinbeck presciently warned over half a century ago, "the decay spreads over the State, and the sweet smell is a great sorrow on the land."[3]

CHILD CARE AS A HUMAN RIGHT

Most industrialized democracies have recognized the importance of creating a "positive state" for women and children through the provision of strong family support policies[4] that incorporate child care as a key social citizenship right (see Chapter 1). However, attempts to create a legal right to child care in the United States through litigation have been largely unsuccessful, and state constitutional provisions that grant children the right to a public education have not been extended to early education and the right to child care.[5] Davis and Powell argue that because of its failure to offer basic social protections and family supports to its citizens, the United States is an outlier in the international arena and that it is a misguided strategy to rely *only* on domestic law to attempt to establish child care provisions. The absence of child care should not be viewed as another competing demand of a special interest group, but rather, child care should be framed as a fundamental human right, emanating from international human rights standards, and an affirmative obligation of government. By framing child care solely as a domestic policy agenda, women's and children's advocacy groups have actually "abetted the United States policy of exceptionalism."[6]

As discussed in Chapter 1, the affirmative obligation of government to create family support policies and child care provisions is recognized in three international human rights conventions, which the United States has failed to ratify: the Convention on the Rights of the Child (CRC), the Convention on the Elimination of All Forms of Discrimination against Women (CEDAW), and the International Covenant on Economic, Social, and Cultural Rights (ICESCR). The CRC, adopted by unanimous consent at the United Nations in 1989, was implemented in 1990 and has been ratified by 191 countries. In the CRC, children, for the first time, are recognized as "rights bearers," as citizens, and as social actors.[7] The CRC also addresses children's rights to receive care and protection and the promotion of their best interests for "full and harmonious development." Article 18 emphasizes that State Parties must provide "appropriate assistance to parents . . . in the performance of their child-rearing responsibilities" and take " all appropriate measures to ensure that children of working parents have the right to benefit from child-care services."[8] Countries that have ratified the CRC are required to submit periodic reports that are subject to international review and scrutiny. Although the reports and recommendations are not binding, they do serve a critical purpose in creating an international discourse of child care rights that has had the power to shape domestic policy changes in numerous countries that have ratified the Convention.[9]

CEDAW, hailed as an "international bill of rights for women," was adopted by the UN General Assembly in 1979 and entered into force as a treaty in 1981. CEDAW has been ratified by 169 countries, excluding the United States. There is explicit recognition in CEDAW of the links between women's equality, the right to work, family life, and the necessity for government to ensure that these rights and opportunities are upheld by focusing on provisions for the care of children. Article 11 specifically addresses women's "right to work as an inalienable right," including "the right to maternity leave with pay or with comparable benefits." State Parties are enjoined to make it possible to "combine family obligations with work responsibilities and participation in public life . . . through promoting the establishment and development of a network of child-care facilities."[10] Similarly, ICESCR ratified by 145 countries, but not the United States, ensures the "equal right of men and women to the enjoyment of all economic, social and cultural rights" including rights to "fair wages," "a decent living for themselves and their families," paid maternity leave, and adequate social security benefits for working mothers.[11] The U.N. Committee on Economic, Social and Cultural Rights has, according to Davis and Powell, broadly interpreted the Treaty's provisions to also encompass child care, citing as an example the Committee's recommendations to Canada that provisions "such as . . . child care . . . are available at levels that ensure the right to an adequate standard of living."[12]

The United States clearly violates the social and economic rights that are embedded in these three human rights conventions, specifically those that address women's rights and children's rights. From a cross-national comparative perspective, the United States fails on almost all indices of child and family well-being. The U.S. poverty rate is characterized by Gornick and Meyers in their 12-nation comparative analysis as "exceptional" and of particular concern, given high rates of poverty even among two-parent working families. Among single-mother families who are employed, 45% live in poverty in the United States, a dramatic contrast to levels of 8% in Denmark, and 4% in Sweden.[13] The Luxembourg Income Study (LIS), which provides the database for international comparative studies, shows that the United States has the highest average income in the industrialized world (after Luxembourg), yet ranks worst in child poverty rates among 19 rich industrialized nations. LIS studies point to the clear and positive relationship between social spending and poverty reduction, and, as Smeeding and his colleagues state, "The relationship between low wages and poverty is direct and obvious. . . . Not all of the poor can be expected to 'earn' their way out of poverty."[14]

Most of the major industrialized countries have introduced maternity and parental leave provisions so that the work of caring for newborns and the formation of critical early bonds may occur within the family. Major trends in the past two decades have been to extend parental leaves during infancy, so that there is an affordable alternative for families who are permitted to take paid job-protected leaves. Europe has been instrumental in leading this trend, particularly in Scandinavia. As Kamerman documents among OECD countries, only South Korea and Switzerland have no national statutory provisions for parental leave, and the United Sates is one of only three countries that offers no paid leave. In the advanced industrialized nations the norm is 44 weeks, which includes maternity, paternity, and parental leaves, and the average time for a paid leave is 36 weeks. "U.S. Policy," says Kamerman, "exists in dramatic contrast to the policies that exist around the world and especially in our peer countries."[15]

The U.S. Family and Medical Leave Act (FMLA) of 1993 offers only 12 weeks of unpaid leave to employees for childbirth, adoption, or caring for an ill family member and only to those previously employed for a period of 12 months by companies with 50 or more employees, thereby excluding 42% of the private workforce. Low-income parents, particularly single mothers, cannot afford to take unpaid leave, and California is currently the only state that actually provides paid family leave to mothers and fathers.[16] State Temporary Disability Insurance (TDI) is available in five states (California, Hawaii, New York, New Jersey, Rhode Island), which provide partial short-term wage replacement for disabilities (such as pregnancy and childbirth), but these states include only 25% of the nation's population, and in 45 other states women have no rights to any paid leave.[17]

The absence of family support policies, such as paid parental leave, takes a heavy toll on the lives of infants and their struggling-to-make-it parents. The dearth of child care provisions and the developmentally damaging care that so many young poor children are subjected to violate their human rights. Poor women in particular, as solo mothers, as earners, as caregivers of their children, are stripped of their rights to live as fully functioning human beings, when the conditions for living are distorted. Furthermore, welfare "reform" legislation violates poor mother's human rights by wresting from them the fundamental right to care for their own infants, as they are forced into the low-wage workplace in order to avoid destitution. With no paid parental leave and with their infants left alone or subject to the perils of the unregulated license-exempt child care sector, how is it possible for poor women to make decisions in the best interests of their babies and ensure their "full and harmonious development"? Perhaps that is why Billy Delia, in Toni Morrison's chilling novel, *Paradise* (written after the passage of welfare "reform"), describes her world as "A backward noplace ruled by men whose power to control was out of control and who had the nerve to say who could live and who not and where. . . ."[18]

SOCIAL PROTECTIONS AND WOMAN-FRIENDLY STATES

The pejorative discourse in the United States about poor single mothers stigmatizes and disrespects them as mothers and requires those in need of welfare and child care subsidies to run through a series of mazes to seek any public support, all the while enduring the humiliation of the "undeserving poor." In contrast, the European Commission's Report on Social Inclusion in the EU focuses on combating poverty and social exclusion and supporting parents "so they are not financially disadvantaged" and addresses the wide variety of supports available to lone- (single) parent and two-parent families, including minimum-income guarantees, parental-leave entitlements, and flexible working patterns. All member states of the EU highlight the importance of making it possible to combine working and studying with parenting and emphasize that "in addition to parental leave entitlement, one of the most important factors is therefore the availability of child care." Based on the 2002 European Council of Barcelona recommendations, explicit targets were set for large-scale expansion of national child care provisions and facilities serving infants through school-age children.[19]

Not only has early childhood education been declared a top priority throughout the countries of the EU, but in the Organization for Economic Co-operation and Development (OECD) countries as well. As the labor force participation of women continues to increase, the focus on reconciling family and work and creating equality of work opportunities among men and women have become priority agendas. Kamerman emphasizes that there is widespread international acceptance of the need to ensure the provision of high quality child care and early educational experiences, in particular to mitigate early disadvantages that a sizable proportion of young children experience. It is notable that

OECD countries (the United States excepted) have pledged to expand early childhood educational services by 2010, with a target of enrolling at least 90% of children 3 years old through school age, and 33% of the under 3's; extend paid parental leaves that support the role of parents during the first months of life, which also reduces the need for infant and toddler care; and recognize the importance of transferring child care services under the auspices of education, so that both care and pedagogy are seen as integral to early childhood. The French and Scandinavian systems of care, consistently evaluated as high quality in the international arena, have long-established traditions of integrating both care and pedagogy into their early childhood curricula. Kamerman points out that there is an emergent trend in EU countries to view child care as a right for all children, and these rights have been recognized in the proposed EU constitution. The CRC forms the basis for the recognition of children's rights, and, says Kamerman, "acknowledging this right may become a major trend in the future."[20]

In Scandinavia, family policies have focused on promoting social and gender equality and have often been described as "woman-friendly" with strong investments in the well-being of children.[21] Universal policies with national systems of child care, health care, generous maternity and parental leave provisions, and universal child allowances enable mothers (and fathers) to stay home with their infants during the early months, returning to paid employment when their infants enter the child care system. Denmark's long-standing commitment to the provision of child care for working parents was initiated in 1919 and has produced a high quality system of universal care for children from 6 months through school age. Denmark currently has the highest rate of coverage for the under 3's among EU countries (50%), and over 80% of children 3–6 years old are in center-based care. Denmark's high quality system of child care is distinctive in its social-pedagogical focus, which emphasizes both social development and play-based education. With a well-trained teacher corps in both the preschools (*børnehaver*) and the infant centers (*vuggestuer*), and family day care homes (*dagpleje*) that are regulated, supervised, and educationally supported through staff development and supervision, child care is an integral and vital component of the social democratic infrastructure of the Danish welfare state. With its long tradition of universal family support policies, chronic family and child poverty has largely been alleviated, and universal child care enables women to reconcile full-time paid employment with motherhood in what has been characterized as a dual-breadwinner society, designed to ensure the social equality of single-mother and two-parent families.[22] Both Denmark and Sweden have consistently been cited as the most progressive in terms of universal social policies that promote dual-earner societies, with the best egalitarian outcomes for women and high quality care for children.[23]

Like Denmark, Sweden's welfare state is also characterized by generous entitlements, including a well-developed public child care system and an even more expansive set of maternity and parental leave and sick-child provisions. High expenditures on child care and other family benefits in both countries are in marked contrast to expenditures in the United States. Denmark and Sweden spend $1,822 and $1,417 a year per child (1.5% and 1.6% as share of GDP respectively) in family cash benefits, in contrast to the United States, which spends a meager $650 per child (0.5% of GDP).[24]

In Sweden day nurseries and kindergartens were also initiated in the early 20th century, but it was Sweden's National Preschool Act of 1975 that dramatically expanded the public child care system as part of a new Swedish welfare model designed to promote gender and social equality.[25] In 1990, Sweden ratified the CRC, and in 1995, the Social Welfare Act was amended to require all municipalities to provide child care places for preschool and school-age children.[26] Because of the generous leave provisions, very few children under the age of one were enrolled in public child care, but by 1998 the public child care system enrolled 59% of 1–2-year-olds and 78% of 3–6-year-olds in a preschool (*förskola*) or family day care home (*familjedaghem*).[27] Despite the unemployment crisis of the 1990s and the postindustrial restructuring of the Swedish welfare state, the child care system actually expanded during the period of retrenchment and still enjoys widespread popular support. The stated goals of Swedish child care are to promote greater social equality and enable women "to form and maintain an autonomous household," as well as to educate and support the development of children.[28] Until recently, the public child care system in Sweden primarily served the infants and children of employed parents, those pursuing education, and children with special needs. The policy was amended in 2001 as the Social Democrats expanded the state's equality provisions to encompass employment status and ethnic background, so that the children of vulnerable groups would not be shut out of child care.[29] In a recent OECD evaluation, Sweden's system of public child care was rated as outstanding, with the report concluding that "nothing honors Sweden more than the way it honors and respects its young."[30]

France is another example of a European nation that has invested heavily in a universal child care system that enjoys broad public support. As far back as the 1880s France initiated public child care provisions for poor working parents and developed one of the earliest public child care systems, which supported mothers' employment with an extensive and generous array of social programs.[31] With income supplements, universal public child care for 3-6-year-olds provided through the *écoles maternelles*, subsidized infant care, housing assistance, and medical care, female labor force participation has been far higher than women in many other European countries, and child poverty levels have been kept low. While free, public preprimary education is universal, serving all 3–6-year-olds in the *écoles maternelles*, a well-regulated, subsidized public *crèche* system is available for the under-3's, but demand for infant and toddler spots far outstrips supply. Because the crèche system has suffered from recent welfare-state restructuring, resulting in retrenchment and budget cuts (which the *écoles maternelles* escaped), only 9% of infants and toddlers are enrolled in crèche care, with another 13% in subsidized and regulated family day care homes.[32] Since the 1980s, during a period of high unemployment, state policy has encouraged greater flexibility in work schedules and the reduction of the work week to 35 hours. This led to a variety of care choices for the parents of infants and toddlers, such as the expansion of maternity leaves and generous family benefits to encourage mothers to leave the labor force and care for their own infants. Although such policies have provided women with care choices, the move away from expanding the public crèche system threatens to compromise gender equality, with possible adverse consequences for the labor market attachment of women with young children.[33]

However, in all three countries described–Denmark, Sweden, and France–access to high quality public child care and early education radically alters the life chances of children. Child care and parental leave are seen as vital and fundamental components of social citizenship rights that serve to strengthen and stabilize families and their communities and promote social cohesion. Such social citizenship rights are strongest in the Nordic countries but widely recognized in all wealthy industrialized democracies as part of an affirmative obligation of government. Public responsibility for families engenders the capability for private responsibility. Yet the United States has not joined the community of nations in acknowledging or affirming these rights. Rather the family's viability is essentially a private problem entailing private solutions, so other people's toddlers may end up in filthy basements, but that is *their* problem, not *ours.* The right to care and development must be purchased on the free market, and as with any commodity, you get what you pay for. Hence, tragically for a young child, *to have is to be.* The affirmative obligation of government to assume a fundamental public responsibility for supporting families and children, and thereby ensuring their rights to care and to be cared for, is not part of the current discourse.

THE QUALITY DEBACLE:
WHERE DO OUR CHILDREN SPEND THEIR DAYS?

Despite what national and international research findings tell us, and despite the success of exemplary programs of early childhood education here in the United States, the country has failed to live up to its peer nations in creating a national child care system that is held to high standards and provides both quality and access. The current patchwork of child care provisions for children under 5 with employed mothers includes almost one-quarter of children in organized child care facilities (including centers, preschools, and a very small percentage in Head Start programs); an additional 17.3% in nonrelative care, including 13.4% in family day care; and another 24.8%, in relative care (see Figure 8.1). Children enter child care facilities as young as 6 weeks and may be in care for 40 hours a week until they enter school. Only 14% of the children eligible for child care subsidies receive assistance, and child care costs more than college tuition at most public universities, ranging from $4,000–10,000 a year,[34] and reaching as high as $15,000 at the "baby Ivies."[35]

There is no federal regulation of private child care, and it is up to the states to set minimum standards for child care centers, but minimum translates to less than minimal in terms of regulating the quality of care provided for young children. Standards of best practice have been developed by the National Association for the Education of Young Children (NAEYC) and include ten major program standards and related criteria that define "quality" for child care, preschools, and kindergarten programs and focus on both structural and pedagogical/process factors. The standards broadly encompass relationships; staffing that includes small group size and high adult-child ratios; developmentally appropriate and culturally sensitive curricula; responsive teaching; assessment; children's health, nutrition, and safety; supervision and leadership; community linkages; and a developmentally enriching indoor and outdoor physical environment.[36] However, with 12 million children under 5 in child care,

Figure 8.1. Primary Child Care Arrangements of Preschoolers with Employed Mothers, 2002

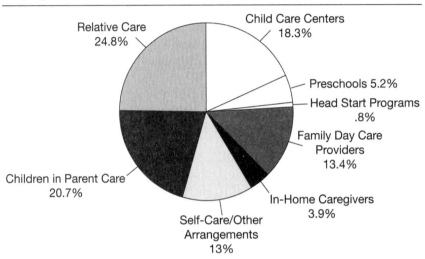

Source: Adapted from Table 3, *Who's Minding the Kids? Child Care Arrangements: Winter 2002.*
U.S. Census Bureau. See also Children's Defense Fund, 2005b.

Definitions of Child Care Settings:
Child Care Centers: Care provided in nonresidential facilities, usually for 13 or more children.
Family Child Care Providers: Care provided in a private residence other than the child's home.
In-home Caregivers: Care provided in the child's home, by a person other than a parent or relative.
Relative Care: Care provided by an individual related to the child.

there are only 11,456 NAEYC accredited programs nationally that actually meet these standards![37]

Standards are deplorably low across the nation; only 21 states require licenses for all child care centers, 12 states exempt religiously-affiliated centers, and 20 states exempt part-day centers. In over half of the states there are minimal or no staff-training requirements—in 37 states, "teachers" without any training in child development or education are permitted to work in child care centers. High ratios of children to staff, a clear indicator of poor quality, are permitted in 20 states, and 18 states permit a ratio of 5 infants to one caregiver.[38] Group sizes and staff turnover due to low wages and bad working conditions are also critical indicators of stability and quality. Many for-profit chains, with their standardized classroom routines that manage large groups of children in rigid and inflexible environments, draw on a pool of untrained and unqualified child care workers who are easily replaceable. Such centers commonly hire low-wage workers to cut costs and increase revenues and are far more likely to produce inferior care.[39]

Regulating and monitoring family day care homes constitutes an even greater quality control issue. Large family day care homes, which may enroll as many as 20 children, have minimal licensing requirements that pertain to health and safety standards, and usually the owner/provider is only required to possess a high school diploma or GED. However, most family day care homes are small operations, where one provider cares for one or more children, and many states exempt such providers from any regulations. Only eleven states require that small family day care homes be licensed. Nineteen states require no regulation, six regulate those receiving public funds, and fourteen permit one provider to care for nine or more children! The majority of states require no training whatsoever or, at best, a minimum of six hours a year, with no prior qualifications or experience necessary for caregivers. In most states, small and large family day care homes may employ providers as young as 18 years, and in some states, providers may be just 16 years old. Helburn and Bergmann conclude that 30 states have inadequate regulation of small family day care home providers.[40]

As demonstrated throughout this book, low-income families in general encounter greater difficulties accessing higher quality care as lack of resources diminishes choices, there is less access in poor neighborhoods to higher quality care, and unstable odd-hour work schedules make child care arrangement very difficult. Vandell and Wolfe report that one-third of employed mothers with incomes below the poverty line and more than 25% of employed mothers with incomes below $25,000 have nontraditional hours and rotating schedules, including weekends.[41] Consequently, mothers must rely on makeshift and multiple care arrangements that create further instability in a young child's life. As discussed in Chapter 2, Chaudry's ethnographic study of low-income mothers in New York City illustrates that the child care they were able to access was largely custodial, and the challenge was not only finding, but also maintaining, stable care arrangements where mothers had few options other than the cheapest of inferior care.[42] The fact that large numbers of poor children end up, not just in bad licensed care, but in the largely invisible underworld of unregulated care is alarming. Helburn and Bergmann estimate, on the basis of a rough approximation of Census data, that about one-third of children in child care from birth to 5 are in the unregulated sector.[43]

The appalling conditions that exist nationwide for millions of vulnerable young children in their most formative stages of development constitute an assault of young children's rights to grow and develop in supportive and nurturing landscapes. There are a multitude of studies in the current literature on early development pointing to the critical links between healthy development and child care quality; yet the existing professional knowledge appears to hold little sway as the overall national crisis of child care continues to worsen. Public policies, such as welfare "reform," have only exacerbated the acute demand for care by low-income mothers, and major social spending cuts further limit access to care.

CHILD CARE QUALITY AND EARLY DEVELOPMENT

The positive outcomes of high quality early education are particularly significant for poor children and for those children whose mothers lack a high school education. Comprehensive long-term studies conducted in recent decades in the United States (see Introduction) include the well-known High/Scope Perry Preschool Project, the Carolina Abecedarian Project, the Chicago Child Parent Center Studies I and II, and the Cost Quality and Child Outcomes Study.[44] All point to significant cognitive gains from high quality early education, as well as increased academic achievement and improved social relationships with teachers and peers. The NICHD findings from the Study of Early Child Care indicate that the quality of care in the first three years of life is associated with improved language and cognitive abilities, and when child care programs meet recommended standards of quality, children exhibit fewer behavioral problems and demonstrate greater school readiness.[45] Barnett's review of 38 long-term studies, including exemplary model programs, examined the long-term effects of early childhood education on economically disadvantaged children through at least third grade and, in some studies, through high school and beyond. Barnett's analysis confirms the strong evidence that already exists: high quality early childhood programs result in long-term gains in learning and school success and less time spent in special education.[46]

However, while the positive outcomes are significant, the converse must also be emphasized: the serious negative impact that poor quality child care has on low-income, young children. The Cost Quality and Outcomes Study (CQO) conducted during the early 1990s, made site visits to a total of 521 state-licensed preschool classrooms and 228 infant/ toddler licensed centers in four states, using environmental rating scales and classroom observations[47] to evaluate the day-to-day quality of care for children, and researchers interviewed directors, teachers, and parents. The results, based on *licensed* child care centers, were sobering. The researchers concluded that most child care in the United States was poor to mediocre, with only 14% of centers providing quality care that promotes healthy development; and only 8% of the infant and toddler settings were rated as good quality, with over 40% providing less than minimal quality care![48] The authors concluded that widespread substandard care was sufficiently bad to impair children's emotional and cognitive development. The CQO follow-up in June 1999 tracked the children four years later as they moved into second grade.[49] "At-risk" children and those whose mothers had lower educational levels were far more sensitive to the negative effects of bad child care. Such experiences only exacerbate the developmental obstacles that children in poverty encounter, as they continue on to public school and experience greater academic difficulties and are most likely to experience developmental delays.[50] However, the CQO study also shows the lasting impact of good child care was far more significant for low-income children where "high quality child care experiences, in terms of both classroom practices and teacher-child relationships, enhance children's abilities to take advantage of the educational opportunities in school."[51]

The large number of infants and toddlers in child care is of particular concern because they are most susceptible to the harmful effects of bad care. Seventy-three percent of the infants and toddlers of employed mothers (about 6 million children under 3) spend much of their waking hours in child care in both the formal and informal sector, and 39% are in full-time care.[52] In the well-known study conducted by the Families and Work Institute, Galinsky and her coresearchers studied regulated and nonregulated family day care home providers, as well as relative care providers for young children 10 months and older.[53] Only 9% of the family day care homes in the study were rated as good, 56% were rated as adequate/custodial, and 35% were rated as inadequate and "growth-harming." In addition, 81% of the day care homes were illegally "nonregulated"–caring for more children than state regulations permitted. Even more disturbing was the fact that over 50% of the children in care were assessed as insecurely attached to their caregivers. In general, providers serving higher-income families had more years of formal education and were rated as more responsive and sensitive caregivers. Children in low-income and minority families were more likely to receive inadequate care where "the lower the child's family income, the lower the quality of the child care home in which he or she is enrolled."[54]

Most low-income children experience multiple child care arrangements during their earliest years, and those in single-mother families spend almost double the amount of hours in outside care than do the children of two-parent families. Center care is used more widely by African-American (30%) and White working mothers (24%), than by Hispanic mothers (10%), whose use of relative care is far higher (39%). The children of higher-income families tend to enroll in child care centers in greater numbers, whereas relative care is most common for children in poor and low-income families.[55]

With infants and toddlers spending so many hours in child care every week, their relationships with their caregivers becomes a formative factor in their early development. The development of stable and secure attachments to their child care providers is critical, and the degree to which the infant's environment is stimulating, attentive, and nurturing, or indifferent and harmful, has lasting consequences. Early language, preoperational cognition, and social-emotional development have their origins in the first two years of life—and the quality of that early environment, says Thompson, enhances and enriches development or creates vulnerability to harm:

> The irreducible core of the environment during early development is people. Relationships matter. They provide the nurturance that strengthens children's security and well-being, offer the cognitive challenges to exercise young minds, impart many essential catalysts to healthy brain growth, and help young children discover who they are and what they can do.[56]

THE DISCOURSE OF COSTS AND BENEFITS

While the centrality of good quality child care has been recognized and operationalized in national child care provisions in the wealthy industrialized nations that have ratified the Convention on the Rights of the Child, a discourse about the *right* to child care is still not part of a national conversation in the United States. Prevailing policy arguments for child care as a national need are made largely on instrumental grounds, focusing not on rights, but on productivity and prevention. Investing in child care accrues value because doing so avoids the negative consequences to society caused by "dysfunctional" poor children; for "their" development threatens "ours" in terms of skewed developmental outcomes. The cost-benefit analysis for investing in poor children's early education is frequently entangled with the developmental literature on children, child care, and the early years, where the childhoods of the poor and the different become the terrain for cold-hearted and crass calculations of economic returns, premised not on the right to an enriched and protected early childhood experience, but on what yields the best returns for the least invested.

The Committee for Economic Development: The Productivity Argument

Heckman and Masterov represent the dominant cost–benefit productivity discourse that is embedded in a disturbing set of assumptions about low-income family environments, stating that "dysfunctional and disadvantaged families are major producers of cognitive and behavioral deficits that lead to adverse teenage and adult social and economic outcomes."[57] Heckman and Masterov claim that additional public spending on schools has not yielded good returns; therefore they favor investing in preschool for disadvantaged children, asserting that early childhood interventions are far more cost-effective than interventions in adolescence or adulthood. They recommend the redirection of funds targeted to early childhood interventions for children under five living in poverty, arguing that such redirection of resources "is a sound investment in the productivity and safety of our society."[58]

Citing a litany of social ills caused by poor parenting and the "constellation of pathologies . . . associated with less educated mothers and teenage mothers,"[59] these two prestigious economists (one a Nobel Laureate) largely sideline the impacts of the structural conditions that shape poverty, the distorted market politics of distribution, and uncritically embrace the gendered and racialized assumptions about single mothers and their children, viewing any variants to a traditional family structure as dysfunctional. The detailed cost-benefit analyses they produce, citing the major early intervention studies, are viewed favorably only because they are seen as "cost effective remedies for reducing crime and the factors that breed crime,"[60] yielding large social benefits and taxpayer savings, with net public benefits worth billions of dollars. These economic calculations are part of the distorted public policy analyses that have fueled the arguments for economic investment in preschool, of which the High/Scope Perry Pre-school Project is the most widely cited. How, one wonders, do poor, po-tential child criminals stand up against the children of Enron plunderers Ken Lay and Jeffrey Skilling, who presumably as white-collar criminals also must breed intergenerational crime that costs taxpayers millions of dollars? What "family improvement policy" would be "a successful anti-crime policy" for their families? Such instrumental policies demean poor children's lives; for their lives are only deserving of investment *if* there are clear economic payoffs. Their existential and social distress count for little. In short, within this productivity framework, children are reduced to unwanted public goods.

Child Care as an Economic Development Strategy

Another argument that has gained currency in recent years is one that promotes strengthening the child care industry as a sound economic de-velopment strategy, with impacts on local, regional, and national econo-mies. The "National Economic Impacts of the Child Care Sector"[61] study examined the substantial contributions that child care makes to the econ-omy, focusing on expenditures on licensed child care, employment in the child care industry, child care as a necessary infrastructure that enables the employment and productivity of parents, and the value of investing in quality child care in terms of future educational achievement and pro-ductivity of the work force. In 2001, $38 billion a year was spent on li-censed child care programs alone, creating enough income to support 2.8 million jobs, with one-third of those jobs in the child care industry. The child care sector also generates $9 billion in tax revenues a year. More Americans, in fact, are employed in the child care sector—934,000—than are employed as public secondary school teachers. By enabling parents to work, the formal child care sector accounts for over $100 billion in an-nual earnings. Every dollar spent in the formal child care sector generates $15.25 in additional earnings by parents. Child care services, it is argued, are thus an essential part of the work force, enabling parents to work. Projections indicated that by 2010, 85% of the labor force will be parents, and the number of working women is expected to exceed the number of working men.[62]

Cornell University's "Linking Economic Development and Child Care Research Project" has been a leading force in framing a more pro-gressive rationale for economic development strategies to promote child care quality.[63] Warner argues that planners and policymakers need to "understand the complexity of child care as a market sector," involving not only the needs of working families but also land use, transportation, and private and public financing, and that child care should be recognized and supported as a key social infrastructure for development.[64] Countering the conservative refrain that child care is a private problem to be solved by individual families, Warner analyzes the structural problems in the economy and existing public policy deficits: jobs that do not pay a living wage, workplace policies that do not support the roles of parents as workers, the failure of planners and policy makers to recognize these critical realities faced by working parents, and the lack of an adequate infrastructure of child care provisions.

The child care industry is not an undeveloped market, argues Warner, as much as it is a problem of "market failure," which entails the need for "government regulation and investment" to ensure quality and promote the professionalization of the child care sector.[65] Because competition erodes quality in child care due to cost pressures (reducing the ratios of staff to children, for example), Warner asserts it is essential that government underwrite high quality care through adequate child care subsidies to parents and direct subsidies to providers. Warner views child care as both a private and public good. As a public good, it supports parents by enabling them to be productive members of the work force and contributes to expanding the earnings of working parents, and, she argues, the entire society benefits from the human capital investment in children–the future work force.[66]

PRAGMATIC PROPOSALS THAT ADDRESS
THE CHILD CARE CRISIS: WHAT WOULD IT TAKE?

Multiple proposals for creating a nationwide, quality child care system have been floated in the decades since the Comprehensive Child Care Development Act was vetoed by former President Nixon in 1973. In the mid-1990s, Edward Zigler, the founder of Head Start, wrote that the state of child care had reached a crisis "placing millions of the nation's young children at developmental risk because we are letting them grow up in child care environments that are inadequate and fail to provide a level of quality that promotes healthy development and learning."[67] A decade later, many more millions of low-income mothers with young children are in the work force, and the crisis has only been exacerbated by the increased welfare-to-work requirements that generate more urgent demands for infant care and child care. With drastic cuts in social spending under the current Bush Administration and a race to the bottom by states to provide child care subsidies that support the cheapest of care, who will care for our children?

Three comprehensive proposals that deserve consideration are discussed in this section. Although the proposals are economically instrumentalist in conception, building on existing child care market provisions and using public monies and facilities already in place in the states, these three proposals are also pragmatic attempts to address the urgent need for quality child care provisions for all children.[68]

Schools of the 21st Century

Schools of the 21st Century (21C), a proposal developed by Zigler and Finn-Stevenson, embodies a community school model that promotes the growth and development of children through the provision of high quality child care and related family and community services.[69] The Plan calls for using the public schools as a hub to create full-day, year-round child care for all 3- and 4-year-olds, as well as after-school programs for school-age children, operating from 6:00 a.m. to 6:00 p.m., with some buildings open into the evening hours. Using public schools to provide child care services builds on existing facilities and public infrastructures already in place. Child care services would be provided in partnership with local providers and subsidized by parent tuition based on sliding scale fees, state Department of Education funds, local school district funds, and private foundation grants, as well as federal Title 1 funds. In Kentucky and Connecticut, statewide legislation has already been influenced by the 21C Plan, creating Family Resource Centers for child care and family supports, and San Diego's 6-to-6 program has been a significant benefit for families, including Kathy's, described in Chapter 7. The 21C guiding principles are based on current best practice models in the early childhood field and promote the use of trained early childhood professionals and paraprofessionals with adequate compensation and wage supports. The Plan relies on existing public funding, as well as grants from private foundations. To date, variations of the model have been implemented in 1,300 schools across the United States. Although described as universal, the Plan, in its current configuration, provides a higher quality alternative choice to parents in the existing patchwork service provisions. It is a good demonstration model that could be expanded and adopted on a broader scale if adequate state and federal funds were invested to sustain it. However, the 21C Plan does nothing to address the critical need for infant and toddler care and tiptoes around the huge, unregulated private child care industry, positioning the Plan as "another option for parents."[70]

The Institute for Women's Policy Research and Universal Preschool

The Institute for Women's Policy Research (IWPR) has developed a model for estimating the cost of designing a universally accessible, state-based, high quality preschool program that would serve 3–5 year olds.[71] The model emphasizes teacher training, credentials, and adequate compensation as key factors in designing a high quality program. Teachers would be required to have bachelor's degrees in early childhood education, and in many states would also need to meet requirements for state certification. The model includes technical assistance, assessment and evaluation, and facilities costs and basically builds on the existing early childhood service provisions that exist in each state. Estimates for additional program costs incorporate the quality-assurance criteria built into the model. The model includes both a full-day (10 hours) year-round program and a part-day (3 hours) school-year option.

Based on a fictional state scenario, IWPR has developed cost estimates for universal preschool for the state, starting with the assumption that a state prekindergarten program already exists. Direct unit costs per child in this model are assessed at $9,536 a year for full-time full-year care, almost $4,000 more per child in comparison to existing full-day preschool programs. That estimate does not include the costs of upgrading staff credentials, or the renovation of facilities and program-evaluation costs. The model develops cost estimates over a 10-year period for full- and part-day programs, with the total population of children served increasing each year. In Year 1, the annual cost of universal preschool is projected to be $136,860,694, serving only 10% of the projected population (23,500 children). By Year 10, when the entire projected population (235,000 children) of the state is served, the annual cost estimate is projected to be $967,090,620.[72]

The IWPR model is a useful tool for estimating the real costs of a universally accessible, high quality prekindergarten program and places a premium on staff qualifications and training. However, the children served are primarily 3- and 4-year-olds, leaving the under-3's behind, as well as the children who need before- and after-school care. In addition, quality standards vary enormously across the states, and the IWPR model does not adequately account for this wide variation in quality and the increased regulatory problems caused by multiple prekindergarten partners delivering services.

Currently 38 states offer state-funded prekindergarten, which served 800,000 children during 2004–2005. However, that figure represents only 17% of the nation's 4-year-olds and 3% of 3-year-olds. Despite an overall pattern of growth (Florida's new pre-K program initiative is likely to add 100,000 4-year-olds), 11 states actually reduced enrollment as part of budget cuts and retrenchment, and in some cases 3-year-olds were cut from pre-K programs in order to maintain 4-year-old enrollments.[73] Oklahoma is currently the only state with near-universal prekindergarten coverage, with 90% of 4-year-olds enrolled in pre-K, Head Start or special education and community preschool programs. Georgia has the second highest coverage, with 67% of 4-year-olds enrolled. However, 21 states have minimal educational standards for teachers, and do not even require their pre-K teachers to hold at least a bachelor's degree. The IWPR model assumes that a high quality preschool system can be built from existing child care and prekindergarten provisions in the states, but what exists is a shaky foundation that has neither quality standards nor an embedded culture of early childhood professionalism. As Barnett and his colleagues point out, "Unlike children in the K–12 education system, preschoolers are not guaranteed any education at all, much less a high quality education."[74] This set of low expectations for what constitutes a quality early education is pervasive and is a key obstacle confronting changes in state preschool education.

The Helburn and Bergmann Proposal
for Affordable Care and Improved Quality

Helburn and Bergmann, building on the present market-based system of child care, propose three child care subsidy plans: an *Interim Plan*, an *Affordable Child Care at Improved Quality Plan*, and a *Free Universal Care Plan*.[75] The Interim Plan involves an expansion of current existing programs and fully funding state programs now in place that are funded by the Child Care and Development Fund (CCDF) and by state appropriations. Fully funding current state plans would cost $12.8 billion a year in new funding for a total cost of $25.8 billion. This plan would increase the number of children who receive child care subsidies from 2 million to 10 million. The Universal Plan would provide free child care to all children irrespective of family income. There would be no co-pays for care, and the annual net cost would be \$122.5 billion a year, requiring \$102.5 billion in new funds.

However, Helburn and Bergmann argue on pragmatic grounds that Plan Two, The Affordable Child Care at Improved Quality, is the strongest proposal to push forward towards implementation. Plan Two lays out a comprehensive national program that would provide all families access to affordable care, requiring families to pay "no more than 20% of that part of [their] income that is above the poverty line" as co-pays for child care.[76] This formula would provide free care to those families at or below the federal poverty line and would benefit middle-class parents as well, serving 17 million children, including infants and children up to 12 years old.

In order to upgrade quality, only licensed child care centers, family day care homes, and public school programs would be eligible for voucher reimbursement, although licensed nannies and licensed relative providers would be included. The Plan offers base reimbursement for average quality fees and higher reimbursement incentives (\$2,000 per child) to those child care settings that meet good quality care standards,[77] as determined by accreditation and the percentage of staff that are trained and credentialed. Included in their budget costs are additional quality-control measures such as adequate compensation and wages and staff training. Annual costs for this Plan would be \$46.4 billion, with \$26.4 billion of new funding required. In addition, if all 4-year-olds gain access to free full-time prekindergarten, that would add another \$9 billion to the cost, for a total of \$56 billion a year. They propose that the needed new funds for a \$50 billion-a-year federal program could be obtained by reallocation of funds, by taxation, by borrowing, or by using a budget surplus. Although Helburn and Bergmann acknowledge such a large federal program is unlikely in the current political climate, they point to other examples of questionable federal outlays and expenditures that total billions of taxpayer dollars.

An obvious example of distorted priorities and the politics of skewed resource distribution is the escalating costs of the invasion and occupation of Iraq, when juxtaposed against the fundamental rights of young children to child care. The latest estimates for the final cost of the war are calculated to be between \$1 and \$2 trillion by Bilmes and Stiglitz in their report to the Annual Meeting of the American Economic Association. These costs include not only combat operations but also the costs required in government payments to veterans for years to come, and, "even more fundamentally," say Bilmes and Stiglitz, "there is the question of whether we needed to spend the money at all."[78] Yet why not $50 billion a year for child care? It ultimately is a question of priorities, and Helburn and Bergmann assert that the federal government must take responsibility for financing a national child care system, as it certainly belongs on our list of national needs, stating that "the goal of affordable care for every American child cannot be reached without a federal effort."[79]

The Helburn and Bergmann Plan is a comprehensive attempt to create affordable care for all children from infancy through age 12; but the quality assurances are problematic. Leaving quality to an incentive-based system in the child care market is a wild card. As most existing child care is less than good, such a plan would mean that low-income children's care would be somewhat improved as many children would shift from the unregulated sector to licensed care, but the incentive system would mostly benefit higher quality centers and higher-income children. The existing segregated system of care would be difficult to overcome without additional interventions and regulations, and the problematic upgrading so essential in family day care homes would be left to market forces.

All three proposals–21C, IWPR, and the Helburn/Bergmann Plan 2–are significant and comprehensive proposals with the well-being of children a central concern and serious efforts made to resolve the quality debacle. However, while progressive in orientation, the proposals are firmly embedded in the market-based system of child care. Helburn and Bergmann's third option, the Free Universal Care Plan, which comes closest to serving all children and is the costliest, is not even given serious consideration. In the case of IWPR, the underfunded state provisions for prekindergarten, which relies on contracting out services in the child care market, make it an unlikely candidate for success. As such, all proposals are subject to the exigencies of the market and to the frequent downturns that result in federal and state cuts to social and educational services. Investing in children's early education and well-being always makes good sense in any society. Building their social capital through high quality early education, good schools, after-school networks of care, and fostering community can, indeed, alter destinies.[80] But that takes a nationwide public commitment to serve *all* our children, and to serve them well. Ultimately the question of child care belongs on a different terrain and must be reframed in terms of a new conception of rights.

ORGANIZING AND MOBILIZING FOR HUMAN RIGHTS

Civil rights, educational rights, poverty, welfare rights, and union rights have been the flashpoints for large-scale mobilization around fundamental wrongs in the past century, fighting for rights denied to those who lack the fundamentals for a fully functioning life. More recently, a grassroots coalition of economic and social justice groups in the United States have mobilized to create an international forum for bringing poverty to international visibility, and used international human rights law to argue that poverty is a violation of human rights.

The Kensington Welfare Rights Union (KWRU) has long been the leading force behind the grassroots coalition of the Poor People's Economic Human Rights Campaign (PPEHRC), with a focus is on housing, low-wage work, and economic justice. The Economic Human Rights Documentation Project documents domestic violations of rights laid out in the Universal Declaration of Human Rights and submits reports to the United Nations. In 1999, lawyers for the Center on Economic and Social Rights worked with the KWRU to file a petition with the Inter-American Commission on Human Rights, challenging U.S. welfare policy as a violation under the International Covenant on Civil and Political Rights (ICCPR). Once again, the attempt to use international human rights treaties and principles to assert domestic rights within the United States is, as Davis notes, a "paradigm shift." By looking beyond state and national borders, community activists are linking their struggles to the global struggle for human rights, and faced with a shredded social safety net, and federal hostility in ratifying international human rights treaties, domestic activists are documenting the U.S. failure to enforce human rights at home. Child care as a human right is now an integral part of that struggle.[81]

Large-scale militant demonstrations organized by the KWRU have drawn attention to the lack of social and economic rights for the poor. Illegal takeovers of abandoned HUD housing units in Philadelphia and "Bushville" tent encampments drawing media attention to conditions reminiscent of the Great Depression serve to cast poverty as a social and economic rights violation. The KWRU also attended and represented poor people's coalitions at the recent 2005 World Social Forum in Brazil. By framing U.S. poverty as a global human rights issue, one that policymakers and legislators continue to ignore, emergent grassroots campaigns have been effective in building a nascent national movement to end poverty. The PPEHRC has also used international forums such as the Olympic Games in Salt Lake City in 2002 and the Republican Convention in 2004 as high-visibility events to expose and shame the United States in the international arena for its failure to address egregious human rights violations such as poverty, hunger, and homelessness on the domestic front.[82]

Such human rights organizing has its origins in local resistance and community-based coalitions. For the women chronicled in *Who Cares for Our Children?* a welfare advocacy group in Iowa, and economic and racial justice advocacy coalitions in New York City, empowered women such as Kim (Chapter 3) and Carmina and Danielle (Chapters 2 and 4) to fight for their rights to obtain public benefits and child care. In Miewald's study of poor women in Appalachian Kentucky, a local grassroots coalition mobilized to fight the restricted access to higher education imposed on welfare mothers, challenging the violation of their rights to attend postsecondary education and receive child care. Their story of resistance represents "only one small part of a much larger story of women fighting back against punitive public assistance policies."[83]

In her book, *Radical Possibilities*, Anyon similarly urges educators to mobilize as allies with poor communities against the deeply embedded social and economic injustices that undergird educational inequality. Anyon argues that we should no longer tolerate a system that allows the poor to pay disproportionately to support wealth concentration for the most privileged and powerful, and that combating poverty calls for "cross-place collaboration" with progressive labor unions, the living-wage movement, activist youth, and other grassroots community-based coalitions to create a forceful mobilization for educational, social, and economic rights.[84]

Child care is a vital part of the struggle for human rights, and there is a potentially powerful constituency of millions of mothers in the work force waiting to be mobilized. Documenting before the United Nations the deplorable conditions of young American children in squalid internments in the unregulated child care sector would indeed bring further disgrace to the United States' policy of deprivation and violation of children's rights.

CHILDREN AS RIGHTS BEARERS

The Convention on the Rights of the Child confers rights on children so that children, too, are agents and "rights bearers," and should be treated as ends not means, for each has "a life to live, deserving of both respect, and resources."[85] Not so, not yet, in the United States. Unique in its unparalleled wealth and global dominance, and too, in its obdurate violations of domestic human rights whose first and primary victims are always children—the United States increasingly has come to occupy its own singular and eroded human rights milieu.

Poverty in a land of plenty is a moral disgrace; so too is the consequential child care crisis among America's millions of low-wage families. Many other countries take seriously the fundamental care gaps that must be filled in order for children and their mothers to remain healthy and stable, by developing carefully crafted social protections aligned with the key international human rights treaties. There is a stark contrast in assumptions and sensibilities about how poor children are viewed in Europe and the United States. Viewed instrumentally, children have no rights to care, to early education, to housing, to health care, and to adequate nutrition. As dubious public goods, their young lives are cheap. And it is cost–benefit analyses of young children's lives that dominate the cold-hearted discourse about the child care crisis, and enable the deplorable perennial question about whether investing in child care and early education is worth it. This privatized tunnel vision results in a shameful indifference, where "individuals become angry at even the notion of the public good,"[86] with often brutal consequences for young children and their families.

Unequal life circumstances and the lack of fundamental social and economic rights entrap poor women and entangle their lives in a web of resource deficits that diminishes their own development as human beings, and profoundly alters their own children's life chances. Children's distress, their fears, their shaken sense of trust and security that ensue when child care harms, when it does not work, when it is not there when needed—must be heeded and attention must be paid. There are seeping wounds and developmental scars that are readily produced in socially toxic landscapes. Consigning young children to overcrowded, unsafe, indifferent spaces, where opportunities for discovery, imaginative play, active learning, and the formation of stable relationships are absent, or worse, twisted into harsh regimens of compliance—is a violation of their human rights to grow and develop.

And it is always poor children whose lives count for less, who inhabit the dreary landscapes; while their mothers, denied autonomy and choice in making decisions that ensure the best interests of their children, must settle for less—and worse than less, and the existential terrors that come with no good place to choose.

What will be the consequences when human capabilities are interrupted? Diminished? Cut down? How are daily lives corroded and futures positioned by such public policy neglect? So many shameful losses spread among childhood's ruins, amid the pernicious public policies that make for social suffering and then normalize its reality. As Martin Luther King, Jr. succinctly put it forty-two years ago: "There is no deficit in human resources; the deficit is in human will."[87]

The will to care for *all* our children is, as yet, an unrealized possibility. But bearing witness, recording, documenting the rights that are always products of wrongs, resisting and mobilizing with allies to form linkages and partnerships for transformative action herald hope. Child care as a human right exists in many other countries alongside social and economic rights. Child care will yet see its day in the United States.

> Tomorrow, we shall have to invent,
> once more,
> the reality of this world.

>   —Elizabeth Bishop, *January First*[88]

Notes

Introduction

1. John Dewey, 1915, p. 7
2. 13.5 million children live in poverty (below $16,600 for a family of three); 29.2 million live in low-income families (defined as 200% of the poverty threshold or $33,200). See U.S. Department of Health and Human Services, 2006; National Center for Children in Poverty, 2006a.
3. Michael Katz, 1989
4. The major part of the material for this section on the history of child care is drawn from Sonya Michel's *Children's Interests/Mothers' Rights,* 1999, as well as Margaret O'Brien Steinfels' *Who's Minding the Children,* 1973.
5. Michel, 1999, p. 45
6. See Michel, 1999, Chapter 1, for a detailed discussion of the use of orphanages/orphan asylums as boarding institutions.
7. "Origins of Day Nursery Work," cited in Steinfels, 1973, p. 40
8. Constitution and By-laws of the Infant School Society, Boston, 1828, cited in Steinfels, 1973, p. 36
9. For detailed discussion of the racial and class division, see Michel, 1999, chapters 1 and 2.
10. Michel, 1999, pp. 50–51
11. "The Day Nursery discussed by Miss Addams," cited in Michel, 1999, p. 72
12. The social welfare reformers were influential and also successfully lobbied for the passage of the short-lived Sheppard-Towner Maternity and Infancy Protection Act of 1922, which guaranteed health care for woman and infants.
13. Garfinkel & McLanahan, 1986
14. The ideology of separate spheres was embraced by domestic feminists such as Catherine Beecher in the 1800s. Women were encouraged to withdraw from the public sphere and to create a domestic sphere under women's control for which they were eminently and biologically suited in their calling as wives and mothers. See Welter, 1978.

15. Michel, 1999, p. 110

16. Steinfels, 1973

17. See Michel's extensive discussion in chapter 4 of the New Deal and wartime policies; see also James Hymes, 1995, for a description of the Kaiser wartime nurseries.

18. The work of Sigmund Freud and his daughter Anna, Helene Deutsch, and John Bowlby helped shape the discourse of a motherhood-at-home in the United States.

19. Amott & Matthaei, 1991

20. See the report of the Interdepartmental Subcommittee of the Women's Bureau, Children's Bureau, and the Bureaus of Employment Security and Public Assistance, as well as the Women's Bureau Report, "Employed Mothers and Child Care," all cited in Michel, 1999, pp. 175–178.

21. Robert Cooke, Project Head Start, quoted in Wrigley, 1989, p. 428

22. In FY 2004, Head Start's enrollment was: 52% 4-year-olds; 34% 3-year-olds; 50% of all eligible children were served in 2003, and less than 3% of infants and toddlers in Early Start. See Children's Defense Fund, 2005c.

23. "Excerpts from Nixon's veto message," 1971, p. 20

24. Reagan, quoted in Gilliam, 1999

25. Kelly, 2003; Kamerman & Kahn, 1987

26. Kelly, 2003, p. 607

27. U.S. Department of Labor, 2005

28. Gornick & Meyers, 2003, p. 8

29. For a discussion of the care deficit and the cultural frameworks of care, see Hochschild, 1995.

30. While the federal law required mothers with infants over 12 months to meet mandatory work requirements, states were permitted to set their own requirements and implement even stricter work-activation requirements: Massachusetts, Michigan, Wisconsin, Ohio, and New York implemented 12-week requirements.

31. Mink 1998, p. 103. See also Kahn & Polakow, 2000a

32. Children's Defense Fund, 2005b

33. Blank, Schulman, & Ewen, 1999; Barnett et al., 2005

34. *Child Care* as used in this book includes all forms of nonparental care provided to infants, toddlers, preschool and school-age children in licensed child care centers, licensed family child care home providers, unlicensed/license exempt family child care home providers, in-home caregivers where care is provided by a nonrelative in the child's home, and relative care providers. When care is provided by public prekindergarten, public preschool, and Head Start programs, all typically part-day, they are designated as such. Higher quality licensed care centers are typically associated with the term *preschool,* and the quality of the early childhood program is largely dependent on the educational philosophy, edu-

cational levels, training, and staff–child ratios of the facility. Some high quality child care centers are accredited by the National Association for the Education of Young Children, which is a coveted and hard-won accreditation for a generally top quality facility.

35. The reimbursement rates are pegged at the 75th percentile of local market rates, but most states have not updated their market surveys. Michigan's current subsidy rates, for example, are based on a 1999 survey and 66% of subsidy expenditure is in the unlicensed informal care sector. See Kahn et al., 2006. Also see Schulman and Blank's report on *Child Care Assistance Policies 2005.*

36. Center on Budget and Policy Priorities, 2005, 2006

37. Gornick & Meyers, 2003

38. Goldman, 2003

39. Carlson & Sharf, 2004

40. See Jonathan Kozol's work, in particular *Savage Inequalities* (1992) and his latest book, *The Shame of the Nation: The Restoration of Apartheid Schooling in America* (2005), for compelling documentation of inequality, racism, and resegregation in our public schools.

41. Bernstein, 2004

42. See the critique of a cost–benefit rationale, Chapter 8.

43. Campbell et al., 1998; Helburn, 1995; NICHD Early Child Care Research Network, 2000, 2002; Peisner-Feinberg et al., 1999; Schweinhart, 2004

44. Folbre, 1994

45. Gornick & Meyers propose the earner/carer model; see also Mahon, 2002.

46. Grubb & Lazerson, 1988, p. 52

47. Doctorow, 1994, p. 67

48. The narratives in the book are based on qualitative interviews conducted with low-income mothers during 2003 and 2004. I initially interviewed 50 individuals (including two single fathers) across four states: Michigan, Iowa, New York, and California. The selection of these states was based on ease of access, availability (or lack) of child care services, waiting lists for child care subsidies, ethnic and educational diversity of low-income mothers, rural-urban differences, and specific state policies pertaining to mandatory work requirements for welfare recipients. I contacted low-income nonprofit advocacy networks and agencies that primarily serve low-income parents and children. Using these networks and snowball sampling techniques, I invited interested participants to meet with me for one or more interviews (these were initially open-ended, followed by semi-structured interviews) that focused on participants' experiences with child care: affordability, accessibility, quality, availability of subsidies, and perception of children's comfort and well-being. Interviews were audio taped and transcribed. All identifying characteristics were deleted in order to maintain anonymity. In certain instances, I changed minor background details to preserve confidentiality

of participants. The 21 mothers selected for inclusion in this book were chosen because of the richness of their narratives and the extended time I spent with them as they shared their experiences with me.

Chapter 1

1. High school drop-out rates are now estimated to be 30%. See Barton, 2005, who critiques the lower rates reported by the National Center for Education Statistics.

2. Work First, Michigan's welfare-to-work program, requires mothers who are welfare applicants to attend mandatory orientation and job search for 40 hours a week when their infants reach 12 weeks in order to become eligible for any cash benefits.

3. The Michigan 4C (Community Coordinated Child Care) Association is a statewide network of 16 regional 4C offices covering all 83 counties in Michigan and dedicated to improving services and child care for children and their families. Funded by state contracts and private foundation grants, the 4C regional agencies offer professional development training, scholarships for low-income parents, free referrals to licensed facilities, and consumer information for assessing quality, as well as financial assistance. See http://www.mi4c.org.

4. Low-income families are disproportionately represented in the informal-care sector where, generally, child care is rated at its worst. See Galinsky et al., 1994; Helburn & Bergman, 2002.

5, See Davis, 2003, and Gornick & Meyers, 2003, who discuss U.S. "exceptionalism" in the context of international human rights.

6. Nussbaum, 2000, p. 5

7. From T. S. Marshall's 1949 Cambridge Marshall lecture "Citizenship and Social Class," pp. 98, 72, 107

8. Hobson & Lister, 2002

9. Esping-Anderson, 1990

10. Hobson & Lister, 2002. Feminists have leveled a strong critique against the gender-blind welfare state envisioned by Marshall and the later gendered assumptions in Esping-Anderson's concept of social rights.

11. Mahon, 2002, p. 13

12. Kahn & Polakow, 2000a; Kittay, 1998; Lewis, 1997; Mink, 1998

13. Gornick & Meyers, 2003, p. 269

14. OECD, 2005. The OECD comprises 30 member nations that cooperate on economic, social, scientific, educational, and trade issues, with a stated commitment to democratic government and a market economy.

15. Gornick, quoted in Mahon, 2002, p. 3

16. See Boushey & Wright, 2004; and Helburn & Bergmann, 2002, who quote even higher figures.

17. Children's Defense Fund, 1996, 2002; Ebb, 1994; Helburn, 1995; Helburn & Bergmann, 2002; Schulman, 2000; U.S. General Accounting Office, 1993

18. Sunstein, 2004, p. 3

19. Roosevelt's State of the Union delivered by radio address to the nation in 1944, cited in Sunstein, 2004, p. 12.

20. Sunstein, 2004, p. 95

21. Roosevelt, quoted in Sunstein, 2004, pp. 28, 90

22. Sunstein, 2004, p. 2

23. Nussbaum, 2000, p. 1

24. Nussbaum, 2000, p. 65

25. Human Development Report, 1997, cited in Nussbaum, 2000

26. Nussbaum, 2000, pp. 1, 3

27. Nussbaum, 2000, p. 62

28. Nussbaum, 2000, p. 73

29. Sunstein, 2004

30. Gornick & Meyers, 2003, p. 9

31. Davis, 2003; Davis & Powell, 2003

32. European Commission, 2004

33. CRC, 1989, Preamble, Article18(3); Davis, 2003

34. Muriel Rukeyser's "Käthe Kollwitz," 2005, p. 463

Chapter 2

1. Michigan's Department of Human Services (DHS) does not pay the full cost of care. According to the income-eligibility scale, which ranges from 0 income to a gross monthly income of $1607 for a family size of two, subsidies will cover between 70% and 95% of the maximum rates for child care, which are considerably lower than the market costs of child care. DHS reimbursement rates are typically paid up to the 75th percentile of market rates in each county, based on an outdated market survey of 1999. See Introduction, note 35.

2. Michigan's Department of Human Services (DHS) has undergone several name changes. Under former Republican Governor Engler, the department was renamed the Family Independence Agency (FIA). Under curent Democratic Governor Granholm, the department reverted back to its former name but retained the name Family Independence Program (FIP) for the welfare cash grant program. The irony, of course, is that the punitive program, with its meager and hard-to-access benefits, fosters neither family stability nor independence.

3. See Kahn & Polakow, 2000b, for further documentation of unreasonable delays in accessing child care subsidies. See also Carlson & Sharf, 2004; Schulman & Blank, 2004.

4. Annette's child care co-pay would be calculated as follows: Her gross earnings are $1,548 a month. With a family size of two (she and the baby), she is

technically eligible for 80% of the maximum DHS rate of $2 an hour for infants in her shelter area, which comprises several counties in southeast Michigan. 80% of $2 an hour = $1.60; therefore, the subsidy covers $64 a week. But the provider charges $150 a week. So in addition, Annette must pay the difference in the cost of care, which is $86 a week or $344 a month.

5. 50,000 adults have been denied access because of massive budget cuts. Former Republican Governor Engler decimated adult education, and in 2003, Democratic Governor Granholm cut the budget from $77.5 million to $20 million, claiming the cuts were necessary in order to protect education funding for K–12 students. See Moses, 2003.

6. Kahn & Polakow, 2000b

7. Annette, like thousands of other single mothers in Michigan, was forced into a mandatory work placement when her baby reached the age of 3 months in order to access benefits.

8. NACCRRA and Michigan 4C, 2006; 75% estimate supplied by Mark Sullivan, Executive Director of Michigan 4C.

9. Michigan 4C, 2006. Costs in that county average $158 a week.

10. See Urban Institute, 1999

11. See Moses, 2003

12. Women's earnings and income increase as their educational level rises, and postsecondary education has a dramatic impact on employment, wages, and family well-being for single mothers in poverty. See Gittell et al., 1996; Kahn et al., 2004; Kates, 2004.

13. *Reynolds v. Giuliani.* The Welfare Law Center won a comprehensive federal injunction in a class-action suit that stopped the city's unlawful policy of denying welfare recipients access to food stamps, Medicaid, cash assistance, and emergency assistance. The Court ruled that these polices violated state and federal rules. See National Center for Law and Justice, 2006.

14. Carlson & Scharf, 2004. The Welfare Law Center in its latest damning report *Lost in the Maze* calls for radical structural changes and leadership from New York City Mayor Bloomberg in the delivery of child care services to low-income parents, in order to fix a chaotic system with competing agencies and thousands of children falling through the cracks.

15. For a detailed discussion, see Carlson & Scharf, 2004; Chaudry, 2004

16. Chaudry, 2004

17. Children's Defense Fund, 2003a; Galinsky et al., 1994; Helburn, 1995; Schulman, 2000

18. Chaudry, 2004, p. 14

19. *Davila v. Eggleston,* a recent settlement in a class-action lawsuit, protects the rights of single parents to attend school and count that as a "work activity." See Legal Aid Society, 2003.

20. DeParle, 1998, pp. 52, 53

21. DeParle, 1998, p. 54
22. Cited in Ratner, 2004
23. Mink, 1998
24. Kafka, 1925/1953, p. 235
25. See Bell & Strege-Flora, 2000; Kahn & Polakow, 2004; Ratner, 2004
26. Bell & Strege-Flora, p. 3
27. Piven, 1998; Piven et al., 2002
28. Mink, 1998, p. 133
29. See Presser & Cox, 1997
30. Presser & Cox, 1997, p. 32
31. Chaudry, 2004; Children's Defense Fund, 2002; Galinsky et al., 1994
32. See Polakow et al., 2004, for an analysis of welfare "reform" and its impact on low-income student mothers pursuing postsecondary education and documentation of their experiences across the states.

Chapter 3

1. Under the 1996 PRWORA legislation there are individual work requirements that welfare-reliant individuals must meet, and there are aggregate work-participation rates imposed on the states. The Temporary Assistance to Needy Families (TANF) program that replaced the former Aid to Families with Dependent Children (AFDC) program embeds a work-first philosophy, which has demarcated a 5-year lifetime limit for welfare assistance and severely restricts college options for welfare-reliant clients. Postsecondary education is not specified as an allowable work activity under PRWORA, although up to 30% of working participants are permitted to enroll in time-limited vocational education. States do have some discretion in permitting college attendance as a work activity; however, few have elected to do so. (See Jones-DeWeever & Gault, 2006; Kahn et al., 2004). Iowa's Department of Human Services does permit a 24-month postsecondary education waiver in lieu of work requirements. Child care subsidies are provided to those enrolled in the Promise Jobs Program, which requires full-time student enrollment or a minimum of 28 hours of work per week (or some combination thereof). Child care assistance is prioritized according to income level: at or below the federal poverty line, below 140% of the poverty line, below 200% of the poverty line, and when a member of the family has a child with special needs. See Iowa Department of Human Services, 2003, 2005.

2. Iowa is one of a handful of states that permits time-limited full-time enrollment in a college degree. With the exception of Maine's model Parents-as-Scholars Program, the other states (California, Kentucky, Illinois, and Wyoming) only permit 24 months.

3. According to the posted regulations, the minimum is now 28 hours a week;

see Iowa Department of Human Services, 2003.

4. Although the Iowa Department of Human Services states 28 hours of work as the minimum requirement, all the Iowa student mothers interviewed for this study (10 of them) had been informed that if they combined work with school, they needed to work a minimum of 20 hours a week.

5. Iowa Department of Human Services, 2003, 2005

6. Bloom, 2005, p. 24

7. Levine & Nidiffer, 1996

8. Heller & Bjorklund, 2004, pp. 134–135

9. Heller & Bjorklund, p. 132

10. Strawn, 2000; Heller & Bjorklund, 2004

11. Kahn & Polakow, 2000b; Kahn et al., 2004

12. Brauner & Loprest, 1999; Kahn et al., 2004; Institute for Women's Policy Research (IWPR), 1998; Sherman et al., 1998

13. Kahn et al., 2004; U.S. Department of Health and Human Services, 2003

14. Toner & Pear, 2002, p. A18

15. IWPR, 1998; Kahn et al., 2004

16. Deprez, Butler, & Smith, 2004

17. For further details, see the recent IWPR report by Jones-DeWeever & Gault, 2006.

18. Kahn et al., 2004; Spalter-Roth & Hartmann, 1991; U.S. Department of Labor, Bureau of Labor Statistics, 1997

19. Jones-DeWeever & Gault, 2006; U.S. Department of Commerce, Bureau of the Census, 2005

20. Deprez, Butler, & Smith, 2004; Gittell, Schehl, & Fareri, 1990; Gittell et al., 1996; Kates, 2004

21. Haveman & Wolfe, 1994, p. 99

22. American Psychological Association, 1998, p. 15

Chapter 4

1. Harrington, 1971, p. 188

2. Bernstein, 2004

3. See the Economic Policy Institute's (EPI) report by Boushey et al., 2001

4. National Center for Children in Poverty, 2006a, 2006b

5. Boushey, quoted in EPI Press Release, July, 2001a

6. The Children's Defense Fund (2005a) lists the annual income eligibility cutoff for child care assistance for a family of three as $35,100 in 2004. With a family of five, Hannah and Thomas technically should be eligible as a working poor family. However, approximately 48% of child care funds in the state are targeted for CalWORKs welfare recipients. The remaining funds are for low-income

families who are not part of the CalWORKs program. Parents participating in CalWORKs are guaranteed child care, but low-income families not participating in CalWORKs find themselves on long waiting lists with restricted access.

7. In April 2003, after years of intensive lobbying by advocacy coalitions, the New York City Council passed the Coalition for Access to Training and Education Law (Local Law 23), permitting city residents receiving public assistance to enroll in postsecondary or vocational education, with those hours counting towards the mandatory work requirements.

8. See Carlson & Scharf, 2004

9. The Children's Defense Fund (2005d) lists the annual cost of center-based care in New York as $8,060. Goldman (2003) reported that costs may run as high as $15,000 at the "Baby Ivies." The income eligibility cutoff for assistance for a family of three was $31,340 in 2004.

10. Ehrenreich, 2001, pp. 196, 199

11. Ehrenreich, 2001, p. 27

12. Katz, 1989

13. Bernstein, 2001

14. Smeeding, Rainwater, & Burtless, 2000. I am indebted to my colleague Peggy Kahn for the knowledge and insights she has shared with me in conversations about this issue.

15. Federal poverty guidelines (often called the federal poverty line) are issued by the Department of Health and Human Services and determine eligibility for public benefits. The guidelines are updated in spring of each current year, so they are more current than the threshold, which is updated the following year. For a more detailed explanation of the difference between poverty thresholds and poverty guidelines, see Economic Policy Institute, 2001b.

16. National Center for Children in Poverty, 2006a

17. Boushey et al., 2001

18. EPI, 2001b. Family budgets are based on self-sufficiency standards originally developed by Diana Pearce and Wider Opportunities for Women (WOW).

19. Allegretto, 2005, p. 1

20. Allegretto, 2005

21. EPI, 2005

22. U.S. Department of Health and Human Services, 2006

23. "Heartless Marriage Plans," 2004, p. 14

Chapter 5

1. See Chapter 2, note 1, regarding child care subsidies.

2. Lollipop Learning Center, a pseudonym for a private, for-profit child care business, has had complaints about ratios and other inappropriate practices

dating back twenty years; eighteen years ago the center was placed on proba-
tion by the licensing board.

3. The maximum income eligibility for a family of two (one parent and one child) is a monthly gross amount of $1,607. Chiquila's gross monthly income at $13.68 an hour is $2,188. See Michigan Department of Human Services, 2005.

4. Presser & Cox, 1997, p. 33

5. Garbarino, 1995, p. 155

6. See the discussion of the accumulation of risk model in Vorrasi & Garba-rino, 2000.

7. Garbarino, 1992

8. Albee, quoted in Garbarino, 1992, p. 27

9. Garbarino, 1992, p. 42

10. Schulman, Blank, & Ewen, 2001

11. 12% of Head Start children served are diagnosed with disabilities. See Children's Defense Fund, 2005b, 2005c.

12. Polakow, 1993; Swadener, 1995

13. These policies have been identified as a growing source of racial bias and lack of due process for public school students. See Harvard's Advancement and Civil Rights Project, 2000, for extensive documentation on disproportionate ex-pulsions based on race and gender; also Zweifler & DeBeers, 2002.

14. Kozol, 1992, 2005; Orfield & Lee, 2005

15. Gilliam, 2005

16. Blank, 1997; Espinosa, 2003; Fuller & Kagan, 2000; Peisner-Feinberg et al., 1999; Salisbury & Smith, 1993; Wolery, Brashers, & Neitzel, 2002

17. See Smith, 1988; personal communication with Sarah Ginsberg

18. Wolery, Brashers, & Neitzel, 2002

19. See Polakow, 1982, 1993, for such documented observations.

20. Garbarino, 1995

Chapter 6

1. Matthews & Ewen, 2006

2. Capps et al., 2005

3. All of the interviews in this chapter were conducted in Spanish (with the exception of Marabel's) and translated and transcribed with the help of Spanish-speaking research assistants.

4. Passel, Capps, & Fix, 2004

5. See Chapter 4, note 6. For low-income families not participating in Cal-WORKs, there are long waiting lists with restricted access, which may be why Maria was told (incorrectly) that her family income was too high to qualify. For further details, see California Legislative Analyst's Office, 2006; Children's De-fense Fund, 2005a.

6. CalWORKs (California Work Opportunity and Responsibility to Kids) is California's welfare-to-work program established in 1997, after the passage of the federal welfare legislation PRWORA in August 1996. CalWORKs permits vocational education and training as an allowable work activity and up to 24 months of postsecondary education at community colleges; most students are also required to work 20 hours per week. See California Department of Social Services, 2004.

7. California has two distinct child care programs: Title 22 (the voucher program), which serves the majority of low-income children, including those whose parents are in the CalWORKs program, and the California Department of Education (CDE) direct-contract system (Title 5), which contracts directly with child care centers and requires adherence to higher educational training and accountability standards. The Title 22 programs include license-exempt providers (relatives, friends, neighbors) who are *not* subject to any accountability standards, training, or adult–child ratios. The Title 22 FCCH-licensed providers are not required to meet any educational or child care development standards, either. However, they are required to pass a fingerprint criminal background check, meet minimal health and safety standards, and have an adult–child ratio of 1:6, with a site visit every five years. Title 22 centers require teachers to have a CDA (Child Development Associate) credential or 12 hours of college credit in early childhood development, whereas Title 5 regulations require 40 hours of college credit and a child-development teacher permit. See California Legislative Analyst's Office, 2006.

8. Children's Defense Fund, 2005a

9. Capps et al., 2005

10. Capps et al., 2005; Tumlin & Zimmermann, 2003

11. Capps et al., 2005

12. Capps et al., 2005

13. Passel, Capps & Fix, 2004

14. Matthews & Ewen, 2006; Takanishi, 2004; Urban Institute, 2006

15. Matthews & Ewen, 2006

16. Capps et al., 2005

17. Nussbaum, 2000, p. 65

18. Galinsky et al., 1994; Helburn, 1995; Helburn & Bergmann, 2002

19. For a discussion about ethnic and cultural differences in parental choices, see Johnson et al., 2003.

Chapter 7

1. Child Care Access Means Parents in School Program (CCAMPIS) grants support the participation of low-income student parents by providing child care services on campus through the federal Office of Postsecondary Education.

Average awards in 2005 were $47,491 for one year, with just over 200 awards given annually to higher education institutions.

2. My impressions of the program, and discussion with the director, corroborated the glowing descriptions by the student parents.

3. Mathur, 2004

4. Michel, 1999, used the term to describe the strategies and resources that working mothers throughout history have developed to cover the child care deficit in their lives.

5. Overturf Johnson, 2005

6. Guzman, 1999; Overturf Johnson, 2005; Reschke, 2006

7. Guzman, 1999

8. Jendrek, 1993

9. Heymann & Earle, 2000; U.S. Department of Labor, Bureau of Labor Statistics, 2005

10. Bernstein, 2004, p. 4

11. Heymann & Earle, 2000

12. Children's Defense Fund, 2003b

13. Overturf Johnson, 2005

14. Snyder & Sickmund, 1999

15. Maeroff, 1998, p. 16

16. Posner & Vandell, 1994; See also Children's Defense Fund, 2003b, for a summary of the research evaluating outcomes from national and statewide after-school programs, pp. 96–99.

17. Maeroff, 1998

18. To protect the confidentiality of the mothers and their children, the Indian reservation has not been identified and is only noted by its affiliation as part of the Ojibwe tribe.

19. I visited the program in 2003, and this description is based on my documented observations.

20. The High/Scope Educational Research Foundation, home to the Perry Preschool Early Intervention Study, provides training and certification programs, educational curricula, and assessments using a constructivist philosophy of active discovery learning guided by trained early childhood teachers.

21. Parents who are eligible for state-funded child care subsidies must access them off the reservation at the county FIA office, which many women find difficult and humiliating to do.

22. The Boys and Girls Club of America is a national organization financed by corporate sponsors and provides free daily and weekend educational and recreational services for school-age children who lack access to other community programs. A Columbia University evaluation of The Boys and Girls Club of America's Educational Enhancement Program, Project Learn, points to academic gains and improved school attendance cited in Children's Defense Fund, 2003b.

23. Despite the series of Head Start cuts during the Bush Administration's second term, the tribe has invested in the program and pays about 30% of its costs, according to the current director.

24. Alex at 5 is one of the children caught in the transition year before the program age eligibility was lowered from 8 to 5 years.

25. Merleau-Ponty, 1962, p. 446

Chapter 8

1. Rukeyser, "Ann Burlak," 2005, p. 195
2. Nussbaum, 2000, p. 1
3. Steinbeck, 1939/1967, p. 384
4. Hobson & Lister, 2002
5. See Davis & Powell, 2003, on domestic and international child care rights.
6. Davis & Powell, p. 711; see also Davis, 2003
7. Kilbourne, 1999, p. 27
8. CRC, 1989, Preamble, Article 18(2), (3)
9. Davis & Powell, 2003
10. CEDAW, 1979, Article 11, 1(a) 2(b) 2(c)
11. ICESCR, 1986, Article 3, 7(a) (i) (ii); Article 10(2)
12. Quoted in Davis & Powell, 2003, p. 692
13. Poverty here is defined as income below 50% of the country's median income. See Gornick & Meyers, pp. 74–75.
14. Smeeding, Rainwater, & Burtless, 2000, p. 20
15. Kamerman, 2000, p. 13
16. Davis & Powell, 2003
17. Several states have expanded the eligibility requirements or extended the leave period. See Gornick & Meyers for a discussion of the FMLA and TDI, Chapter 5. See also Kamerman, 2000.
18. Morrison, 1998, p. 308
19. European Commission, 2004. The European Commission is the governing executive body of the EU Polity.
20. Kamerman, 2005, p. 195. See also Kamerman et al., 2003
21. Hernes, 1987; Siim, 1997
22. Siim, 1997
23. Davis, 2003. Also see cross-national and OECD comparisons discussed in Gornick & Meyers, 2003; Michel & Mahon, 2002; Plantenga & Hansen, 1999.
24. See Gornick & Meyers, Table 2.1, p. 41
25. Bergqvist & Nyberg, 2002
26. Davis, 2003
27. Bergqvist & Nyberg, 2002
28. Orloff quoted in Bergqvist & Nyberg, p. 298
29. In up to 40% of Swedish municipalities children lost their places when

a parent became unemployed. See Bergqvist & Nyberg, 2002; see also Davis, 2003, on Sweden's expanded social equality provisions in response to the criticism by the Report of the UN Convention on the Rights of the Child.

30. OECD, quoted in Bergqvist & Nyberg, p. 296

31. Bergmann, 1996

32. Morgan, 2002

33. See Morgan's discussion on the impact of diversification of types of child care and extended leave.

34. Children's Defense Fund, 2005b

35. Goldman, 2003

36. National Association for the Education of Young Children, 2005a, 2005b

37. National Association for the Education of Young Children, 2006

38. See Helburn & Bergmann, 2002, Chapter 6; see also Children's Defense Fund, 2005c

39. Helburn & Bergmann, 2002

40. Helburn & Bergmann, Chapter 6

41. Vandell & Wolfe, 2000

42. Chaudry, 2004

43. See Helburn & Bergmann, 2002, Chapter 7

44. Barnett, 1998; Campbell et al., 1998; Helburn, 1995; Schweinhart, 2004

45. NICHD Early Childcare Research Network, 2000, 2002

46. For a detailed discussion of the 38 studies, which include the High/Scope Perry Preschool Project and the Carolina Abecedarian studies, see Barnett, 1998.

47. See *The Early Childhood Environment Rating Scale* (ECERS-R), Harms, Clifford & Cryer, 2005; *The Infant/Toddler Environment Rating Scale* (ITERR), Harms, Cryer, & Clifford, 2006

48. Helburn, 1995

49. Peisner-Feinberg et al., 1999

50. Duncan & Brooks-Gunn, 1997

51. Peisner-Feinberg et al., 1999, p. 2

52. Ehrle, Adams, & Tout, 2001

53. Galinsky et al., 1994. Target children in the study averaged 26.3 months.

54. Galinsky et al., p. 90

55. See Ehrle, Adams, & Tout, 2001; Phillips & Adams, 2001. The fact that a disproportionate number of poor children are ethnic minorities and children of color may also shape the limited choices parents have placing their children in the licensed sector. Dealing with an untrained caregiver who shares the same ethnic background and speaks your native language may create an ethnic comfort zone; hence fictive kin for African-American children and *comadrazgo* (co-mothering) may, on the surface, appear as more attractive options. See Johnson et al., 2003.

56. Thompson, 2001, p. 30

57. Heckman & Masterov, 2004, p. 7

58. Heckman & Masterov, 2004, p. 3

59. Heckman & Masterov, 2004, p. 17

60. Heckman & Masterov, 2004, p. 7

61. National Child Care Association, 2002

62. All of these figures and projections are drawn from *The National Economic Impacts of the Child Care Sector* report, National Child Care Association, 2002.

63. See Warner, 2006; Warner et al., 2005; Warner & Stoney, 2005

64. Warner, 2006, p. 1

65. Warner, 2006, p. 5

66. Warner, 2006

67. Zigler & Finn-Stevenson, 1995, p. 215

68. I have greatly benefited from discussions with my colleague Peggy Kahn about these proposals and their ramifications.

69. Zigler & Finn-Stevenson, 1995, 1996

70. Zigler & Finn-Stevenson, 1996, p. 119

71. Golin & Mitchell, 2004

72. Golin & Mitchell, 2004

73. Barnett et al., 2005

74. Barnett et al., 2005, p. 6

75. For details of the three plans, see Helburn & Bergmann, 2002, Chapters 2, 9, and Appendix A

76. Helburn & Bergmann, 2002, p. 215

77. Average would be defined as a standard midway between minimally adequate and good, according to standard rating scales such as ECERS-R (Harms, Clifford, & Cryer, 2005).

78. Bilmes & Stiglitz, 2006

79. Helburn & Bergmann, 2002, p. 217

80. Maeroff, 1998

81. Davis, 2003, 2005

82. Neubeck, 2006

83. Miewald, 2004, p. 182

84. Anyon, 2005, p. 165

85. Nussbaum, 2000, p. 65

86. Morrison, 1995, p. 760

87. King, 1964

88. Bishop, 1983, p. 273

References

Advancement and Civil Rights Project. (2000, June). *Opportunities suspended: The devastating consequences of zero tolerance and school discipline policies.* Cambridge, MA: The Civil Rights Project, Harvard University. Available at: http://www.civilrightsproject.harvard.edu/research/discipline/opport_suspended.php#fullreport

Allegretto, S. A. (2005, September 1). *Basic family budgets: Working families' incomes often fail to meet living expenses around the U.S.* (No. 165). Washington, DC: Economic Policy Institute. Available at: http://www.epi.org/content.cfm/bp165

American Psychological Association. (1998). *Making "welfare to work" really work: Report of the task force on women, poverty, and public assistance.* Washington, DC: Author.

Amott, T., & Matthaei, J. (1991). *Race, gender & work: A multicultural economic history of women in the United States.* Boston: South End Press.

Anyon, J. (2005). *Radical possibilities: Public policy, urban education, and a new social movement.* New York: Routledge.

Barnett, W. S. (1998). Long-term effects on cognitive development and school success. In W. S. Barnett & S. S. Boocock (Eds.), *Early care and education for children in poverty: Promises, programs, and long-term results* (pp. 11–44). Albany, NY: State University of New York Press.

Barnett, W. S., Hustedt, J. T., Robin, K. B., & Schulman, K. L. (2005). *The state of preschool: 2005 preschool yearbook.* New Brunswick, NJ: National Institute for Early Education Research. Available at: http://nieer.org/yearbook/pdf/yearbook.pdf

Barton, P. (2005). *One-third of a nation.* Washington, DC: Policy Information Center. Available at: http://ets.org/Media/Education_Topics/pdf/onethird.pdf

Bell, L., & Strege-Flora, C. (2000, May). *Access denied.* Washington, DC: National Campaign for Jobs and Income Support. Available at: http://www.nwfco.org/05-01-00_NWFCO_Access_Denied.pdf

Bergmann, B. R. (1996). *Saving our children from poverty: What the United States can learn from France.* New York: Russell Sage.

Bergqvist, C., & Nyberg, A. (2002). Welfare state restructuring and child care in Sweden. In S. Michel & R. Mahon (Eds.), *Child care policy at the crossroads: Gender and welfare state restructuring* (pp. 287–307). New York: Routledge.

Bernstein, J. (2001). *Let the war on the poverty line commence.* New York: Foundation for Child Development. Available at: http://www.ffcd.org

Bernstein, J. (2004). The low-wage labor market: Trends and policy implications. In A. Crouter & A. Booth (Eds.), *Work–family challenges for low-income parents and their children* (pp. 3–34). Mahwah, NJ: Lawrence Erlbaum Associates.

Bilmes, L., & Stiglitz, J. (2006, January 17). War's stunning price tag. *The Los Angeles Times.* Available at: http://www.latimes.com/news/opinion/commentary/la-oe-bilmes17jan17,0,7038018.story?coll=la-news-comment-opinions

Bishop, E. (1983). *The complete poems, 1927–1979.* New York: Farrar, Straus and Giroux.

Blank, H. (1997, January). *Helping parents work and children succeed.* Washington, DC: Children's Defense Fund.

Blank, H., Schulman, K., & Ewen, D. (1999, September). *Seeds of success: State prekindergarten initiatives, 1998–1999.* Washington, DC: Children's Defense Fund.

Bloom, L. R. (2005, May). *Staying in school after welfare reform: How Beyond Welfare, Inc. supports student mothers in higher education.* Ann Arbor, MI: Center for the Education of Women, University of Michigan. Available at: http://www.umich.edu/~cew/PDFs/pubs/bloom05.pdf

Boushey, H., Brocht, C., Gundersen, B., & Bernstein, J. (2001). *Hardships in America: The real story of working families.* Washington, DC: Economic Policy Institute. Available at: http://www.epinet.org/content.cfm/books_hardships

Boushey, H., & Wright, J. (2004, May 5). *Working moms and child care* (No. 3). Washington, DC: Center for Economic and Policy Research. Available at: http://www.cepr.net/publications/child_care_2004.pdf

Brauner, S., & Loprest, P. (1999, May). *Where are they now? What states' studies of people who left welfare tell us* (No. A-32). Washington, DC: Urban Institute. Available at: http://www.urban.org/UploadedPDF/anf32.pdf

California Department of Social Services. (2004). *CalWORKs welfare to work program.* Available at: http://www.dss.cahwnet.gov/cdssweb/Welfare-to_172.htm

California's Legislative Analyst's Office. (2006, February). *Analysis of the 2006–07 budget bill: Child care.* Available at: http://www.lao.ca.gov/analysis_2006/education/ed_10_anl06.html

Campbell, F. A., Helms, R., Sparling, J. J., & Ramey, C. T. (1998). Early childhood programs and success in school: The abecedarian study. In W. S. Barnett & S. S. Boocock (Eds.), *Early care and education for children in poverty: Promises, programs and long-term results* (pp. 145–166). Albany, NY: State University of New York Press.

Capps, R., Fix, M. E., Reardon-Anderson, J., Ost, J., & Passel, J. S. (2005, February 8). *The health and well-being of young children of immigrants* (No. 6). Washington, DC: Urban Institute. Available at: http://www.urban.org/url.cfm?ID=311139

Carlson, B. C., & Scharf, R. (2004, February). *Lost in the maze: Reforming New York*

City's fragmented child care subsidy system. New York: Welfare Law Center. Available at: http://www.nclej.org/contents/childcare/LostInTheMaze.pdf

Center on Budget and Policy Priories. (2005). *Federal budget outlook.* Washington, DC: Author. Available at: http://www.cbpp.org/budget-slideshow.htm

Center on Budget and Policy Priorities. (2006, March 27). *Five-year discretionary caps would be unwise at this time: Proposed caps would lead to overly deep cuts and could hinder enactment of large scale deficit reduction.* Washington, DC: Author. Available at: http://www.cbpp.org/3-27-06bud2.htm

Chaudry, A. (2004). *Putting children first: How low-wage working mothers manage child care.* New York: Russell Sage Foundation.

Children's Defense Fund. (1996). *The state of America's children: Yearbook 1996.* Washington, DC: Author.

Children's Defense Fund. (2002, September 5). *Low-income families bear the burden of state child care cutbacks.* Washington, DC: Author.

Children's Defense Fund. (2003a). *Infants and toddlers are particularly vulnerable: Good child care and early education can play a vital role in their development.* Washington, DC: Author. Available at: http://www.childrensdefense.org/site/DocServer/keyfacts2003_infant.pdf?docID=587

Children's Defense Fund. (2003b). *School-age child care: Keeping children safe and helping them learn while their families work.* Washington, DC, Author. Available at: http://campaign.childrensdefense.org/earlychildhood/schoolagecare/keyfacts2003_schoolagecare.pdf

Children's Defense Fund. (2005a, March). *California: Early childhood development facts.* Washington, DC, Author. Available at: http://campaign.childrensdefense.org/earlychildhood/statefacts/CA.pdf

Children's Defense Fund. (2005b, April). *Child care basics 2005.* Washington, DC: Author. Available at: http://www.childrensdefense.org/site/DocServer/child_care_basics_2005.pdf?docID=282

Children's Defense Fund. (2005c, March). *Head start basics 2005.* Washington, DC: Author. Available at: http://www.childrensdefense.org/site/DocServer/headstartbasics%202005.pdf?docID=616

Children's Defense Fund. (2005d, March). *New York: Early development facts.* Washington, DC: Author. Available at: http://campaign.childrensdefense.org/earlychildhood/statefacts/NY.pdf

Convention on the Elimination of all Forms of Discrimination Against Women (CEDAW). (1979). *United Nations Division for the Advancement of Women.* Available at: http://www.un.org/womenwatch/daw/cedaw/cedaw.htm

Convention on the Rights of the Child (CRC). (1989, November 20). *United Nations Office of the High Commissioner for Human Rights.* Available at: http://www.unhchr.ch/html/menu3/b/k2crc.htm

Davis, M. (2003, June). Child care as a human right: A new perspective on an old debate. *"Women working to make a difference." IWPR's Seventh International Women's Policy Research Conference.* Washington, DC. Available at: http://www.iwpr.org/pdf/Davis_Martha.pdf

Davis, M. (2005). International human rights from the ground up: The potential for subnational, human rights-based reproductive health advocacy in the United States. In W. Chavkin & E. Chesler (Eds.), *Where human rights begin: Health, sexuality, and women in the new millennium* (pp. 235–266). New Brunswick, NJ: Rutgers University Press.

Davis, M., & Powell, R. (2003, August). The International Convention on the Rights of the Child: A catalyst for innovative child care policies. *Human Rights Quarterly, 25*(3), 689–719.

DeParle, J. (1998, December 20). What welfare-to-work really means? The *New York Times*, pp. 50–59, 70–72, 88–89.

Deprez, L. S., Butler, S., & Smith, R. J. (2004). Securing higher education for women on welfare in Maine. In V. Polakow, S. Butler, L. S. Deprez, & P. Kahn (Eds.), *Shut out: Low income mothers and higher education in post-welfare America.* (pp. 217–236). Albany, NY: State University of New York Press.

Dewey, J. (1915). *The school and society* (rev. ed.). Chicago: University of Chicago Press.

Doctorow, E. L. (1994). *The waterworks.* New York: Random House.

Duncan, G. J., & Brooks-Gunn, J. (Eds.). (1997). *Consequences of growing up poor.* New York: Russell Sage Foundation.

Ebb, N. (1994, January). *Child care tradeoffs: States make painful choices.* Washington, DC: Children's Defense Fund.

Economic Policy Institute. (2001a, July 24). *One in three families with young children can't afford basics like food, housing, and health care.* Washington, DC: Author. Available at: http://www.zmag.org/amerpoverty.htm

Economic Policy Institute. (2001b, August). *Poverty and family budgets.* Washington, DC: Author. Available at: http://www.epinet.org/issueguides/poverty/poverty_issueguide.pdf

Economic Policy Institute. (2005, September). *Basic family budget calculator.* Washington, DC: Author. Available at: http://www.epi.org/content.cfm/datazone_fambud_budget

Ehrenreich, B. (2001). *Nickel and dimed: On (not) getting by in America.* New York: Metropolitan Books.

Ehrle, J., Adams, G., & Tout, K. (2001). *Who's caring for our youngest children? Child care patterns of infants and toddlers* (No. 42). Washington, DC: The Urban Institute. Available at: http://www.urban.org/UploadedPDF/310029_occa42.pdf

Esping-Anderson, G. (1990). *The three worlds of welfare capitalism.* Cambridge, UK: Polity Press.

Espinosa, L. (2003, March). *High-quality preschool: Why we need it and what it looks like.* Available at: http://nieer.org/resources/factsheets/1.pdf

European Commission. (2004, May). *Joint report on social exclusion.* Brussels: Employment and Social Affairs. Available at: http://ec.europa.eu/employment_social/publications/2005/keaq04001_en.pdf

Excerpts from Nixon's veto message. (1971, December 10). The *New York Times*, p. 20.

Folbre, N. (1994, May). Children as public goods. *American Economic Review,* *84*(2), 86–90.

Fuller, B., & Kagan, S. L. (2000). *Remember the children: Mothers balance work and child care under welfare reform.* Growing up in poverty project: Wave 1 findings. Princeton, NJ: Mathematica Policy Research.

Galinsky, E., Howes, C., Kontos, S., & Shinn, M. (1994). *The study of children in family care and relative care: Highlights of findings.* New York: Families and Work Institute.

Garbarino, J. (1992). *Children and families in the social environment* (2nd ed.). New York: Aldine de Gruyte.

Garbarino, J. (1995). *Raising children in a socially toxic environment.* San Francisco, CA: Jossey-Bass.

Garfinkel, I., & McLanahan, S. (1986). *Single mothers and their children: A new American dilemma.* Washington, DC: Urban Institute Press.

Gilliam, F. D. (1999, Summer). The "welfare queen" experiment. *Nieman Reports,* *53*(2). Available at: http://www.nieman.harvard.edu/reports/99-2NRsummer99/Gilliam.html

Gilliam, W. (2005, May). *Prekindergarteners left behind: Expulsion rates in state prekindergarten programs* (No. 3). New York: Foundation for Child Development. Available at: http://www.fcd-us.org/PDFs/ExpulsionFinalProof.pdf

Gittell, M., Schehl, M., & Fareri, C. (1990). *From welfare to independence: The college option: A report to the Ford Foundation.* New York: Howard Samuels State Management and Policy Center.

Gittell, M., Vandersall, K., Holdaway, J., & Newman, K. (1996). *Creating social capital at CUNY: A comparison of higher education programs for AFDC recipients.* New York: Howard Samuels State Management and Policy Center.

Goldman, V. (2003, January 12). The baby Ivies: Preschool pedagogy for up to $15,000. The *New York Times,* p. 22.

Golin, S. C., & Mitchell, A. W. (2004). *The price of school readiness: A tool for estimating the cost of universal preschool in the states* (No. G713). Washington, DC: Institute for Women's Policy Research. Available at: http://www.earlychildhoodfinance.org/handouts/CostingOutConferenceCallPublication.pdf

Gornick, J., & Meyers, M. (2003). *Families that work.* New York: Russell Sage.

Grubb, W. N., & Lazerson, M. (1988). *Broken promises: How Americans fail their children.* Chicago: University of Chicago Press.

Guzman, L. (1999). *The use of grandparents as child care providers* (No. 84). Madison, WI: Center for Demography and Ecology, University of Wisconsin-Madison. Available at: http://www.ssc.wisc.edu/cde/nsfhwp/nsfh84.pdf

Harms, T., Clifford, R., & Cryer, D. (2005). *The early childhood environment rating scale* (ECERS-R) (Rev. ed.). New York: Teachers College Press.

Harms, T., Cryer, D., & Clifford, R. (2006). *The infant/toddler environment rating scale* (ITERS-R) (Rev. ed.). New York: Teachers College Press.

Harrington, M. (1971). *The other America: Poverty in the United States* (Rev. ed.). Baltimore, MD: Penguin Books.

Haveman, R., & Wolfe, B. (1994). *Succeeding generations: On the effects of investments in children.* New York: Russell Sage Foundation.

Heartless marriage plans [Editorial]. (2004, January 17). The *New York Times,* p. 14.

Heckman, J. J., & Masterov, D. V. (2004, October 4). *The productivity argument for investing in young children* (No. 5). Washington, DC: Committee for Economic Development. Available at: http://www.ced.org/docs/report/report_ivk_heckman_2004.pdf

Helburn, S. W. (Ed). (1995, June). *Cost, quality and child outcomes in child care centers.* Technical Report (ED 386 297). Denver, CO: Center for Research on Economic and Social Policy, Department of Economics, University of Colorado.

Helburn, S. W., & Bergmann, B. (2002). *America's child care problem: The way out.* New York: Palgrave MacMillan.

Heller, D., & Bjorklund, S. (2004). Student financial aid and low income mothers. In V. Polakow, S. Butler, L. S. Deprez, & P. Kahn (Eds.), *Shut out: Low income mothers and higher education in post-welfare America* (pp. 129–148). Albany, NY: State University of New York Press.

Hernes, H. M. (1987). *Welfare state and woman power. Essays in state feminism.* Oslo: Norwegian University Press.

Heymann, J., & Earle, A. (2000, Winter). Low-income parents: How do working conditions affect their opportunity to help school-age children at risk? *American Educational Research Journal, 37*(4), 833–848.

Hobson, B., & Lister, R. (2002). Citizenship. In B. Hobson, J. Lewis, & B. Siim (Eds.), *Contested concepts in gender and social politics* (pp. 23–54). Cheltenham, UK: Edward Algar. Available at: http://portal.unesco.org/shs/en/file_download.php/995815fd94412ec1556af27aa39e71b8citizenship.pdf

Hochschild, A. (1995, Fall). The culture of politics: Traditional, post-modern, cold modern and warm modern ideals of care. *Social Politics, 2*(3), 331–346.

Hymes, J. (1995). The Kaiser Child Service Centers–50 years later: Some memories and lessons. *Journal of Education, 177*(3), 23–38.

International Covenant on Economic, Social, and Cultural Rights (ICESCR). (1966, December 16). *Office of the United Nations High Commissioner for Human Rights.* Available at: http://www.unhchr.ch/html/menu3/b/a_cescr.htm

Institute for Women's Policy Research (IWPR). (1998, April). Welfare reform and postsecondary education: Research and policy update. *Welfare Reform Network News, 2*(1), 1–10.

Iowa Department of Human Services. (2003, October 21). *Child care assistance.* Available at: http://www.dhs.state.ia.us/policyanalysis/PolicyManualPages/Manual_Documents/Master/13-g.pdf

Iowa Department of Human Services. (2005). *Promise Jobs.* Available at: http://www.dhs.state.ia.us/dhs2005/dhs_homepage/reports_pubs/results_based/PJ.html#search='promise%20jobs%20are%20assistance

Jendrek, M. P. (1993). Grandparents who parent their grandchildren: Effects on lifestyle. *Journal of Marriage and the Family, 55*, 609–621.

Johnson, D. J., Jaeger, E., Randolph, S. M., Cauce, A. M., Ward, J., & The NICHD Early Child Care Research Network. (2003, October). Studying the effects of early child care experiences on the development of children of color in the United States: Towards a more inclusive research agenda. *Child Development, 74*(5), 1227–1244.

Jones-DeWeever, A., & Gault, B. (2006, April). *Resilient and reaching for more: Challenge and benefits of higher education for welfare participants and their children* (No. D466). Washington, DC: The Institute for Women's Policy Research. Available at: http://www.iwpr.org/pdf/D466.pdf

Kafka, F. (1925/1953). *The trial.* Harmondsworth: Penguin Books.

Kahn, P., Butler, S., Deprez, L. S., & Polakow, V. (2004). Introduction. In V. Polakow, S. Butler, L. S. Deprez, & P. Kahn (Eds.), *Shut out: Low income mothers and higher education in post-welfare America* (pp. 1–17). Albany, NY: State University of New York Press.

Kahn, P., & Polakow, V. (2000a). Mothering denied: Commodification and caregiving under new U.S. welfare laws. *SAGE Race Relations Abstracts, 25*(1), 7–25.

Kahn, P., & Polakow, V. (2000b, May). *Struggling to stay in school: Obstacles to post-secondary education under the welfare-to-work restrictions in Michigan.* Ann Arbor, MI: Center for the Education of Women, University of Michigan. Available at: http://www.umich.edu/~cew/PDFs/pubs/PolakowKahn2000. pdf

Kahn, P., & Polakow, V. (2004). That's not how I want to live: Student mothers fight to stay in school under Michigan's welfare-to-work regime. In V. Polakow, S. Butler, L. S. Deprez & P. Kahn (Eds.), *Shut out: Low income mothers and higher education in post-welfare America* (pp. 75–96). Albany, NY: State University of New York Press.

Kahn, P., Ruark, P., McHugh, R., & Doig, J. (2006, May 18). *Impacting poverty: Current trends and issues.* A presentation to the National Association of Social Workers/MI. Lansing, MI.

Kamerman, S. B. (2000). Parental leave policy: As essential ingredient of early childhood care policies. *Social Policy Report, 14*(2), 3–19. Available at: http:// www.childpolicy.org/SocialPolicyReport-2000_v14n2.pdf

Kamerman, S. B. (2005, November). Early childhood education and care in advanced industrialized countries: Current policy and program trends. *Phi Delta Kappan, 87*(3), 193–195.

Kamerman, S. B., & Kahn, A. (1987). *The responsive workplace: Employers and a changing labor force.* New York: Columbia University Press.

Kamerman, S. B., Neuman, M., Waldfogel, J., & Brooks-Gunn, J. (2003). *Social policies, family types and child outcomes in selected OECD countries.* Paris: OECD. Available at: http://www.oecd.org/dataoecd/26/46/2955844.pdf

Kates, E. (2004). Debunking the myth of the failure of education and training for welfare recipients: A critique of the research. In V. Polakow, S. Butler, L. S.

Deprez, & P. Kahn (Eds.), *Shut out: Low income mothers and higher education in post-welfare America* (pp. 19–43). Albany, NY: State University of New York Press.

Katz, M. (1989). *The undeserving poor.* New York: Pantheon Books.

Kelly, E. L. (2003, November). The strange history of employer-sponsored child care: Interested actors, uncertainty, and the transformation of law in organizational fields. *American Journal of Sociology, 109*(3), 606–649.

Kilbourne, S. (1999, Spring). Placing the convention on the rights of the child in an American context. *Human Rights, 28*(2), 27.

King, M. L., Jr. (1964, December 11). *The quest for peace and justice.* Nobel lecture. Available at: http://nobelprize.org/nobel_prizes/peace/laureates/1964/king-lecture.html

Kittay, E. F. (1998, April). Welfare, dependency, and a public ethic of care. *Social Justice, 25*(1), 123–146.

Kozol, J. (1992). *Savage inequalities: Children in America's schools.* New York: Harper Perennial.

Kozol, J. (2005). *The shame of the nation: The restoration of apartheid schooling in America.* New York: Crown Publishing Group.

Knitzer, J., & Lefkowitz, L. (2006, January). *Pathways to early school success: Helping the most vulnerable infants, toddlers, and their families.* New York: National Center for Children in Poverty. Available at: http://www.nccp.org/media/pew06e_text.pdf

Legal Aid Society. (2003). *Attention single parents on welfare! Know your rights to go to school!* New York: Author. Available at: http://www.nycetc.org/pdf/Educ%20and%20Training%20Rights%20(Advocates).pdf

Levine, A., & Nidiffer, J. (1996). *Beating the odds: How the poor get to college.* San Francisco, CA: Jossey-Bass.

Lewis, J. (Ed.). (1997). *Lone mothers in European welfare regimes: Shifting policy logics.* London: Jessica Kingsley Publishers

Maeroff, G. (1998). *Altered destinies: Making life better for schoolchildren in need.* New York: St. Martins Griffin.

Mahon, R. (2002). Gender and welfare state restructuring: Through the lens of child care. In S. Michel & R. Mahon (Eds.), *Child care policy at the crossroads: Gender and welfare state restructuring* (pp. 1–27). New York: Routledge.

Marshall, T. H. (1963). Citizenship and social class. In *Sociology at the crossroads and other essays* (pp. 66–127). London: Heinemann.

Mathur, A. (2004). Credentials count: How California's community colleges help parents move from welfare to self-sufficiency. In V. Polakow, S. Butler, L. S. Deprez, & P. Kahn (Eds.), *Shut out: Low income mothers and higher education in post-welfare America* (pp. 149–170). Albany, NY: State University of New York Press.

Matthews, H., & Ewen, D. (2006, January). *Reaching all children? Understanding early care and education participation among immigrant families.* Washington, DC: Center for Law and Social Policy. Available at: http://www.clasp.org/publications/child_care_immigrant.pdf

Merleau-Ponty, M. (1962). *Phenomenology of perception.* New York: Routledge & Kegan Paul.

Michel, S. (1999). *Children's interests/mothers' rights: The shaping of America's child care policy.* New Haven, CT: Yale University Press.

Michel, S., & Mahon, R. (Eds.). (2002). *Child care policy at the crossroads: Gender and welfare state restructuring.* New York: Routledge.

Michigan 4C Association. (2006, April). *Cost of care.* Available at: http://www.mi4c.org/aboutus/costofcare.xls

Michigan's Department of Human Services. (2005, October 1). *CDC income eligibility scale, maximum hourly rates and shelter areas.* Available at: http://www.mfia.state.mi.us/olmweb/ex/prt/270.pdf

Miewald, C. (2004). "This little light of mine": Parent activists struggling for access to post-secondary education in Appalachian Kentucky. In V. Polakow, S. Butler, L. S. Deprez, & P. Kahn (Eds.), *Shut out: Low income mothers and higher education in post-welfare America* (pp. 171–187). Albany, NY: State University of New York Press.

Mink, G. (1998). *Welfare's end.* Ithaca, NY: Cornell University Press.

Morgan, K. (2002). Does anyone have a "Libre choix"? Subversive liberalism and the politics of French child care policy. In S. Michel & R. Mahon (Eds.), *Child care policy at the crossroads: Gender and welfare state restructuring* (pp. 143–167). New York: Routledge.

Morrison, T. (1995, May). Racism and fascism. *The Nation, 260*(21), 760.

Morrison, T. (1998). *Paradise.* New York: Knopf.

Moses, A. R. (2003, September 6). Survey: Adult education cuts mean thousands can't enroll. *The Detroit News.*

National Association of Child Care Resource and Referral Agencies (NACCRRA) and Michigan 4C Association. (2006, February). *2006 child care in the state of Michigan.* Available at: http://www.naccrra.org/docs/data/MI.pdf

National Association for the Education of Young Children. (2005a). *NAEYC early childhood program standards.* Washington, DC: Author. Available at: http://www.naeyc.org/accreditation/standards/

National Association for the Education of Young Children. (2005b). *Early childhood program standards and accreditation criteria: The mark of quality in early childhood education.* Washington, DC: Author.

National Association for the Education for Young Children. (2006). *Summary of NAEYC-accredited programs for young children.* Washington, DC: Author. Available at: http://www.naeyc.org/accreditation/center_summary.asp

National Center for Children in Poverty. (2006a, January). *Basic facts about low-income children: Birth to age 18.* New York: Author. Available at: http://www.nccp.org/

National Center for Children in Poverty. (2006b, January). *Low-income children in the United States: National and state trend data, 1994–2004.* New York: Author. Available at: http://www.nccp.org/media/nst06_text.pdf

National Center for Law and Justice. (2006). *2005 highlights.* New York: Author. Available at: http://www.nclej.org/

National Child Care Association. (2002, Fall). *The national economic impacts of the child care sector.* Washington, DC: Author. Available at: http://www.nccanet. org/NCCA%20Impact%20Study.pdf

Neubeck, K. J. (2006). *When welfare disappears: The case for economic and human rights.* New York: Routledge.

NICHD Early Child Care Research Network. (2000, July/August). The relation of child care to cognitive and language development. *Child Development, 71*(4), 960–980.

NICHD Early Child Care Research Network. (2002). Early childcare and children's development prior to school entry. *American Educational Research Journal, 39*(1), 133–164.

Nussbaum, M. (2000). *Women and human development: The capabilities approach.* Cambridge, UK: Cambridge University Press.

Orfield, G., & Lee, C. (2005, January). *Why segregation matters: Poverty and educational inequality.* Cambridge, MA: The Civil Rights Project, Harvard University. Available at: http://www.civilrightsproject.harvard.edu/research/deseg/Why_Segreg_Matters.pdf

Organization for Economic Co-operation and Development (OECD). (2005, March). *Income distribution and poverty in OECD countries in the second half of the 1990s.* OECD Social, Employment and Migration Working Papers. Paris: Author. Available at: http://www.oecd.org/dataoecd/48/9/34483698.pdf

Overturf Johnson, J. (2005, October). *Who's minding the kids? Child care arrangements: Winter 2002* (No. P70-101). Washington, DC: U.S. Census Bureau. Available at: http://www.census.gov/prod/2005pubs/p70-101.pdf

Passel, J. S., Capps, R., & Fix, M. (2004, January 12). *Undocumented immigrants: Facts and figures.* Washington, DC: Urban Institute. Available at: http://www.urban.org/url.cfm?ID=1000587

Peisner-Feinberg, E. S., Burchinal, M. R., & Clifford, R. M., Culkin, M., Howes, C., & Kagan, L. (1999, June). *The children of the cost, quality, and outcomes study go to school: Executive summary.* Chapel Hill, NC: Frank Porter Graham Child Development Center, University of North Carolina at Chapel Hill. Available at: http://www.fpg.unc.edu/ncedl/PDFs/CQO-es.pdf

Phillips, D., & Adams, G. (2001, Spring/Summer). Child care and our youngest children. *The Future of Children, 11*(1), 35–51. Available at: http://www.future-ofchildren.org/information2826/information_show.htm?doc_id=79342

Piven, F. F. (1998, Spring). Welfare and work. *Social Justice, 25*(1), 67–81.

Piven, F. F., Acker, J., Hallock, M., & Morgen, M. (2002). *Work, welfare and politics: Confronting poverty in the wake of welfare reform.* Eugene: University of Oregon Press.

Plantenga, J., & Hansen, J. (1999). Assessing equal opportunities in the European Union. *International Labour Review, 138*(4), 351–379.

Polakow, V. (1982). *The erosion of childhood.* Chicago: University of Chicago Press.

Polakow, V. (1993). *Lives on the edge: Single mothers and their children in the other America.* Chicago: University of Chicago Press.

Polakow, V., Butler, S., Deprez, L. S., & Kahn, P. (Eds.). (2004). *Shut out: Low income mothers and higher education in post-welfare America.* Albany, NY: State University of New York Press.

Posner, J., & Vandell, D. L. (1994, April). Low-income children after-school care: Are there beneficial effects of after-school programs? *Child Development, 65*(2), 440–456.

Presser, H., & Cox, A. G. (1997, April). The work schedules of low-educated American women and welfare reform. *Monthly Labor Review, 120*(4), 25–34.

Ratner, L. (2004). Failing low income students: Education and training in the age of welfare reform. In V. Polakow, S. Butler, L. S. Deprez, & P. Kahn (Eds.), *Shut out: Low income mothers and higher education in post-welfare America* (pp. 45–74). Albany, NY: State University of New York Press.

Reschke, K. (2006, April). *Grandmothers as child care providers for rural, low-income mothers.* St. Paul, MN: Rural Families Speak Project, Department of Family Social Science. Available at: http://fsos.che.umn.edu/img/assets/16501/April_ChildCare_FactSheet.pdf

Rukeyser, M. (2005). "Ann Burlak." In J. E. Kaufman & A. F. Herzog (Eds.), *The collected poems of Muriel Rukeyser* (pp. 191–195). Pittsburgh, PA: University of Pittsburgh Press.

Rukeyser, M. (2005). "Käthe Kollwitz." In J. E. Kaufman & A. F. Herzog (Eds.), *The collected poems of Muriel Rukeyser* (pp. 460–464). Pittsburgh, PA: University of Pittsburgh Press.

Salibury, L. C., & Smith, B. J. (1993). *Effective practices for preparing young children with disabilities for school* (No. ED 358 675). Reston, VA: ERIC Clearinghouse on Handicapped and Gifted Children. Available at: http://www.ericdigests.org/1993/practices.htm

Schulman, K. (2000). *The high cost of child care puts quality care out of reach for many families.* Washington, DC: Children's Defense Fund.

Schulman, K., & Blank, H. (2004, September). *Child care assistance policies 2001– 2004: Families struggling to move forward, states going backward.* Washington, DC: National Women's Law Center. Available at: http://www.nwlc.org/pdf/childcaresubsidyfinalreport.pdf

Schulman, K., & Blank, H. (2005, September). *Child care assistance policies 2005: States fail to make up lost ground, families continue to lack critical supports.* Washington, DC: National Women's Law Center. Available at: http://www.nwlc.org/pdf/ChildCareSubsidyReport_September2005.pdf

Schulman, K., Blank, H., & Ewen, D. (2001, November). *A fragile foundation: State child care assistance policies.* Washington, DC: Children's Defense Fund.

Schweinhart, L. J. (2004, November). *The High/Scope Perry preschool study through age 40: Summary, conclusions, and frequently asked questions.* Ypsilanti, MI: High/Scope Educational Research Foundation. Available at: http://www.highscope.org/Research/PerryProject/PerryAge40_SumWeb.pdf

Sherman, A., Amey, C., Duffield, B., Ebb, N., & Weinstein, D. (1998, December). *Welfare to what: Early findings on family hardship and well-being.* Washington, DC: Children's Defense Fund and National Coalition for the Homeless.

Siim, B. (1997). Dilemmas of citizenship in Denmark: Lone mothers between work and care. In J. Lewis (Ed.), *Lone mothers in European welfare regimes: Shifting policy logics* (pp. 140–170). London: Jessica Kingsley Publishers.

Smeeding, T. M., Rainwater, L., & Burtless, G. (2000, September). *United States poverty in a cross-national context* (No. 244). Syracuse, NY: Syracuse University. Available at: http://www.lisproject.org/publications/liswps/244.pdf

Smith, B. J. (1988, March). *Does early intervention help?* (No. ED 295 399). Reston, VA: ERIC Clearinghouse on Handicapped and Gifted Children. Available at: http://www.ericdigests.org/pre-928/help.htm

Snyder, H., & Sickmund, M. (1999). *Juvenile offenders and victims: 1999 national report.* Washington, DC: U.S. Department of Justice, Office of Juvenile Justice and Delinquency Prevention. Available at: http://www.ncjrs.gov/html/ojjdp/nationalreport99/toc.html

Spalter-Roth, R. M., & Hartmann, H. I. (1991). *Increasing working mothers' earnings.* Washington, DC: Institute for Women's Policy Research.

Steinbeck, J. (1939/1967). *The grapes of wrath.* New York: Penguin Books.

Steinfels, M. O. (1973). *Who's minding the children? The history and politics of day care in America.* New York: Simon & Schuster.

Strawn, J. (2000). *Workforce development for the unemployed and low wage workers: The role of postsecondary education.* Washington, DC: Center for Law and Policy. Available at: http://www.clasp.org

Sunstein, C. R. (2004). *The second bill of rights: FDR's unfinished revolution and why we need it more than ever.* New York: Basic Books.

Swadener, B. B. (1995). Stratification in early childhood social policy and programs in the United States: Historical and contemporary manifestations. *Educational Policy, 9*(4), 404–425.

Takanishi, R. (2004, Summer). Leveling the playing field: Supporting immigrant children from birth to eight. *The Future of Children, 14*(2), 61–79. Available at: http://www.futureofchildren.org/usr_doc/takanishi.pdf

Thompson, R. A. (2001, Spring/Summer). Development in the first years of life. Caring for infants and children [Special Issue]. *The Future of Children, 11*(1), 21–33.

Toner, R., & Pear, R. (2002, February 27). Bush urges work and marriage programs in welfare plan. The *New York Times*, p. A18.

Tumlin, K. C., & Zimmermann, W. (2003, October 20). *Immigrants and TANF: A look at immigrant welfare recipients in three cities* (No. 69). Washington, DC: Urban Institute. Available at: http://www.urban.org/publications/310874.html

Urban Institute. (1999). *Child care in Michigan: A short report on subsidies, affordability, and supply.* Washington, DC: The U.S. Department of Health and Human Services. Available at: http://aspe.hhs.gov/hsp/Child-Care99/mi-rpt.htm

Urban Institute. (2006, May). *Children of immigrants: Facts and figures.* Washington, DC: Author. Available at: http://www.urban.org/UploadedPDF/900955_children_of_immigrants.pdf

U.S. Department of Commerce, Bureau of the Census. (2005, March). *Table A-3.*

Mean earnings of workers 18 years and over, by educational attainment, race, Hispanic origin, and sex: 1975 to 2003. U.S. Census Bureau, Current Population Survey. Washington, DC: Author. Available at: http://www.census.gov/population/socdemo/education/tabA-3.pdf

U.S. Department of Health and Human Services. (2003). *Temporary assistance for needy families: Total number of families and recipients July–September 2002.* Washington, DC: Author. Available at: http://www.acf.hhs.gov/

U.S. Department of Health and Human Services. (2006). *The 2006 HHS poverty guidelines.* Washington, DC: Author. Available at: http://aspe.hhs.gov/poverty/06poverty.shtml

U.S. Department of Labor, Bureau of Labor Statistics. (1997, December). *A profile of the working poor, 1996* (No. 918). Washington, DC: Author. Available at: http://www.bls.gov/cps/cpswp96.htm

U.S. Department of Labor, Bureau of Labor Statistics. (2005, May). *Women in the labor force: A databook* (No. 985). Washington, DC: Author. Available at: http://www.bls.gov/cps/wlf-databook-2005.pdf

U.S. General Accounting Office. (1993). *Review of health and safety standards at child care facilities.* Washington, DC: U.S. Department of Health and Human Services.

Vandell, D. L., & Wolfe, B. (2000, November). *Child care quality: Does it matter and does it need to be improved?* (No. 78). Madison, WI: Institute for Research on Poverty. Available at: http://www.irp.wisc.edu/publications/sr/pdfs/sr78.pdf

Vorrasi, J., & Garbarino, J. (2000). Poverty and youth violence: Not all risk factors are created equal. In V. Polakow (Ed.), *The public assault on America's children: Poverty, violence, and juvenile injustice* (pp. 59–77). New York: Teachers College Press.

Warner, M. (2006, January/February). *Child care and economic development: The role for planners.* Chicago: American Planning Association. Available at: http://government.cce.cornell.edu/doc/pdf/pasmemo0106.pdf

Warner, M., Adriance, S., Barai, N., Halla, J., Markeson, B., Morrissey, T., & Soref, W. (2005). *Economic development strategies to promote quality child care.* Ithaca, NY: Cornell University Department of City and Regional Planning. Available at: http://government.cce.cornell.edu/doc/pdf/EconDevStrat.pdf

Warner, M., & Stoney, L. (2005). *Economic development strategies to promote quality child care.* Ithaca, NY: Cornell University. Available at: http://government.cce.cornell.edu/doc/pdf/EconDevStratBrochure.pdf

Welter, B. (1978). The cult of true womanhood 1820–1826. In M. Gordon (Ed.), *The American family in social-historical perspective* (2nd ed.). New York: St. Martin's Press.

Wolery, M., Brashers, M. S., & Neitzel, J. C. (2002). Ecological congruence assessment for classroom activities and routines: Identifying goals and intervention practices in childcare. *Topics in Early Childhood Special Education, 22*(3), 131–142.

Wrigley, J. (1989). Different care for different kids: Social class and child care policy. *Educational Policy, 3*(4), 421–439.

Zigler, E. F., & Finn-Stevenson, M. (1995, Fall). The child care crisis: Implications for the growth and development of the nation's children. *Journal of Social Issues, 51*(3), 215–231.

Zigler, E. F., & Finn-Stevenson, M. (1996, Summer/ Fall). Funding child care and public education. Financing Child Care. *The Future of Children, 6*(2), 104–121. Available at: http://www.futureofchildren.org/usr_doc/vol6no2ART6b.pdf

Zweifler, R., & DeBeers, J. (2002, Fall). How zero tolerance impacts our most vulnerable youth. *Michigan Journal of Race and Law, 8*(1), 191–220.

Index

About the Author

Valerie Polakow is Professor of Educational Psychology and Early Childhood at Eastern Michigan University. She has been active in advocacy organizations that support access to high quality child care for low-income families, as well as welfare rights and postsecondary educational access for low-income women. As a writer and researcher, Polakow is committed to an engaged and activist scholarship that "bears witness," documents, and points the way to social transformation. She has written extensively about women and children in poverty, homelessness, educational inequality, and family and child care policies in national and international contexts. She was a Fulbright scholar in Denmark and the recipient of the Distinguished Faculty Award for Scholarship at Eastern Michigan University. She is the author of *The Erosion of Childhood, Lives on the Edge: Single Mothers and Their Children in the Other America* (winner of the *Kappa Delta Pi* book of the year award in 1994), *Diminished Rights,* and *Tab af Rettigheder* (with T. Halskov and P. Schultz Jørgensen); editor of *The Public Assault on America's Children: Poverty, Violence, and Juvenile Injustice*; and co-editor of *International Perspectives on Homelessness* (with C. Guillean) and *Shut Out: Low Income Mothers and Higher Education in Post-Welfare America* (with S. Butler, L. S. Deprez, and P. Kahn).